Of Irony and Empire

SUNY series

EXPLORATIONS

in

POSTCOLONIAL STUDIES

Emmanuel C. Eze and Arif Dirlik, Editors

A complete listing of books in this series can be found at the end of this volume.

Of Irony and Empire

Islam, the West, and the Transcultural Invention of Africa

LAURA RICE

State University of New York Press

Published by
State University of New York Press, Albany

Printed in the United States of America

Chapter 2 is a modified version of the article "African Conscripts/European Conflicts: Race, Memory, and the Lessons of War" *Cultural Critique* 45 (Spring 2000): 109–149.

Chapter 2 includes excerpts from Léopold Sedar Senghor's "Liminary Poem," "The Enlisted Man's Despair," and "To the Senegalese Soldiers Who Died for France" from *The Collected Poetry of Léopold Sedar Senghor* by Melvin Dixon, ed. (Charlottesville: University of Virginia Press, 1991). These are reprinted with permission of the University Press of Virginia.

Chapter 4 includes segments from "Of Heterotopias and Ethnoscapes: The Production of Space in Postcolonial North Africa" *Critical Matrix* 14 (Fall 2003): 36–75, and from the chapter "The Maghreb of the Mind in Mustapha Tlili, Brick Oussaïd, and Malika Mokeddem" in the collection *Maghrebian Mosaic: A Literature in Transition*, edited by Mildred Mortimer, pp. 119–150 (Boulder: Lynne Rienner, 2001).

For information, contact State University of New York Press, Albany, NY
www.sunypress.edu

Production by Diane Ganeles
Marketing by Anne M. Valentine

Library of Congress Cataloging-in-Publication Data

Rice, Laura.
Of irony and empire : Islam, the West, and the transcultural invention of Africa / Laura Rice.
p. cm. — (Suny series, explorations in postcolonial studies)
Includes bibliographical references and index.
ISBN 978-0-7914-7215-6 (hardcover : alk. paper)
ISBN 978-0-7914-7216-3 (pbk. : alk. paper)
1. Africa—Intellectual life. 2. Islamic countries—Intellectual life. 3. Africa—Relations—Europe. 4. Europe—Relations—Africa. 5. Imperialism in literature. 6. Irony in literature. 7. Imperialism in literature. 8. War in literature. 9. African literature—20th century—History and criticism. 10. Islamic literature—Africa—History and criticism. I. Title.

DT14.R495 2007
960—dc22

2006037450

10 9 8 7 6 5 4 3 2 1

For Karim

his intellect, an oasis

his imagination, wind in the palms

Contents

Acknowledgments

This book is the fruit of the labor of many people who helped me turn over and plow through the rich soil of irony and transcultural invention on two continents. In both the U.S. and Tunisia, many colleagues offered steadfast support for work in postcolonial studies. Joseph Krause, chair of Foreign Languages and Literatures, and Tracy Daugherty, chair of English, have supported comparative literature through thin times. Tracy read the entire manuscript of a very early version as did Alan Thomas of University of Chicago Press. Jack Van de Water and Chris Sproul from International Programs visited me in Tunisia to encourage my research, and provided continuous support in more than one way; Lisa Ede, Betty Campbell, Anita Helle, Vicki Tolar Burton, Jennifer Cornell, Tina Carnegie, Marjorie Sandor, and Heidi Brayman-Hackel shared their critical acumen; Chris Anderson read an early version of a chapter; Richmond Barbour discussed with me our common interest; Rich Daniels and Bob Wess provided political commentary. The late Jim Draper, a dear friend sorely missed, was a model of engaged activism. I acknowledge the financial support from Fulbright and the American Institute for Maghreb Studies (AIMS) to conduct field research in North Africa. Oregon State University supported me through various research awards. David Robinson and Wendy Madar at the Center for the Humanities provided a wonderful place to work. In Tunisia, among the many colleagues whose insights have enriched my life, I would like to thank especially Monia and Leila Hejaiej, Khadija Arfaoui and Samira Mechri, as well as Jim Miller, director of the Centre d'études maghrébines à Tunis (CEMAT). Many of the ideas that went into shaping this book came not from academia, but from my extended family and friends from southern Tunisia. Their expertise at irony, mastery of Joha stories, and commentary on global politics were invaluable. My own experts of irony, at home with me on both continents, are precious and their insights run throughout this book; it is with love and gratitude that I thank Karim, Rob, and John, my fellow travelers.

CHAPTER ONE

Prologue

Of Irony and Empire

> One day a poor man who had only a piece of bread to eat was walking by a restaurant in the village. In front of the restaurant, barbecues were smoking away cooking mechoui for the noon meal. The poor fellow looked longingly at the lamb roasting on the grills. Famished, he held his dry bread in the smoke over the meat to give it a hint of the smell before he ate it.
>
> The restaurant owner, furious, rushed out to demand payment for the smell of the meat. But the poor man was broke. The case was taken to Joha, acting village judge. The restaurant owner explained the theft.
>
> After some thought, Joha took three dinars from his pocket, cupped them in his hands and jingled them together by the restaurant owner's ear.
>
> "Case closed," said Joha.
>
> "How do you figure that?" asked the restaurant owner.
>
> "The smell of meat paid for by the sound of money," answered Joha. Now go back to work.

In villages across North Africa and the Middle East, Joha stories are told as families sit on the terrace on hot summer evenings or around the *kanoun* wrapped in blankets on cold winter nights. They are told in coffee shops early in the morning, and it doesn't take a great stretch of the imagination to characterize the poor man as a peasant or a worker, the restaurant owner as a colonial official, a comprador capitalist, or a World Bank expert, and Joha as the "Arab street." As narrative expressions of a Muslim social imaginary, these stories reflect ideas of distributive justice, offer examples of the folly of humankind, and with their ironic turns, string the audience along only to make them laugh at their own assumptions in the end. In the story of the smell of meat and the sound of money, Joha metes out a form of justice that is exactly fit to the case, using irony as an equalizer. For better or for worse, we all belong to the tribe of *Beni Adam* (Everyman).

But irony does not always inhabit the land of wisdom. In imperial hands, irony was a tool of contempt, sarcasm, or ridicule. Employed by speakers who thought they lived at a distance from this world, irony was used to target the victims of their scrutiny and abuse. The fathers of colonial ethnopsychiatry, such as Antoine Porot in North Africa and British-trained South African J. C. Carothers in Kenya, maintained that the natives were incapable of the kind of reflection upon which irony depends. "The normal African" in Carothers' view, was a "lobotomized European" (Fanon, *The Wretched of the Earth* 302) and in Porot's view "the native of North Africa . . . is a primitive creature whose life [is] essentially vegetative and instinctive" (300), and Joha and his Muslim tribe were found, by a subsequent generation of French experts in psychological warfare, to "[lack] a critical spirit" and to be unable to "tolerate irony" (Keller 281).[1]

Negative irony, that satirical detachment associated with imperial power, is largely unironic given its lack of self-reflexivity. I argue here that irony as the trope based on dialectical relationships is able to translate the relativity of our epistemologies, and by that very fact, opens the way to new understandings. The dialectical framework used in this study is not a teleological Hegelian form based on some ultimate unity, rather it is an open system of the sort Fanon embraced. As Ato Sekyi-Otu explains in his study of Fanon's prose, this dialectical thought process brings into question both the tropes we use and the social imaginaries[2] in which they occur, thus opening the way for continual reassessment and new possibilities. To the question, "What then does it mean to read Fanon's texts as if they constituted a dialectical dramatic narrative?" Sekyi-Otu replies:

> It means, first, that relationships between utterance and proposition, representation and truth, enacted practice and authorial advocacy, are rendered quite problematic. It means, furthermore, that an utterance or a representation or a practice we encounter in a text is to be considered not as a discrete and conclusive event, but rather as a strategic and self-revising act set in motion by changing circumstances and perspectives, increasingly intricate configurations of experience. (5)

Of Irony and Empire looks at how our social imaginaries—our ways of making sense of the practices of our societies—are shaped by the rhetorical figures we use. It examines the transcultural experience of modernity, both linguistic and material, as it has invented that part of contemporary Africa which includes the largely Muslim countries surrounding the Sahara desert and the people who inhabit this region.[3] The histories of colonialism, resistance, nationalism, and postcolonial globalization in these countries, from 1914 to the present, provide illustrative cases of what Frantz Fanon called "sociogeny," the social origin of things often attributed to individual invention, on the one hand, or natural causes, on the other. The social imaginary of this region is grounded in Muslim codes of behavior and conduct, as Jean Déjeux explained in his study *Le Sentiment religieux dans la littérature maghrébine de langue française*:

> Most Maghrebian writers, born into Muslim families, consider themselves Muslim in this sense of (shared) "Islamness," without this having any eventual bearing on their possible faith in a transcendent God, in their indifference to or their involvement in religious practice. Their unconscious mind and imagination were steeped and formed in a Maghrebian cultural context that is Islamic and not French or otherwise. (27)[4]

Muslim social imaginaries, while varied across this region of Africa, for example, provide a reservoir of beliefs that shapes attitudes at an unspoken level, gives legitimacy to certain ways of thinking about and assigning legitimacy to things, and is tied to historical developments, in the same ways a Western social imaginary anchored in a Protestant work ethic might be. In explaining the title of his recent book *Muslim Narratives and the Discourses of English*, Amin Malak provides the following useful insight into how a social imaginary provides the background (what Kenneth Burke has called the "scene" as we shall see later in this chapter) in a way that is quite distinct from this or that practice of religion by an individual or religious group.

> *Muslim* is derived from the Arabic word that denotes the *person* who espouses the religion of Islam or is shaped by its cultural impact, irrespective of being secular, agnostic, or practicing believer. The term *Islamic* emphasizes the *faith* of Islam. It denotes thoughts, rituals, activities, and institutions specifically proclaimed and sanctioned by Islam or directly associated with its theological traditions. Such a crucial distinction is often missed or ignored, particularly in mediocre writing, sensational reporting, or calumnious descriptions. (5–6)

Of Irony and Empire explores the dynamics of the transcultural invention of Muslim Africa. As a tool of imperial expansion in which one social imaginary attempts to wipe out another, the invention of Muslim Africa was the outcome of a unilateral deployment of the imagination. Irony, the trope based on dialectical thinking, provides a way of understanding how competing social imaginaries interacted to create transcultural inventions of Muslim Africa. Irony, as we shall see, is double-edged: while it has often been the weapon of exclusion, derision, and humiliation, it also has, when used as a corrective to imperial instincts, the power to protect and the potential to transform.

Empire and *irony* are strange bedfellows. *Empire* is about domination based on "a relationship, formal or informal, in which one state controls the effective political sovereignty of another people. It can be achieved by force, by political collaboration, by economic, social or cultural dependence. Imperialism is simply the process or policy of establishing or maintaining an empire" (Doyle 45). When Edward Said built on this definition in the early 1990s, colonialism and imperialism seemed relatively discrete chronologically [whereas for us today in 2006, they are unfortunately once again superimposed]: "In our time, direct colonialism has largely ended; imperialism . . . lingers where it has always been, in a kind of general cultural sphere as well as in specific political, ideological, economic and social practices (Said, *Culture* 45). *Irony* is much more wedded to the ideas of revolution and transformation. It is affirmation through denial. It demystifies. Through mockery, it unmasks petty error and encourages analysis of the scheme of things. Yet through paradox and reconciliation, irony at its best affirms by opening our structuring of the world to transformation. In his study *L'Ironie*, Vladimir Jankélévitch finds irony to be the very basis of good conscience: "True revolution is not found in the violence of detail or excess of language or clothing, but in the profound conversion of a will refusing the traditional order" (128). Throughout *Of Irony and Empire*, the trope of irony provides a lens that valorizes the dialectical, reciprocal, and empathetic open systems over closed system analyses.[5] It asks how Muslim African self-representation is refracted through the detour of the other, and how Western self-representation is refracted through the mirror of other social imaginaries. Irony is the figurative trope that focuses our attention on the suspicious, subversive, creative distortions that occur in the gap between our intentional acts, linguistic and otherwise, and the world in which they take place. Irony gives the lie to the closed system of empire, to the system that relegates to the margins all input that challenges its world vision. Irony turns our attention rather to the open system of alternative social imaginaries operating within a shared environment. "Irony, then, saves what's worth saving. Wisdom begins where the cynicism [associated with] analysis no longer denies us the simple pleasure of synthesis" (Jankélévitch 194). Granted, any synthesis in an open system is temporary and will be subject to further ironic investigation, but irony, as the trope most linked to moral perception and dialectical analysis, is also linked to therapeutic and empathetic outcomes.

In this prologue, I begin with a close look at stable and unstable forms of irony and their connections to empire. Next I consider the particular ironies involved in the "provincialization" of Western modernity in the section on "Alternative Modernities and Transcultural Invention." I analyze the role of transcultural experience in bringing about a focus on irony as central to discourse in the section "The Linguistic, Spatial, and Social Turns/Modernity and its Malcontents." At the end of the chapter, I return to the insights of Kenneth Burke and Frantz Fanon on the apotropaic (protective) and therapeutic (curative) potentials they saw in irony. In the section "Human Rights, Secularism, and Recognition: the Importance of Being Ironic," I consider irony for its potential to give us insights into how competing social imaginaries have shaped human rights discourse and how irony might open this arena to a more productive transcultural invention.

In the subsequent chapters of the book, I examine the comparative poetics that shape Western and Muslim African social imaginaries. Chapters 2 through 5 apply the theories set forth in the prologue to particular cases that illustrate how social imaginaries compete. "African Conscripts/European Conflicts: Race, Memory, and the Lessons of War" illustrates the dissonance between European and African social imaginaries as clear situational ironies emerge around the conscription of the colonized (both Muslim and non-Muslim Africans) and their insertion into the metropole during the period of the two World Wars. In both wars, intra-European hatred seemed, at the time, irreversible and irremediable, yet these European enemies have managed, time and again, to reunite and turn on the perennial enemy: the cultural and racial Other from Africa. Moving on to the era of independence, I do a close reading of Cheikh Hamidou Kane's semi-autobiographical novel *Ambiguous Adventure*, focusing on the competing cultural understandings that the literary conventions used in this novel encourage. "*Heimlich un-Heimlich:* Of Home as Heterotopia" looks at how Tayeb Salih (Sudan), Mustapha Tlili (Tunisia), and Malika Mokeddem (Algeria) each negotiate the particulars of their postcolonial identities as expatriate authors working in transnational contexts. This study of "home as heterotopia" in the postcolonial novel investigates the uncanny ways falsehood and truth, the *heimlich* (at-homeness) and the *unheimlich* (exile at home), cohabit in these aesthetic and political transcultural inventions of Muslim Africa. "The Ends of Irony," the epilogue to *Of Irony and Empire*, argues for the continuing value of irony in a post-9/11 world. There is a need for a new humanism that offers a transfigurative vision to replace our current landscape of war and terror. The active engagement of public intellectuals such as the writers studied in this book has become more pressing than ever in the struggle to counter the humorless and self-important global plans of ideologues. By discussing international agreements based on a just recognition of the rights of individuals to be protected from violence, public intellectuals speak for and defend the rights of peoples to manage their resources and express their cultures.

From Stable to Unstable Irony: The links between irony and empire

> As an over-all ironic formula here, and one that has a quality of inevitability, we could lay it down that "what goes forth as A returns as non-A." This is the basic pattern that places the essence of drama and dialectic in the irony of the "peripety," the strategic moment of reversal.
>
> —Kenneth Burke, "Four Master Tropes," *A Grammar of Motives*

> It will be seen that the black man's alienation is not an individual question. Beside phylogeny and ontogeny stands sociogeny . . . let us say this is a question of sociodiagnostics.
>
> —Frantz Fanon, *Black Skin, White Masks*

The essays that make up *Of Irony and Empire* are illustrative rather than definitive; they investigate the power of irony to cure and to transform. For this reason, the title begins with "of." Just as Shakespeare's Touchstone in *As You Like It* appreciated the rhetorical flexibility of "if" in human relations—"Your If is the only peacemaker; much virtue in If" (5.4.96–97), much virtue is found in "of" for its ambiguity, for its insistence on dialectic. As Adam Smith noted in his *Lectures on Rhetoric and Belles Lettres—Considerations concerning the First Formation of Languages*:

> Ask any man of common acuteness, What relation is expressed by the preposition *above*? He will readily answer, that of *superiority*. By the preposition *below*? He will as quickly reply, that of *inferiority*. But ask him, what relation is expressed by the preposition *of*, and, if he has not beforehand employed his thoughts a good deal upon these subjects, you may safely allow him a week to consider of his answer. . . . The preposition *of*, denotes relation in general, considered in concrete with the corelative object. . . . We often apply it, therefore, to express the most opposite relations; because, the most opposite relations agree so far that each

> of them comprehends in it the general idea or nature of a relation. . . . The word *of*, however, serves very well to denote all those relations, because in itself it denotes no particular relation, but only relation in general; and so far as any particular relation is collected from such expressions, it is inferred by the mind, not from the preposition itself. (Smith)

Of and *irony* both turn our attention to the question of relationship. The preposition *of* and the trope *irony* encourage us to decide how what is implied by the writer connects to what is then inferred by the audience. Wayne Booth has noted that stable irony is built on four traits (5–6), and by extrapolating a bit for this study, we might explain them as follows: *intentionality* (the author has in mind a particular audience), *slippage* (the overt surface meaning gives way to a covert, submerged meaning), *commonality* (intelligibility is based on a set of shared attitudes and expectations), and *legitimacy* (the reconstructed, hidden meaning leaves us finally on a solid intellectual footing). Stable ironies happen in closed systems. Unstable ironies imply open systems, alternative social imaginaries, dialectical relationships. In such open systems, the four traits of stable irony are all called into question: authorship no longer means authority over the text, slippage is continuous rather than limited, commonality is cross-cut by difference, and legitimacy depends upon a particular frame of reference rather than upon some universal or transcendent ethical measure. Unstable ironies are the stuff of decolonization because they challenge authority, undercut stability, insist on the local and the particular, and demystify false claims to legitimacy.

"We are all here on earth to help others; what on earth the others are here for, I don't know" (Auden). This observation, which leftist poet and social critic W.H. Auden was fond of repeating,[6] has been traced to a 1923 recording, "The Parson Addresses His Flock," by the English music-hall and radio comedian John Foster Hall (1867–1945), popularly known as the Revd. Vivian Foster, the Vicar of Mirth (Mendelson). The Vicar of Mirth's remark contains the doubled features that define irony, a rhetorical figure that "say[s] one thing and mean[s] the opposite" (Booth 34). Appearance gives way to a putative reality as the audience senses the dissonance between the universal moral imperative the Vicar parrots, and the Vicar's self-centered, unreflective gloss on this law of morality. The required "peripety" or drama of reversal as abstracted in Kenneth Burke's formula for irony is there: what goes forth as A (the obligation to help others) returns as non-A (an ethnocentric dismissal of "others"—be they the Victorian workhouse poor or those another Burke [Edmund] referred to as the "great unwashed masses of humanity"). Mirroring the stolid mentality of the Victorian period, the Vicar's words mark the end of the long nineteenth century (1789–1914). During this period, the colonial officials of Britain and France, sharing the "white man's burden" to carry out their "civilizing mission" in Africa, found no ironic dissonance between the "rights of man" and the establishment of colonial empires, rather they thought of the combination as "progress."

World War I and its aftermath bring us into the highly ironic context of our contemporary age (1914 to the present). Today, irony exercises "its imperialistic wanderings through the whole of man's discourse" (Booth 33). "Ours joins just about every other century in wanting to call itself the 'age of irony,'" as postmodern theorist Linda Hutcheon pointed out in 1994, "and the recurrence of that historical claim in itself might well support the contention of contemporary theorists from Jacques Derrida to Kenneth Burke that irony is inherent in signification, in its deferrals and in its negations" (9). Yet the irony that permeates contemporary issues of personal identity, interpersonal relations, and cross-cultural exchange differs significantly from eighteenth-century wit delivered from under powdered wigs in elegant salons, and from nineteenth-century romantic irony with its infinite ideal forever escaping the lyric poet's finite embrace. Language and experience shape the world as they describe and inscribe it. We have entered the era of unstable ironies in which transcendent meaning has become one discursive regime among others.

Irony demystifies discourse. Working through a dialectic that has no totalizing end point, the unstable irony of our age gives the lie, on a linguistic level, to the ontological bad faith that did not distinguish between an unreachable reality and our representation of that reality. Thus, as Paul de Man has commented in "The Rhetoric of Temporality" from his *Blindness and Insight*, the value of irony is its instability: "Curiously enough, it seems to be only in describing a mode of language which does not mean what it says that one can actually say what one means" (211). *Of Irony and Empire* takes this discussion of irony's new importance beyond the frame of European cultural and literary history addressed by de Man in *Blindness and Insight* and Hayden White in *Tropics of Discourse* and *Metahistory* to look at what part colonial and postcolonial relations played in identifying destablizing irony as the major philosophical and epistemological mode of figuring the world.

Up through the nineteenth century, intellectual locations were strongly associated with rhetorical analysis:

> From Aristotle until the nineteenth century, treatises on rhetoric as the art of persuasion always included an account of the intellectual "locations" that could provide such points of agreement. Once found, these locations—what the Greeks called *topoi*, the Latins *loci*, and the English *places*—were used almost literally as platforms on which speaker and listener could securely stand while conducting an argument. (Booth 34)

The trope of stable irony, Booth explains, requires two platforms: "the reader is asked simply to move from one platform, on which the speaker pretends to stand, to another one, on which he [sic] really stands—one that is somehow 'opposite,' across the street, as it were. But perhaps the implied intellectual motion is really 'downward,' 'going beneath the surface' to something solider or more profound; we rip up a rotten platform and probe to a solid one" (34–35). By the early twentieth century, the epistemological platform upon which speaker and listener "could securely stand" has been undermined. Instability arises not only from the recognition of the role of intentionality in language, but also from the absence of a shared cultural location, a shared social imaginary. Competing social imaginaries and alternative experiences of modernity lead to instability. The formula in stable irony, moving from false to true, from rotten to solid, becomes dialectical in unstable irony, a movement from same to other and back.

Unstable irony is a trope keenly aware of its own figurative distortions. As Hayden White notes in *Metahistory*:

> Irony represents a stage of consciousness in which the problematical nature of language itself has become recognized. . . . The trope of irony . . . provides a linguistic paradigm of a mode of thought that is radically self-critical with respect not only to a given characterization of the world of experience but also to the very effort to capture adequately the truth of things in language. It is, in short, a model of the linguistic protocol in which skepticism in thought and relativism in ethics are conventionally expressed. (37–38)

Postcolonial irony, like postcolonial empire, sometimes seems like a descent into the bottomless pit of infinite regressions and pointless dialectic. While some would like to return to a world of stable ironies, and thus think of empire as "the sort of enlightened foreign administration once provided by self-confident Englishmen in jodhpurs and pith helmets" (Porter 31), contemporary American imperialism has rather given us Paul Bremer running around Iraq in suits and combat boots, and the toastmaster of cognitive litotes, Donald Rumsfeld declaiming, on the one hand, the "known unknowns and unknown knowns" and on the other that, "We don't do empire." The irony in our time is unstable in that it allows us no purchase on an agreed-upon reality. Abstract debates over the discursive nature of truth and the rule of law fill the halls of justice while violations of human rights are pressed into the flesh around the world in jails like Abu Ghraib. Theories envisioning a "clash of civilizations" ratchet Manicheism up to a global level. But these binary views are challenged by dialectical theories positing "alternative modernities," which provincialize Western modernity.[7]

Without gainsaying the violence of empire or the epistemological instability of human knowledge, *Of Irony and Empire* argues that we must also keep in the mix the more comic notion of irony's powers to create more just interactions among peoples. And although irony is certainly "transideological," serving both liberal and conservative causes, Hayden White's assertion that "as a basis of a world view, irony tends to dissolve all belief in the possibility of positive political actions" (*Metahistory* 38) is a claim that needs careful scrutiny if it is to be applied to the colonial and postcolonial experience. By the same token, so does Paul de Man's provisional conclusion to "the Rhetoric of Temporality," which claims that

> irony divides the flow of temporal experience into a past that is pure mystification and a future that remains harassed forever by a relapse within the inauthentic. It can know this inauthenticity but can never overcome it. It can only restate and repeat it on an increasingly conscious level, but it remains endlessly caught in the impossibility of making this knowledge applicable to the empirical world. It dissolves in the narrowing spiral of a linguistic sign that becomes more and more remote from meaning, and it can find no escape from this spiral. (222)

The work of social critics and cultural studies founders such as Kenneth Burke, Frantz Fanon, and Edward Said reassures us that irony, while oppositional, is not merely destructive. Fanon, for example, questions the way language is used to shape and create the colonial environment, peopling it with actors, attitudes, and relationships. By dramatizing and revealing its performative aspect, Fanon challenges the normative and descriptive role rhetoric is traditionally assigned. In this spirit, for example, Fanon shows how it is that the settler creates the native, first by displacing him, and then by attributing his own fear of displacement to the hostile mentality of the native: "Their first encounter was marked by violence and their existence together—that is to say the exploitation of the native by the settler—was carried on by dint of a great array of bayonets and cannons. . . . In fact, the settler is right when he speaks of knowing 'them' well. For it is the settler who has brought the native into existence and who perpetuates his existence. The settler owes the fact of his very existence, that is to say, his property, to the colonial system" (*The Wretched of the Earth* 36). Having brought the native into being through displacement, the settler must deal with the social inequalities he has instituted: "The colonized man is an envious man. And this the settler knows very well; when their glances meet he ascertains bitterly, always on the defensive, 'They want to take our place'" (*The Wretched of the Earth* 39). The ironic peripety this kind of dramatization depends upon is best captured in the Arab proverb: "He hit me and he cried, then ran ahead and complained." By mimicking the colonial perspective, Fanon demonstrates that the native and his desire are not brute facts of nature; they are a result of the colonial relationship—they are made not born. As Hussein Abdulahi Bulhan noted in his study, *Frantz Fanon and the Psychology of Oppression*, the first step toward ending oppression is to locate its sociogenesis:

> Basic concepts such as freedom, responsibility, violence, madness, and death lose much of their crucial import if not placed in a historical and social context. For to conceive of freedom only as the absence of restraint, responsibility simply as the avoidance of punishment, violence merely as the personal intent to harm, madness as only the private travails of an individual, or death merely as physical mortality limits our understanding of oppression and serves to narrow our vision of human possibilities. The social foundation of violence, madness, death, and liberty require further consideration.
>
> We must find a way of placing biography in history, the crisis of personal identity in communal uprooting, clinical symptoms in relational systems. (13–14)

Fanon highlights the ironic context of the colonial project by dramatizing the discourse of the colonizer. Performance, which is always on the epistemological fence between individual speech (a doing/a subject) and the typical discourse that defines a given role (a thing done/an object), provides Fanon with a way to place the unironic monologue in a highly ironic world.

Often through the use of indirect free discourse, the narrative device that allows a character to say one thing in a scene where the author implies the opposite, Fanon lets the settler dramatize the hypocrisy and pathology of the colonial arrangements. The lack of irony found in the colonial period suggests not just a simple investment in the "reality" of the grand narrative of colonialism (progress, evolutionary history, etc.) but a substantial dose of bad faith and denial. The colonial system is "an order of absolute difference and radical irreciprocity which is fixed, made manifest in *space*" (Sekyi-Otu 72). This spatialized colonial relation is antidialectical: "The zone where the natives live is not complementary to the zone inhabited by the settlers. The two zones are opposed, but not in the service of a higher unity" (Fanon, *The Wretched of the Earth* 38). Rather, a manichean allegory is at work in the settler's psyche that, as Abdul JanMohamed put it, transforms "racial difference into moral and even metaphysical difference" (80), as human interactions are reified into a relationship of superior to inferior. The act of decolonization, then, is also a return to dialectic, and an opening for reciprocal, rather than exclusionary, human relationships in Fanon's view:

> Decolonization never takes place unnoticed, for it influences individuals and modifies them fundamentally. It transforms spectators crushed with their inessentiality into privileged actors, with the grandiose glare of history's floodlights upon them. It brings a natural rhythm into existence, introduced by new men, and with a new language and a new humanity. Decolonization is the veritable creation of new men. But this creation owes nothing of its legitimacy to any supernatural power; the "thing" which has been colonized becomes man during the same process by which it frees itself. (*The Wretched of the Earth* 36–37)

Fanon is no fool about the rapidity with which human relations can become reified again and the same old farces of unequal power and nonrecognition be replayed. In "The Pitfalls of National Consciousness" from *The Wretched of the Earth*, he notes that following a revolution, the middle class, instead of putting its technical and intellectual capital in the service of the people and breaking out of the old channels of inequality set up by the colonial system, apes the behavior of the former colonial masters:

> But unhappily we shall see that very often the national middle class does not follow this heroic, positive, fruitful, and just path; rather, it disappears with its soul set at peace into the shocking ways—shocking because anti-national—of a traditional bourgeoisie, of a bourgeoisie which is stupidly, contemptibly, cynically bourgeois.
>
> . . . this incapability to seek out new systems of management will be equally manifested by the bogging down of the national middle class in the methods of agricultural production which were characteristic of the colonial period.
>
> The national economy of the period of independence is not set on a new footing. It is still concerned with the groundnut harvest, with the cocoa crop and the olive yield. In the same way there is no change in the marketing of basic products, and not a single industry is set up in the country. We go on sending out raw materials; we go on being Europe's small farmers, who specialize in unfinished products.
>
> . . . To them, nationalization quite simply means the transfer into native hands of those unfair advantages which are a legacy of the colonial period. (150–152)

Fanon insisted on the centrality of dialectical recognition between people and groups. He did not frame it in Hegel's ideal sense where recognition is not grounded in lived experience. Nor did he imagine it within the frame of Sartre's Hobbesian universe of negative human relations where we each try to make the other an object. Rather Fanon invested recognition with comic possibilities but recognized the tragic or farcical potential of human interaction as well. To challenge conventional social and institutional practices by staging them, is to hope to transform them. Irony is strongly associated with freedom because of its liberating potentials—not the least of which is laughter. Irony is apotropaic; through mockery, it helps the oppressed resist internalizing the evils of injustice: "when the great lord passes the wise peasant bows deeply and silently farts."[8] Irony is also therapeutic as its dialectical tensions prevent reification. In "West Indians and Africans," Fanon calls irony a form of good conscience because it keeps the oppressed from replacing the dishonesty of colonization with self-serving mystifications. "A West Indian, in particular an intellectual who is no longer on the level of irony, discovers his Negritude," Fanon observed in reference to followers of the theories of his Martinican teacher, the poet Aimé Césaire (*Toward the African Revolution* 19); "It is thus that the West Indian, after the great white error, is now living in the great black mirage" (27). A healthy sense of irony would have saved him from this misrecognition.

In thinking through what universal traits connect the self (ontogeny) to others (phylogeny), Frantz Fanon focused on sociogeny as playing a crucial, if often submerged, role. Sociogeny describes the process of how we develop our unspoken assumptions and how our surrounding cultures inculcate within us the social imaginary we are immersed in from birth. Bulhan attributes Fanon's break from Eurocentric psychology to his focus on the social roots of oppression, thus of potential freedom as well. Freud's social imaginary was particular to the Europe of his time: "Freud's theorizing emerged out of a nuclear, patriarchal, and bourgeois family context and within a sexually repressive Victorian Europe. . . . Although he challenged the Victorian mores of his day, Freud was essentially an apologist for the status quo within the bourgeois family and the larger capitalist society" (71). Fanon also criticized Jung's collective unconscious, not for what it revealed about the European social imaginary, but because it was mystified and universalized: "Jung locates the collective unconscious in the inherited cerebral matter. But the collective unconscious, without our having to fall back on the genes, is purely and simply the sum of prejudices, myths, collective attitudes of a given group," Fanon points out in *Black Skin, White Masks* (188); "He wanted to go back to the childhood of the world, but he made a remarkable mistake: He went back only to the childhood of Europe" (190). As Bulhan makes clear, Fanon's critique had to do with the assumption that "bourgeois psychology" was synonymous with the human condition:

> The fragmenting effect of ontogenetic perspective and the ossifying consequences of phylogenetic explanations obscured a fundamental dimension of the human psyche. Because of their conservative thrust, both ontogeny and phylogeny negate man's vocation as a subject of history and

> thus dash any hopes of social change. Ontogeny reveals man the individual—the helpless, hopeless, and isolated object of a repressive and overpowering social structure. Phylogeny points to the futility of man's resistence against a curse that is embedded in an irretrievable past. As consistently argued throughout his writings, it was Fanon's unwavering conviction that the fundamental cause of alienation is first socioeconomic and second the internalization of societal inequity as well as violence. (80)

Fanon critiqued theories like the Oedipus Complex that not only made the mistake of presenting the particular as the universal, but also reduced human reality to the psychic modalities of individual deviations from the norm, and a suspect norm at that.

Sociogeny provided a perspective that focused on the dialectic of individual and group as mutually constructing. Through an examination of the paradoxes of his own social construction and its ironic basis in a European social imaginary that excluded him, Fanon learned to put recognition at the heart of his humanism:

> As a schoolboy, I had many occasions to spend whole hours talking about the supposed customs of the savage Senegalese. In what was said there was a lack of awareness that was at the very least paradoxical. Because the Antillean does not think of himself as a black man; he thinks of himself as an Antillean. The Negro lives in Africa. Subjectively, intellectually, the Antillean conducts himself like a white man. But he is a Negro. That he will learn once he goes to Europe; and when he hears Negroes mentioned he will recognize that the word included himself as well as the Senegalese. (*Black Skin, White Masks* 148)[9]

Fanon, then, hardly bought into the European social imaginary,[10] rather he recognized the dangers of naturalizing the contents of the social imaginary and the benefits of exploring its tensions and ambiguities.

Turning away from reified, essentialist, atomistic, antidialectical notions of who we are as individuals and how we interact and are acted upon as participants in society and across cultures, Burke, like Fanon, used irony as a hermeneutic because its operation as a trope required inclusion of the contextual and the dramatic. Burke's theory of "dramatism" attempted to identify the universal traits we all share, and he called the result his "grammar of motives":

> What is involved, when we say what people are doing and why they are doing it? [*A Grammar of Motives*] is concerned with the basic forms of thought which, in accordance with the nature of the world as all men necessarily experience it, are exemplified in the attributing of motives. These forms of thought can be embodied profoundly or trivially, truth-

> fully or falsely. They are equally present in systematically elaborated metaphysical structures, in legal judgments, in poetry and fiction, in political and scientific works, in news and in bits of gossip offered at random. . . . Any complete statement about motives will offer some kind of answers to these five questions: what was done (act), when or where it was done (scene), who did it (agent), how he did it (agency), and why (purpose). (xv)

Burke's pentad gives us a set of principles to apply in order to understand actual statements of motives—what he calls philosophies, or fragments of philosophies. Thus, for example, scene is a blanket term for the background in which agents and acts are placed: "and we move into matters of 'philosophy' when we note that one thinker uses 'God' as his term for the ultimate ground or scene of human action, another uses 'nature,' a third uses 'environment,' or 'history,' or 'means of production,' etc." (xvi–xvii). Philosophical idioms will differ, and the question of judging which idiom is right, or more right than the next, will always demand further investigation in Burke's view, but a universal grammar of motives sets the common ground for cross-cultural comparison.

At first, Burke tells us, he planned to write a treatise on human relations based on a theory of comedy: "Feeling that competitive ambition is a drastically over-developed motive in the modern world, we thought this motive might be transcended if men devoted themselves not so much to 'excoriating' it as to 'appreciating' it" (xvii). This examination of the basic stratagems we use to outwit each other grew into a more general grammar of motives that retained traces of its "comic" origin, the ironic return to a source with transformational, although not necessarily transcendental, potential:

> A perfectionist might seek to evolve terms free of ambiguity and inconsistency (as with the terministic ideals of symbolic logic and logical positivism) . . . we take it for granted that, insofar as men cannot themselves create the universe, there must remain something essentially enigmatic about the problem of motives, and that this underlying enigma will manifest itself in inevitable ambiguities and inconsistencies among the terms for motives. Accordingly, what we want is *not terms that avoid ambiguity*, but *terms that clearly reveal the strategic spots at which ambiguities necessarily arise.* (xviii)

Burke does not aim to "dispose of" ambiguity but rather to "study and clarify the resources of ambiguity" because "it is in the areas of ambiguity that transformations take place." Imagining that "distinctions . . . arise out of a great central moltenness, where all is merged," Burke sees distinctions as matter "thrown from the liquid center to the surface, where they have congealed."

Ambiguities and ironies cause us to return to this "alchemic center" to emerge with new distinctions: "So that A may become non-A. But not merely by a leap from one state to the other. Rather, we must take A back into the ground of its existence, the logical substance that is its causal ancestor, and on to a point where it is consubstantial with non-A; then may we return, this time emerging with non-A instead" (xix). To investigate that "ground," Burke, like Paul de Man, Hayden White, and Edward Said after him, returned to Vico's description of the source of poetics as being the unhappy marriage between the instability of language and the necessity of explaining ourselves.

In Appendix D to *A Grammar of Motives*, Burke examines the "Four Master Tropes"; Burke takes as his starting point Giambattista Vico's idea in his *New Science* (sections 404–409) that all figurative thought can be reduced to four tropes: metaphor, metonymy, synecdoche, and irony (116–119). Vico claimed (section 34) that the "master key of the Science" is an understanding of the "poetic nature of [the] first men" and that the "sources of all poetic locution" are to be found in two: "poverty of language and necessity to explain and make oneself understood" (19). Whereas Vico privileged metaphor that asserted similitude as the most important trope, contemporary critics privilege irony, defined by Vico (section 408) as being "fashioned by falsehood by dint of a reflection which wears the mask of truth" (118). Citing Vico's observation, deconstructive critics such as Hayden White and Paul de Man see irony as giving rise to endless series of subversive interpretations and slippages that condemn us to a world of scepticism. Burke, on the other hand, aims to trace the master tropes to understand their "role in the discovery and description of 'the truth'" (503). He connects the four master tropes to their literal or "realistic" applications: *metaphor*, seeing something in terms of something else, is equated to *perspective*; *metonymy*, substituting the tangible for the intangible, is equated to *reduction*; *synecdoche*, representing the whole by a part, is equated to *representation*; and *irony*, reversing the meaning so A comes back as non-A, is equated to *dialectic*. Contemporary feminist theory as well as postcolonial and cultural studies have added to Burke's dictum a variation on this theme in the critique of binarism. Thus in binary pairings such as male/female or colonizer/colonized, we discover that the first term has a "positive" value, and the second term exists as a spectral image, like a photographic negative, existing not in its own right but rather to valorize the first. Irony is not simply the rhetorical form that translates exclusion and domination (as in Edward Said's orientalism) or that captures ambiguity (as in Homi Bhabha's postcolonial mimicry), it is also a mode of representation and invention that can protect against the violations of empire (as in James Scott's hidden transcripts) and can engender the new forms of recognition (as in Frantz Fanon's revolutionary humanism).

Vico himself in the early eighteenth century struggled against the closed-system thinking of abstract binaries and cause-and-effect reasoning that were becoming prevalent in his time; he defended "the 'copious' methods of traditional rhetoric . . . against the sterile practices of the Cartesians, then so fashionable in the north": "To introduce geometrical method into practical life . . . is 'like trying to go mad with the rules of reason' [Terence, *Eunuch*, 62–63], attempting to proceed by a straight line among the tortuosities of life, as though human affairs were not ruled by capriciousness, temerity, opportunity, and chance."[11] Vico, whose perspectives would be echoed by Burke, Fanon, and Said, valued the messy unpredictable open system in which human interactions take place, and valued the very messiness of the system as an antidote for reductive imperial thinking. Vico gave empathy the central role on the rhetorical stage: "Humanity is the affection of one man helping another. This is done most effectively through speech—by counseling, warning, exhorting, consoling, reproving—and this is the reason I think that studies of languages are called "humanities" [*studia humanitas*], the more so since it is through languages that humanity is most strongly bound together."[12] Disdain, superiority, and detachment rather than empathy, as we shall see, are features of the stable, colonial brand of irony.

"Irony in the Victorian Age was a pretty rare commodity," according to Paul Fussell ("Initial Shock"). The authors of Western imperial expansion during the long nineteenth century (1789–1914) believed in positivist reasoning, secular institutions, "progressive" outlooks, and instrumental individualism. Their hegemonic beliefs were buttressed by the social transformations that institutionalized industrial market economies, bureaucratically administered states, modes of popular government, and a vastly expanded public sphere.[13] Antipathetic to the scepticism, ironic distance, and mechanistic design with which the Enlightenment thinkers apprehended the world, nineteenth-century Positivists involved in the colonial project (1830–1870) insisted on a "realistic" comprehension of social reality, as Hayden White argued:

> To be a "realist" meant both to see things clearly, as they *really* were, and to draw appropriate conclusions from this clear apprehension of reality for the living of a possible life on its basis. As thus envisaged, claims to an essential "realism" were at once epistemological and ethical. . . .
>
> From our vantage point in the eighth decade of the twentieth century, we can now see that most of the important theoretical and ideological disputes that developed in Europe between the French Revolution and World War I were in reality disputes over which group might claim the right to determine of what a "realistic" position might consist . . . what

> is most interesting about this whole period, considering it as a finished drama of inquiry and expression, is the general authority which the notion of "realism" itself commanded. (*Metahistory* 46)

The colonizers of Africa engaged in a number of critical appropriations: they saw the land and the people through the lens of their own myths of origin, established their political and representational hegemony, and left a legacy of false universalism, which still impacts the production and reception of African texts today.

Modernity is defined here as beginning with World War I, in part because this is the point when colonial subjects were conscripted to take on the duties of citizens but denied the rights of citizenship. The debacle of World War I embodied the situational irony that undermined the myth of the civilizing mission. For Europeans themselves, World War I brought an end to the certainties upon which realism was based and called civilization itself into question; as Ezra Pound put it: "There died a myriad,/And of the best, among them,/For an old bitch gone in the teeth,//For a botched civilization" (64). Paul Fussell noted in *The Great War and Modern Memory*: "Every war is ironic because every war is worse than expected. Every war constitutes an irony of situation because its means are so melodramatically disproportionate to its presumed ends. . . . But the Great War was more ironic than any before or since. . . . It reversed the Idea of Progress" (7–8).

For many people in North Africa and the Middle East, the war was a different kind of wake-up call. Among Arab intellectuals, it is generally agreed that "modernity's shock" began with Napoleon's invasion of Egypt in 1798, but modernity has mainly been associated with events connected with the two World Wars: first, the World War I–era Sykes-Picot Agreement (1916) and Balfour Declaration (1917), which paved the way for "imperialist-installed structures" of dominance that displaced the hope of true self-determination for the Arabs; and second, the post–World War II creation of Israel on Palestinian land in 1948 (Nusseibeh). These events, and the rhetoric that accompanied them, in the context of the sacrifices that had been extracted from the colonized during the two World Wars, heralded a movement among colonized peoples toward renewed resistance to oppression and renewed efforts to claim a more just world. In January 1918, Woodrow Wilson delivered his 14 Point Program to the U.S. Congress, a program that affirmed the principle of self-determination for all peoples:

> We entered this war because violations of right had occurred which touched us to the quick and made the life of our own people impossible unless they were corrected and the world secured once for all against their

> recurrence. What we demand in this war, therefore, is nothing peculiar to ourselves. It is that the world be made fit and safe to live in; and particularly that it be made safe for every peace-loving nation which, like our own, wishes to live its own life, determine its own institutions, be assured of justice and fair dealing by the other peoples of the world as against force and selfish aggression. All the peoples of the world are in effect partners in this interest, and for our own part we see very clearly that unless justice be done to others it will not be done to us. (Wilson)

In the context of Wilson's promises to foster national sovereignty and to extend "the principle of justice to all peoples and nationalities, and their right to live on equal terms of liberty and safety with one another, whether they be strong or weak," Africans had every reason to expect justice at home and in the region. Muslim Africa had a long history of resistance to the colonial powers, a resistance fueled precisely by their experiences, which demonstrated that Western "rules of law" did not result in justice being done. For this reason, political dissidents have challenged the universality of secular Western law and its applicability to their own societies: "They believe that justice, when it is real, is fair, substantive, and equitable rather than procedurally formal. They argue that foreign legal and political systems simply do not fit within the moral order of Islam. They claim that these systems apply the law mechanistically and that they do not achieve substantive justice. They allege that these systems tolerate high levels of inequality, with prevalent racial, ethnic, and economic discrimination" (Laremont 2). While the injustices of the Western system of justice in Africa are well documented in colonial archives, it is their peculiar displacement of moral responsibility that finally brings them under unstable irony's lens. During the heyday of colonialism (1870–1914), the French passed the Warnier Law, which systematically displaced Algerian people from their land, and then passed subsequent laws that held Algerians financially "responsible for the administrative costs of their displacement from their own lands" (43). During World War I, conscription from Algeria alone had sent 120,000 troops to Europe to fight for France, about 25,000 of whom ended up dead or missing; however, these same Muslim conscripts did not enjoy the basic rights of citizenship. The era of unstable irony came about not only because the World War's "means [were] so melodramatically disproportionate to its presumed ends" but because its actual ends were so devastatingly disproportionate to its presumed ends.

The aftermath of World War II repeated the gross inequities that followed World War I—the clear violation of human rights, the double standard applied to Muslims, the appropriation of land. The counter-narratives of liberation written by Africans from World War I to the present foreground issues of recognition and social justice, and challenge the doxa of the Western social imaginary. In "Doxa and Common Life," Pierre Bourdieu observes: "We have spoken too much about consciousness, too much in terms of representation. The social world doesn't work in terms of practices, mechanisms, and so forth" (Bourdieu and Eagleton 268). Rather, the social imaginary is based on all sorts of beliefs that *go without saying*. In speaking of this naturalization of ideas, Bourdieu uses the term *doxa* rather than the much used and abused term *ideology*. A repository of cultural appropriations that could be thought of as those things we assume to be true, doxa operates at a level beneath conscious understanding. Doxa involves *symbolic domination*; that is, the selection of a set of ways of representing reality that conceals other possible representations, thus hiding parts of the same reality. Doxa shapes our experience of the real; it is the imaginative metaphysics by which appropriation happens as we project our needs, interests, and desires on the world around us. Of course, we don't all share the same doxa, but this is often only revealed through transcultural encounters that reveal the cultural specificity of our representational appropriations. We discover doxa through paradox, when what goes without saying is contradicted by another perspective.

Alternative Modernities and Transcultural Invention

The uncertainty, unverifiability, and relativity associated with the making of meaning are translated on the textual level, by what Booth termed unstable irony. In the "post"modern, "post"colonial twenty-first century, we discover that modernity did not die out when the certainties that spawned it were given the lie: "to announce the general end of modernity, even as an epoch, much less as an attitude or an ethos, seems premature, if not patently ethnocentric, at a time when non-Western peoples everywhere begin to engage critically their own hybrid modernities," Dilip Parameshwar Gaonkar argues in *Alternative Modernities* (14). Rather, the "provincialization" of Western modernity has been accompanied by the investigation of alternative modernities:

> To think in terms of "alternative modernities" is to admit that modernity is inescapable and to desist from speculations about the end of modernity. Born in and of the West some centuries ago under relatively specific sociohistoric conditions, modernity is now everywhere. It has arrived not suddenly but slowly, bit by bit, over the *longue durée*—awakened by contact; transported through commerce; administered by empires, bearing colonial inscriptions; propelled by nationalism; and now increasingly steered by global media, migration, and capital. And it continues to

> "arrive and emerge," as always in opportunistic fragments accompanied by utopic rhetorics, but no longer from the West alone, although the West remains the major clearinghouse of global modernity. (1)

Arguing that alternative modernities are site-specific, that they unfold "within a specific cultural or civilizational context," and that "different starting points for the transition to modernity lead to different outcomes," Gaonkar separates the concept of societal modernization from that of cultural modernity. Those who speak of modernization and globalization have too often based their understandings on a theory of convergence: "the inexorable march of modernity will end up making all cultures look alike" (17). The irony, of course, is that "one can provincialize Western modernity only by thinking through and against its self-understandings, which are frequently cast in universalist idioms" (15). In order to capture "the pull of sameness and the forces making for difference," a cultural theory of modernity problematizes *convergence* (usually thought of in terms of the Western institutional arrangements such as a market economy or a bureaucratic state) and *divergence* (thought of "primarily in terms of lived experience and cultural expressions of modernity that are shaped by what is variously termed 'habitus,' or 'background, or the 'social imaginary'") (Taylor, "Two Theories" 188–189). Thinking alternative modernities means focusing on "creative adaptation," which is "not simply a matter of adjusting the form or recoding the practice to soften the impact of modernity: rather, it points to the manifold ways in which people question the present. It is the site where people 'make' themselves modern, as opposed to being 'made' modern by alien and impersonal forces, and where they give themselves an identity and a destiny" (Gaonkar 18).

This view of how creative adaptations engender alternative modernities underscores, in my view, the centrality of "recognition" in transcultural interaction. The "forces making for difference" mean that the lived experience of modernity and its embodied character obviously vary from site to site. The "pull of sameness," however, is exerted not only by abstract global institutions, but also in experiential similarities: experiencing the "ethos of irony" or the "anxiety of mimicry" takes place across alternative modernities, linking them to one another (23). To think modernity in terms of recognition does not allow us to escape from the master trope of irony in social relations, rather it reinscribes it on different philosophical ground. As Scott Lash and Mike Featherstone point out in their introductory essay to the 2002 collection *Recognition and Difference: Politics, Identity, Multiculture*: "The irony is that the issue of recognition has been posed by social and cultural theory precisely at the point in time that recognition is in decline, precisely when the nation-state, the human (as we know it) and the social bond are in perhaps terminal decline" (17). A 1999 article in *The Economist* illustrates this pervasive sense (among the former colonizers) of human isolation generated by the loss of grand narratives of colonialism. The unnamed correspondent noted that British diplomats these days are giving briefings that share a common trait: "They would start with a more or less lucid account of the political and economic situation, followed by a few anecdotes. And then—as often as not—our man, in Manila or Bangkok or wherever, would say of the locals: 'You see they have no sense of irony'" ("Quiet Joke"). Given the current British participation with the "coalition" in Afghanistan and Iraq, it is particularly ironic that the article goes on to note that Mr. Cooper, head of the British Foreign Office's Asia department, commented in 1999: "What else is there left for the citizens of a post-heroic, post-imperial, post-modern society? Provided it is tinged with humanity, irony is not such a bad thing. It suggests a certain modesty about oneself, one's values and one's aspirations. At least irony is unlikely to be used to justify programmes of conquest or extermination" ("Quiet Joke").

As Salmon Rushdie's drunken stutterer Whisky Sisodia puts it in *Satanic Verses*: "The trouble with the Engenglish is that their hiss history happened overseas, so they dodo don't know what it means" (343). The unstable irony that defines postcolonial relations is often based on a play of countervailing forces kept in suspension; for example, we find globalization, on the one hand, and a simultaneous provincializing of the West, on the other. And while the trope of irony is especially well-suited to postcolonial critique of the relationship between the West and the rest, "there is no necessary relationship between irony and radical politics or even radical formal innovation . . . irony can and does function tactically in the service of a wide range of political positions, legitimating or undercutting a wide variety of interests" (Hutcheon 10). Distance is what makes irony function. It is sometimes figured as that conservative, hierarchical "thingification" that Aimé Césaire speaks of as so destructive of human community at the beginning of his *Discourse on Colonialism*. Mary Layoun has instructively analyzed this distance in the conservative use of irony as it plays out in the fiction of V.S. Naipaul:

> In Naipaul's narratives, the ironic stance of the text resolutely distances a chosen narrative subject from the objects, and the objectification, of textual irony. The mechanism of narrative irony in the Naipaulian text produces a last line of defense for the continued survival and dominance of (a particular definition of) the (besieged) narrative subject. It attempts to secure a position for that subject somewhere outside of the "disorderly mess" on which the narrative's ironic gaze is fixed. As for those framed in and by the textual imperium of this irony, there is virtually nothing other

> than entrapment in an endless narrative present—as barbaric and irrational savages caged and on textual display. Narrative irony in *Guerillas* or *A Bend in the River* or *In A Free State* is predicated on a longing, a barely repressed textual desire, for the "simplicity" and "order" of a narrative "once" that was precisely colonialism. (64)

In the Naipaulian view, the new world order turns out to be the same old order, one in which "you see, they have no sense of irony," but "we" do. The violence of this plainly stated craft and statecraft, of this valorized "simplicity" and "order," meets its postcolonial antidote in the Socratic irony of a Michael Moore. Socrates adopted the pose of ignorance in order to "entertain points of view which, upon his continued questioning, turn out to be ill-grounded or to lead to absurd consequences" (Abrams 93); the classical Greek *eiron* was "a 'dissembler' who characteristically spoke in understatement and deliberately pretended to be less intelligent than he was, yet triumphed over the *alazon*—the self-deceiving and stupid braggart" (91). Having won the *Palme d'Or* at Cannes for his *Farenheit 9/11*, a scathing attack on the Bush Administration, which made its case by using documentary footage of the President's own words, the *eiron* Moore commented that he did not harbor a grudge toward the *alazon* Bush: "He's got the funniest lines in the film. I'm eternally grateful" (Corliss).

THE LINGUISTIC, SPATIAL, AND SOCIAL TURNS: MODERNITY AND ITS MALCONTENTS

The Linguistic Turn

> What, then, is truth? A mobile army of metaphors, metonyms, and anthropomorphisms—in short, a sum of human relations, which have been enhanced, transposed, and embellished poetically and rhetorically, and which after long use seem firm, canonical, and obligatory to a people: truths are illusions about which one has forgotten that this is what they are; metaphors which are worn out.
>
> —Nietzsche, "On truth and lies in the extra-moral sense"

The crisis of truth can be traced, in part, to the recognition that, as J. L. Austin argued in his *How to Do Things with Words*, a terrible epistemological mistake has been made: language has been treated as if it were a tool to make constative assertions about the world—statements about the world that are characterizable as true or false—when in actuality, speech acts are rather performative. As Richard Van Oort further explains: "the peculiarity of the performative utterance, in contrast to the constative, is that it does not describe a state of affairs independent of itself, but that it is itself the reality it describes. It is therefore a self-reflexive utterance" (Van Oort). Central to the process of a shift from constative realities to performative enactments, and from the application of unselfconscious paradigms in the human sciences to self-reflexive practices, were Western-trained scholars whose theories were deeply altered by their having lived in North Africa. Robert J. C. Young argues in *White Mythologies* that "If so-called 'so-called poststructuralism' is the product of a single historical moment, then that moment is probably not May 1968 but rather the Algerian War of Independence—no doubt itself both a symptom and a product. In this respect it is significant that Sartre, Althusser, Derrida and Lyotard, among others, were all either born in Algeria or personally involved with the events of the war" (1).[14] More central to the texts and contexts examined in *Of Irony and Empire*, however, is the work of another set of scholars whose North African experiences caused them to ask "tactical questions" about what Western thought "excluded from its discourses": Foucault (philosophy), Fanon (psychiatry), and Bourdieu (sociology/anthropology). Shifting our attention from the constative to the performative is analogous to moving from arguing over "truth claims" to analyzing "discourse": in both cases, a focus on "truth" becomes an attention to trope.

In his *Tropics of Discourse*, which examines how tropes function in the discourses of the human sciences, Hayden White notes that "the word *tropic* derives from *tropikos*, *tropos*, which in Classical Greek meant "turn" (2). The master tropes of metaphor, metonymy, synecdoche, and irony allow human consciousnesses to turn the unfamiliar into the familiar, by encoding "reality" into "discourses," which themselves are always shuttling "to and fro" between previous encodings based on experience and the "clutter of phenomena which refuses incorporation into conventionalized notions of 'reality,' 'truth,' or 'possibility'" (4): "When we seek to make sense of such problematical topics as human nature, culture, society, and history, we never say precisely what we wish to say or mean precisely what we say. Our discourse always tends to slip away from our data towards the structures of consciousness with which we are trying to grasp them; or what amounts to the same thing, the data always resist the coherency of the image which we are trying to fashion of them" (1). So, while discourse and the tactics it employs allow us to "figure out" reality by encoding it, discourse is, at the same time, subject itself to a critique that employs a *linguistic turn*: "Discourse, if it is genuine discourse, [is] as *self*-critical as it is critical of others. . . . It throws all tactical rules into doubt, including those originally governing its own formation. Precisely because it is aporetic, or ironic, with respect to its own adequacy, discourse cannot be governed by logic alone. . . . [E]very discourse is always as much about discourse itself as it is about the objects that make up its subject matter" (4). Discourse then is inherently ironic because it undercuts the very meanings it is in the process of making by questioning its own processes. Philosopher Michel Foucault, in White's view, shares with anthropologist Claude Lévi-Strauss and psychoanalyst Jacques Lacan "an interest in the deep structures of human consciousness, a conviction that study of such deep structures must begin with an analysis of language, and a conception of language," a view originating in the work of linguist Ferdinand de Saussure: that is, "all three proceed on the assumption that the distinction between language on the one side and human thought and action on the other must be dissolved if human phenomena are to be understood as what they truly are, that is to say, elements of a communications system" (230). This linguistic turn in understanding and formulating our study of cultural and cross-cultural meaning has made the study of literary forms preeminent among disciplines. In *Contingency, Irony, and Solidarity*, for example, Richard Rorty argues that "the rise of literary criticism to preeminence within the high culture of the democracies—its gradual and only semiconscious assumption of the cultural role once claimed (successively) by religion, science, and philosophy—has paralleled the rise in the proportion of ironists to metaphysicians among the intellectuals" (82).[15] The advent of the age of irony, experienced by the Western intellectuals Rorty refers to (as well as his somewhat blindly ethnocentric reference to "the democracies"), is intimately tied to the practice of human relations engendered by colonialism, decolonization, and neocolonialism.

The Spatial Turn

> "Docta ignorantia": Bourdieu
> Our "tactics" seem to be analyzable only indirectly, through another society: . . . They return to us from afar, as though a different space were required in which to make visible and elucidate the tactics marginalized by the Western form of rationality. Other regions give us back what our culture has excluded from its discourse.
>
> —Certeau, *The Practice of Everyday Life*

As Bourdieu's *docta ignorantia* suggests and Certeau asserts, it is as though "a different space were required in which to make visible and elucidate the tactics marginalized by the Western form of rationality" (50). And this same spatial turn is what allows us to recognize those tactics in Western thought precisely as "tactics" deployed by power rather than truth *tout court*. Fascinating and compelling, North Africa has been historically a site whose physical proximity encouraged European scholars to map it both as analogue and antipode, as mirror and mystery, as Same and Other. As part of the East, it was at times constructed psychoanalytically: "European culture gained in strength and identity by setting itself off against the Orient as a sort of surrogate and even underground self" (Said, *Orientalism* 3). Yet, at the same time, this site provided the laboratory where ethnologists could work at fathoming the idiosyncracies of the Other. Ethnography "always has been . . . linked with epistemological problems. . . . [Anthropologists] have struggled with the contradictions of a mode of inquiry that appears, by turns, uniquely revelatory and irredeemably ethnocentric" (Comaroff and Comaroff 7). Exposed to Western navies yet resistant to Western narratives, North Africa is an especially rich repository of the discursively unexpected and the politically untoward. Michel Foucault left for Tunisia shortly after publishing *The Order of Things: An Archeology of the Human Sciences*, a history of ideas that undercuts the idea of history itself. Foucault's experience teaching at the University of Tunis between 1966 and 1968 made literal the *spatial turn* his thought had been taking in the 1960s. In an interview with *La Presse de Tunis* he commented: "After having stayed in the French University for long enough to do what had to be done and to be what one has to be, I wandered about abroad, and that gave my myopic gaze a sense of distance, and may have allowed me to re-establish a better perspective on things" (qtd. in Macey, *Lives* 184–185).

Going to a distant place to gain perspective was not, for Foucault, a simple matter of expanding his point of view, but rather of dislodging himself from normalized modes of thought, of moving into a foreign space, a former colony, where self and other interrelate clearly through economies of power. As Foucault would explain this spatial turn later in an interview on "Questions of Geography": "Metaphorizing the transformations of discourse in a vocabulary of time necessarily leads to the utilization of the model of individual consciousness with its intrinsic temporality. Endeavoring on the other hand to decipher discourse through the use of spatial, strategic metaphors enables one to grasp precisely the points at which discourses are transformed in, through, and on the basis of relations of power" (69–70). The unitary evolutionary narrative that formed the basis of colonial discourse is replaced by an analysis of the multiple forces at work in a colonized space. As Fanon argued in *The Wretched of the Earth*:

> The colonial world is divided into compartments. It is probably unnecessary to recall the existence of native quarters and European quarters, of schools for the natives and schools for Europeans; in the same way we need not recall apartheid in South Africa. Yet if we examine closely this

> system of compartments, we will at least be able to reveal the lines of force it implies. This approach to the colonial world, its ordering and its geographical layout will allow us to mark out lines on which a decolonized society will be reorganized. (37–38)

Both Fanon and Foucault were interested in the revolutionary potential of an analysis of human affairs through the lens of spatial metaphors, but neither argued that they were replacing a lying discourse with a true one. Fanon commented that "the problem of truth ought also to be considered. In every age, among the people, truth is the property of the national cause. . . . The native replies to the living lie of the colonial situation by an equal falsehood" (50). Fanon's concern was to replace the alienating and pathogenic context of colonial relations with an affirming one, recognizing that reactive violence to counteract oppressive violence was one temporary moment of truth in this effort focused on decolonization, and eventually dis-alienation.

Foucault's innovative approaches to spatial politics were connected, as we shall see, to his immersion in the politics of struggle and marginalization. While Foucault was living in Tunis, he wrote a lecture on the topic of space in which he developed the concept of heterotopias, "Des espaces autres," and which he delivered in Paris to a group of architects (March 1967). Around the same time, he delivered a lecture in Tunis at the Club Tahar Haddad (4 February 1967) in which he outlined ideas that anticipated *The Archeology of Knowledge*: "Structuralism was not, he argued . . . a 'philosophy,' but the sum of attempts being made to analyze the 'documentary mass' constituted by all the signs, traces and marks which humanity had left behind it and with which it continued to surround itself" (Macey, *Lives* 190). Foucault replaces the temporal focus (history) with the spatialized idea of archaeology. Rather than focusing on "continuities, traditions, influences, causes, comparisons, typologies," Foucault will use this idea of archaeology to locate the *differences* between various epochs of consciousness: "The conventional historian's interest in continuities, Foucault maintains, is merely a symptom of what he calls 'temporal agoraphobia,' an obsession with *filled* intellectual spaces. It is just as legitimate, and therapeutically more salutary of the future of the human sciences, to stress the discontinuities in Western man's thought about his own being-in-the-world" (White, *Tropics*, 234; emphasis added).

This move into synchrony puts Western thought cheek by jowl with the ways other cultures fill their intellectual spaces. Foucault, in his "Introduction" to *The Order of Things* discusses the Jorge Luis Borges' account of the taxonomy of animals found in a Chinese Encyclopedia, *The Heavenly Emporium of Benevolent Knowledge*; categories include: "(a) belonging to the Emperor, (b) embalmed, (c) tame, (d) sucking pigs, (e) sirens, (f) fabulous, (g) stray dogs,

(h) included in the present classification, (i) frenzied, (j) innumerable, (k) drawn with a very fine camelhair brush, (l) *et cetera*, (m) having just broken the water pitcher, (n) that from a long way off look like flies" (xv). Foucault's commentary on this taxonomy puts aside the usual focus on "filled intellectual spaces," in this case the "exotic charm of another system of thought," and homes in on the aporias of Western taxonomy—"the stark impossibility of thinking *that*" (xv). By focusing on synchronic relationships, Foucault can identify the discontinuities between intellectual systems, as well as within them: this spatial rereading is most often ironic as it defamiliarizes data previously "figured" as familiar. This process doesn't move us away from figuration as the way human consciousness makes sense of the world, nor does it replace temporal patterns with spatial ones, rather it brings the two systems into a dialectic and refocuses our attention on the "positivities," which we create as we try to establish meaning, and on the interstices that call these "positivities" into question.

For example, Foucault directs our attention, at the end of *The Order of Things*, to the norms through which men function, the rules that shape their experience and their needs, the systems that presuppose what they are able to signify. He singles out ethnology and psychology/psychoanalysis as the human sciences most likely to reveal unstable ironies:

> Ethnology, like psychoanalysis, questions not man himself, as he appears in the human sciences, but the region that makes possible knowledge about man in general; like psychoanalysis, it spans the whole field of that knowledge in a movement that tends to reach its boundaries. . . . The privilege of ethnology and psychoanalysis . . . must not be sought, therefore, in some common concern to pierce the profound enigma, the most secret part of human nature; in fact, what illuminates the space of their discourse is much more the historical a priori of all the sciences of man—those great caesuras, furrows, and dividing lines which traced man's outline in the Western episteme and made him a possible area of knowledge. It was quite inevitable, then, that they should both be sciences of the unconscious: not because they reach down to what is below consciousness in man, but because they are directed towards that which, outside man, makes it possible to know, with a positive knowledge, that which is given to or eludes his consciousness. (378)

Foucault draws our attention to inclusions and exclusions (boundaries), to standard discourses and their omissions (furrows), and to aporias (caesuras) that mark out particular ways of knowing. These two sciences, aimed at isolating what is "specific, irreducible, and uniformly valid wherever [man] is given to experience" turn out rather to do the opposite, to be "counter-sciences." They are counter-sciences because they "dissolve man"; they "go backwards towards that which foments his positivity"; in the end, "they ceaselessly 'unmake' that very man who is creating and re-creating his positivity in the human sciences" (379). Ethnology is generally conceived of as the science of the Other, of differences. Psychoanalysis could be thought of as the quintessential European science that focuses on the Self, on identity, on the creation of samenesses. Both have focused on positivities that were traditionally essentialized and individualized in a very parochially Western form. The "rise of literary criticism" mentioned by Rorty is part of this undoing of grand colonial narratives. We could think of the counter-sciences as taking us to an analysis of social imaginaries, those culturally specific sets of assumptions that "go without saying" which create "positivities" that could have been constructed otherwise.

The Social Turn

> Truth isn't the reward of free spirits, the child of protracted solitude. . . . Truth is a thing of this world: it is produced only by virtue of multiple forms of constraint. And it induces regular effects of power.
>
> —Michel Foucault, *Power/Knowledge*

Foucault himself, while living in Tunisia 1966–1968, was immersed in the political realm as he was drawn into the student protests that erupted, in an atmosphere of labor unrest, state repression, and the antisemitic riots that broke out around the 1967 Israeli–Arab War (Amin 200). Foucault later noted in an interview: "For those young people, Marxism did not really represent a mode of analyzing reality; it was at the same time a kind of moral energy, an existential act. . . . For me Tunisia in a sense represented an opportunity to reinsert myself into the political debate" (qtd. in Macey, *Lives* 204). The experience of dislocation, of coming face to face with otherness, revealed the heretofore unconscious geography of home: "[Foucault] used his distance from France while working in a postcolonial state the better to develop an ethnological perspective on French culture. Ethnology, for Foucault, was only useful as a study of one's own culture: he regarded its use for the study of other cultures, as in anthropology, as fundamentally misconceived" because ethnology is, "the exercise of a kind of comparative homology between cultures, one based on their all being made to conform to a fundamental Western model" (Young, *Postcolonialism* 396). Foucault noted at the end of *The Order of Things*: "There is a certain position of the Western *ratio* that was constituted in its history and provides a foundation for the relation it can have with all other societies. . . .

Obviously, this does not mean that the colonizing situation is indispensable to ethnology . . . but . . . ethnology can assume its proper dimensions only within the historical sovereignty—always restrained, but always present—of European thought and the relation that can bring it face to face with all cultures as well as with itself" (Foucault, *Order* 377; Young, *Postcolonialism* 396). The shift Foucault makes between *The Order of Things* and *Archeology of Knowledge* is one that complicates alterity, earlier understood either as the objective history of the silenced, putative counter-narratives, or as their subjective experience of the effects of colonialism and domination.

Foucault's focus on discourse is "directed away from any form of textualism, textual idealism, texts as disembodied artifacts, or intertextuality, toward a concept of the materiality of language in every dimension:

> A discourse . . . is primarily the way in which a knowledge is constituted as a part of a specific practice whose knowledge is formed at the interface of language and the material world . . . knowledge is not contained discursively, but exists at the edge between language and the rest of material reality. Discourse is a border concept, a transcultural practice that crosses intellectual and physical boundaries, both because in practical terms knowledge in discourse will be part of everyday practices, and because material conditions will also operate on the conceptual formation of knowledge. (Young, *Postcolonialism* 398–399)

The social turn that Foucault takes here, turning away both from a focus on individuals and their "private" minds and from social science positivities such as "man," and toward interactions and social practice, is mirrored across the human sciences.[16] Indebted to and building upon Foucault's "social turn," Edward Said argued for the "worldliness" of writers and texts, locating them materially out in the world.[17] Said demonstrated repeatedly the ways texts concerning the Middle East and North Africa have operated in, shaped, and been shaped by their larger environment, how private lives and public culture are politically intertwined.

Exploring the notion of the social nature of what we may consider our own private, individual thoughts, Charles Taylor published an essay entitled "Modern Social Imaginaries" in the journal *Public Culture* in 2002 (expanded to a book-length study by the same title in 2004). Taylor's essay, like his earlier "Two Theories of Modernity," was part of an ongoing discussion of "modernity" in the West and of "alternative modernities" in a global frame at the onset of the twenty-first century. Taylor, like Foucault, recognized the unstable ironic ground of the human sciences and focused on the "interface of language and the material world." As indicated at the beginning of this chapter, Taylor argued, "the social imaginary is not a set of ideas; rather it is what enables, through making sense of, the practices of a society" (*Modern Social Imaginaries* 91). The social imaginary of any given group of people is complex. It is enacted through practices and institutions that are real without being necessary—that is, they express relationships that could have been conceived of and enacted otherwise. As Taylor notes, any given social imaginary provides an unstructured, inarticulate background to social practices:

> I am thinking of the ways in which people imagine their social existence, how they fit together with others, how things go on between them and their fellows, the expectations that are normally met, and the deeper normative notions and images that underlie these expectations.
>
> I want to speak of social imaginary here, rather than social theory, because there are important—and multiple—differences between the two. I speak of imaginary because I'm talking about the way ordinary people "imagine" their social surroundings, and this is often not expressed in theoretical terms; it is carried on in images, stories, and legends . . . the social imaginary is that common understanding that makes possible common practices and a widely shared sense of legitimacy. . . .
>
> It incorporates a sense of the normal expectations we have of one another, the kind of common understanding that makes up our social life. This incorporates some sense of how we all fit together in carrying out the common practice. This understanding is both factual and "normative"; that is, we have a sense of how things usually go, but this is interwoven with an idea of how they ought to go, of what missteps would invalidate the practice. ("Modern Social Imaginaries" 106)

The social imaginary, to the extent that it grounds a people in shared, specific practices, suggests that identity is largely social in nature as is a sense of appropriate moral order. It sets a frame not just for what was, is, or should be, but for what is possible. In the case of the texts and events studied in *Of Irony and Empire*, the social imaginaries of the colonized did not disappear when the colonizers arrived. Nor did the Western social imaginary, which was part and parcel of the act of colonization, end when colonial settlements disappeared. Rather they have been drawn into a complex relationship and are acted out in everyday practices and global institutions, resulting in alternative modernities that may define themselves against one another as well as within the historical scope of their own traditions. Examining the social imaginaries at work in the production and reception of texts from Muslim Africa is, then, not just about recuperating past moments or understanding a present one, but about envisioning a future.

Modernity and Its Malcontents

The nineteenth-century Western modernity so closely associated with colonialism has generally been defined as having two faces. As a political philosopher, Taylor describes modernity as a mixture of technical prowess and emotional malaise, as an "historically unprecedented amalgam of new practices and institutional forms (science, technology, industrial production, urbanization), of new ways of living (individualism, secularization, instrumental rationality)," on the one hand, "and of new forms of malaise (alienation, meaninglessness, a sense of impending social dissolution)" on the other ("Modern Social Imaginaries" 91). Rita Felski, a literary critic, in *The Gender of Modernity* highlights the self-contradictory social imaginary that underpinned Western modernity. As she notes, critics have described modernity as double-sided: on the one hand, modernity arises out of a culture of "stability, coherence, discipline and world-mastery," and on the other, it points to a "discontinuous experience of time, space and causality as transitory, fleeting and fortuitous"; for some writers (Matthew Arnold, for example), it involves a "rational, autonomous subject" and an "absolutist, unitary conception of truth," and for others (Charles Baudelaire, for example), it is a "culture of rupture," marked by historical relativism and ambiguity (11). To be modern is to be on the side of progress, reason, and democracy or, by contrast, to align oneself against this bourgeois order by embracing "'disorder, despair and anarchy.' Indeed, to be modern is often paradoxically to be antimodern, to define oneself in explicit opposition to the prevailing norms and values of one's own time" (11). For John Comaroff, an ethnographer, this social imaginary has been conceptualized in terms of its colonizing ethos: "'modernity' has classically been measured in terms of universalist criteria. Its teleology has always involved the removal of difference, the erasure of relativizing systems of value and knowledge in the cause of world historical processes of rationalization. Hence the almost millennial faith, across all the grand theoretical traditions, in the inevitable demise of cultural localism" (162). Despite the conservative prediction by historian Francis Fukuyama that we've reached the "end of history," Comaroff notes, "there seems to be little doubt that ethnic and nationalist struggles—in fact, identity politics *sui generis*—are (re)making the history of our age with a vengeance. . . . The explosive vitality of ethnic and nationalist consciousness has played havoc with the confident prediction—from left, right, and center—that cultural pluralism would wither away in the late twentieth century" (162). At the onset of the twenty-first century, alternative modernities, and the competing social imaginaries in which they are grounded, have led to a series of new debates concerning secularism, human rights, recognition, and justice. The ontological experience of being "the colonized" is an experience of distance—

from oneself, one's community, one's oppressor. The ontological experience of being the oppressor, though perhaps belatedly, is also a matter of acknowledging distance, thus postcolonial critics focus on the rhetoric of ambiguity, anxiety, or disavowal.

"Irony," Fanon argued quoting Jankélévitch, "is one of the forms good conscience assumes"; irony "is a defense mechanism against neurosis" protecting the colonized self from the morbidity of colonial social relations (*Toward the African Revolution* 19). Health lies in a rhetorical approach to experience that allows the "colonized" to reject the "thingification" thrust upon them.[18] Paul de Man, who looks at irony through Baudelaire's critique of the aesthetics of modern life, focuses on the jarring alienation of self-conscious thought that is intra-subjective, dividing an empirical self immersed in daily life from a reflective self existing primarily in language, the pronominal I serving as an inauthentic and unstable unity. Given this more privileged lens of continental malaise, de Man notes: "When contemporary French philosopher V. Jankélévitch entitled a book on irony *L'ironie ou la bonne conscience*, he certainly was far removed from Baudelaire's conception of irony—unless, of course, the choice of the title was itself ironic" (*Blindness and Insight* 214–215). Aligning oneself against the bourgeois order and longing to get "anywhere out of this world," be it through dreaming the exotic while jumping ship at Mauritius and returning to Paris as Baudelaire did, or heading for the colonies and becoming a gun-runner in Abyssinia as Rimbaud did, involves an ironic distancing that bears little comparison with the alienation engendered by colonial relations. Jankélévitch's "good conscience" is a healthy form of moral perception that allows the self to maintain a distance from a reified self. Perhaps the anguish de Man associates with Baudelaire's style of irony is not caused by a distance from self but rather by the inability to maintain that distance from its object—the self. For Jankékévitch, as for Fanon, irony is the enemy of illusion, not the enemy of commitment or empathy. Irony is prophylactic; it protects the colonized from taking the *mission civilisatrice* at face value. Irony also gives us that distance from ourselves, that awareness of the central role performance has in our lives, that allow us to expand our own imagination and to believe enough in the power of transformation to work in solidarity with others.

Human Rights, Secularism, and Recognition: The Importance of Being Ironic

> Secularism is the sacred cow of modernity. It is a revered but unexamined doctrine that has come to mean all things to all men. For the humanist it represents an ideology of tolerance and pluralism;

> for the liberal it denotes the sociology of modernity; the Christian sees in it, somewhat perplexedly, an ecumenical vision of unity; the political scientist construes it as a theory of public order, while the marginalized non-Westerner dismisses it as a stratagem for Western dominance, the fundamentalist condemns it as an idolatry of the state, and the believer curses it for incarnating the lie of atheism!
>
> —Islamic Forum [Online] Review of William Connolly's *Why I am not a Secularist*

> Joha often entertained himself by getting on his old donkey and going to visit neighboring villages. During one trip, he lost his favorite copy of the Qur'an.
>
> He was sitting relaxing under a palm tree in the oasis two weeks later when a goat walked up to him with the Qur'an in its mouth. Joha was astonished. He gently removed his Qur'an from the goat's mouth, and lifting his eyes to the heavens, he exclaimed, "A miracle! Hear ye, hear ye! A miracle!"
>
> "Hardly," said the goat. "Your name is written on the inside cover."

The discourse of rights in Western modernity developed in a way that married equality to exclusion. This social contract, based on false universals, had embedded within it privileged categories of gender, race, and religion. Secularism is sacrosanct for Western modernity because it appears to be a "universal" category, in the sense that it is a necessary component to any serious discussion of international human rights. Those looking at secularism from the perspective of alternative modernities see it as the outcome of a specifically Western cultural context, which is not universal in its assumptions and practices, and which in fact often is caught in the irony of not recognizing its own provincial roots.

As Charles Taylor sees it, the forms of social imaginary that undergirded the rise of Western modernity implied a new moral order, one embodied in seventeenth-century Natural Law:

> The picture of society is that of individuals who come together to form a political entity against a certain preexisting moral background and with certain ends in view. The moral background is one of natural rights; these people already have certain moral obligations toward each other. The ends sought are certain common benefits, of which security is the most important. . . .
>
> In the next three centuries, from Locke to our present day, although the contract language may fall away and be used by only a minority of theorists, the underlying idea of society as existing for the (mutual) benefit of individuals and the defense of their rights takes on more and more importance. (*Modern Social Imaginaries* 4)

This move from an allegorical system based on transcendent religion to one grounded in organic metaphors of growth and maturation led to modes of *this-worldly* narration: the myth of progress; the story of revolution involving a decisive break with older forms that impede or distort the moral order; birth of a nation narratives in which a people "presides over its own political birth" (176).

A human rights discourse implying radical equality was embedded in the secular logic of the French Revolution as well. As the "Bible" of colonial law, *Principes de colonisation et de législation coloniale* by Arthur Girault, explained: "The Revolution had established the equality of all Frenchmen, and the rights which it proclaimed were in its thought the same for all men without distinction of latitude. What could have been more natural . . . ?" (qtd. in Lewis, 134). Girault's text went through six editions between 1895 and 1943, its final version being published in Paris under Nazi occupation. The radical equality of rights has been traced back to the *philosophes* and to Condorcet's claim that "a good law is good for all men, just as a sound logical proposition is sound everywhere" (134–135). Of course, the ironies of situation that gave the lie to this abstract logic abounded: slaves, emancipated by the 1794 Convention, which declared "all men resident in the colonies, without distinction of color, are French citizens and enjoy all the rights assured by the Constitution," were reenslaved under Napoleon I (134–135); Napoleon III in a report from 1858 referred to indigenous Algerians as "an armed and mettlesome nationality which we must extinguish by assimilation," but five years later was declaring: "Algeria is not a colony, but an Arab kingdom . . . I am as much Emperor of the Arabs as of the French" (135).

One problem with this Western narrative of bringing moral order to fruition is that it involves a struggle that was and is, unfortunately, not limited to the Western sites where it originated. It is a moral order that is imperialist in its operations, as Taylor explains:

> But there is also an extension of the imaginary in space. . . .
>
> If we now bring in civility or civilization in its other sense, not as a way of distinguishing one large cultural complex from another, but in the normative sense that contrasts with savagery or barbarism, we can say that in modern times, Europe has often seen itself not only or so much as Christendom, but as the main repository of civilization. And this sense of a supranational order has itself been gradually transformed over the centuries, until one of its principal defining characteristics has come to be democratic rule and respect for human rights. The modern moral order has colonized our understanding of this widest context of all. Since the European state system formed the basis of its extension into a world system, the order has been imaginatively expanded to include all the (properly behaved) members of the global community. (*Modern Social Imaginaries* 178–179)

Secularism, democracy, and human rights operate as rhetorical "universal" categories that often, ironically enough, become reinventions of the nineteenth-century's *mission civilisatrice.*

"Modernity is secular," Taylor notes, "not in the frequent, rather loose sense of the word, where it designates the absence of religion, but rather in the fact that religion occupies a different place, compatible with the sense that all social action takes place in profane time" (194). Thus we might say that secularism is a politically negotiated, dialectically malleable arrangement by which social space is divided between secular and religious activities. "Secularism is incomprehensible without religion," William D. Hart argues in *Edward Said and the Religious Effects of Culture*; "it is often an aspect of religion and always a product of a religious culture" (161). Said invents what he calls "secular criticism" because he defines theological thinking as doctrinaire and dogmatic (whether we are talking about the seminary or the academy). The secular is defined as a sort of corrective to the religious. Said sees "religion as dogmatic, deferential to authority, otherworldly, subservience-compelling, and violence-producing" (45).[19] Hart notes how Said proceeds by ironic reversals of the tropes of Christian discourse as he seeks a form of cultural critique that would avoid the dual pitfalls of the otherworldliness of religion and the ivory tower of textuality:

> Said "tropes" on an important theme in Christian discourse, where worldliness signifies an order that is in open rebellion against the Christian God. . . . Worldliness signifies "this worldliness," secular hopes, secular forms of solace, secular forms of meaning. . . . Said inverts the normative codes of the worldly—otherworldly distinction, with worldly as a positively charged term for a secular disposition and otherworldly as a negatively charged term for a religious disposition. Otherworldliness is characterized by a flight from circumstantial realities that constrain interpretation, provide a referent, and confer meaning. (155)

Rather than accepting this simple reversal, which opposes secularism to religion, Hart argues more attention should be given to "how religion and politics are articulated, how they actually fit together or do not fit together under specific historical conditions" (38).

In fact, Said does consistently provide a nuanced context in his discussions of Islam as an identity and a history of ideas. Hart is puzzled by Said's defense of Islam, given that he is not Muslim. Amin Malak notes that we need to remember that in his treatment of Islam

> Said [was] simply arguing for a sense of fair play when he observed that most of the Orientalists monopolized the power of describing Islam in their own terms and according to their own agendas. His represents the

> Voltairian stance: the fair-minded intellectual may not agree with another's viewpoint but is willing to die to defend the other's right to express that viewpoint. Moreover, as an uprooted Palestinian, Said is quite aware that the majority of his people espouse a religion that is not unusual to see maligned at various levels of Western discourse, which assumed, in some quarters a brazenly Islamophobic tone in the aftermath of the atrocious attack of September 11, 2001. . . .
>
> Thus as "a Christian who is culturally a Muslim" [as Anouar Majid argues (*Unveiling Traditions* 28)], Said's commitment to Islam is at once sincere, secular, and strategic: his erudite, enthusiastic discourse has been instrumental in unmasking the subtle and not-so-subtle slurs that seem to permeate various levels of Euro-American political, social, literary, and scholarly descriptions of Muslims. (4–5)

Religious histories that are culturally specific shape the social imaginaries of all of us, whether or not we practice, whether or not we are believers. Our notions of the fair and the ethical—central concepts in our views of human rights and the politics of recognition—emerge from a background that combines the religious and the secular.

Some argue that the secular Western nation-state is built upon a situational irony: on the one hand, the nation-state is predicated on the ideals of the French revolution and on the universalist claims of Enlightenment rationalism (including the privatization of religion); on the other, the launching of its industrial revolution and its need for expanding capitalist markets to fuel growth, led to its means (capitalist expansion) undercutting its stated ends (liberty, fraternity, equality). Stanley Tambiah has argued in "The Nation-State in Crisis and the Rise of Ethnonationalism,"

> It is relevant to consider that the other side of the Western model of the secular nation-state is its aggressive nationalism, and its imperialist expansion and penetration into what became its colonial dependencies. So it would seem that the liberal democracy at home in Western Europe and the United States could assume the fierce shape of authoritarian rule abroad, the exploitation of native labor and resources and the inferiorization, if not erosion, of the cultures of the colonized. This inferiorization and threat of cultural extinction in large part impels the rise of Islamic fundamentalism . . . and [its] taking a retaliatory attitude to the West—its exercise of economic influence and domination, its political supremacy, its alleged consumerist values, its celebration of sexual eroticism, its erosion of family durability, and so on. (126–127)

In Tambiah's view, ethnonationalism stems, in part, from regional or subregional reactions and resistances to hegemonic states (whether local or foreign).

It also is an outcome of the desire of groups to organize their own sociopolitical formations (128–129). And finally, ethnonationalism stems from the social rejection of "the relegation of religion to the private domain and [earnest commitment] to the idea that religious values and beliefs must necessarily inform politics and economic activities" (130).

Similar to Herder's view of *Volksgeist*, Tambiah sees ethnonationalism as tapping into a social imaginary, not as a reactionary retreat into tribalism or blood loyalties—what he refers to as the "primordialism thesis" popular with some Western scholars. Nor is ethnonationalism explained by the invention of tradition, or by the idea of imagined communities, (the "instrumentalist and constructivist perspective") both of which are too shallow to account for the enduring power of ethnonationalism (139–140). Ethnic behaviors emerge through socialization and participation in a social imaginary; they are not just constructed and essentialized (or imagined and traditionalized) but rather "are inscribed and imprinted simultaneously in our minds and bodies as patterns of ideas and sentiments":

> These inscriptions take effect through the practices of unmarked daily domestic life as well as marked calendrical festivals . . . and rituals of life and death. They take effect through the practices, preferences, and aesthetic valuations related to naming systems and kin terms, cuisine, costume . . . gender relations, courtship customs and marriage preferences, life cycle stages such as initiations, puberty ceremonies, marriages, and funerals as public events. And let us not leave out house styles, the ordering of domestic space, and furnishings.
>
> Let me also remark in this context that recognition of ethnicity may relate not only to the easily recognizable physical features of skin color, hair, eyes, and so on but also to the more subtle telltale evidence of body movements and gestures while walking, speaking, relaxing, dancing, even sleeping. (140–141)

Tambiah has moved here to those assumptions and behaviors that go without saying and that inscribe and reinscribe relations of identity in a community: "Ethnic communities are not merely imagined communities; more vitally, they are participatory communities . . . the local worlds which produce and reproduce . . . sensibilities" (142). The social imaginary is the way we make sense of the relations between tradition and modernity, religion and secularism, historically particular political systems and universal human rights.

The West, like other regions, has struggled to make theology consonant with modernity, and like other regions has faced a fundamentalist counter movement. Progressive interpretations of religion are not limited to the West. However, it is important to highlight the fact that other regions have had the added dimension of direct or indirect control by colonizing powers to deal with, as Ataullah Siddiqui explains in *Christian-Muslim Dialogue in the Twentieth Century*: "Muslims faced the challenge of epistemology and the reinterpretation of Islamic theology on the one hand, and the political and economic control of the Western Powers, who had drastically changed the social fabric of their societies, on the other" (4). In the aftermath of colonialism, the secular ideology central to Western modernism has been critiqued by non-Western societies for the ways this ideology has undermined human rights rather than securing them.

In the West, response to this critique has often been reductive, seeing it as simply an expression of fundamentalist views that pose a threat to human rights. As Anouar Majid comments with reference to John Esposito's *The Islamic Threat*: "At a time when the reigning ideology of capitalism has desacralized all of human life for the sake of destructive acquisitiveness, the need to open up noncapitalist spaces is more urgent than ever. The insistence on establishing an alternative social imaginary makes Islam appear as the perennial threat it has always been, especially since it has become quite clear that the nationalist secularist model of the postindependence period has utterly failed to emancipate the people and is now seen as a dismal failure" (*Unveiling Traditions*, 118).[20] Majid is examining here the idea that from perspectives outside the Western social imaginary, secularism itself is sometimes seen as a form of epistemological imperialism. This perspective has been most thoroughly argued by Abdulwahab Al-Masseri who finds a close link between the Western philosophies of democratic government, *laissez-faire* economics, rationalism and enlightenment-style humanism and an imperialist vision that would dominate the world. That is, imperialism and its crimes are not an aberration in an otherwise humane system, rather they are its logical outcome (403). The threads that weave the seamy underside of Western epistemology to its more attractive designs are individualism, a Hobbesian view of human nature as based on conflict, faith in progress along with a denial of the cost of that same "progress" (406). For Al-Masseri, secularism is not separation of Church and State but rather loss of connection to the other, be it nature, other humans, or the believing self:

> Secularism is not the separation between religion and the state, as propagated in both Western and Arab writing. Rather, it is the removal of absolute values—epistemological and ethical—from the world such that the entire world—humanity and nature alike—becomes merely a utilitarian object to be utilized and subjugated. From this standpoint, we can see the structural similarity between the secular epistemological vision and the imperialist epistemological vision. We can also realize that

> imperialism is no more than the exporting of a secular and epistemological paradigm from the Western world, where it first emerged, to the rest of the world. (403)

The difficulty with "absolute values," of course, is that human access to this repository of truth is ambiguous. Al-Masseri's essay limits itself to a critique of secular Western imperialist epistemologies, rather than going on to lay out alternative non-Western epistemologies. Al-Masseri sees Western imperialist philosophy as culminating in philosophies such as Nietzsche's "will to power" (406–407), but the thoroughly unironic speech acts of George W. Bush—"God loves you, and I love you. And you can count on both of us as a powerful message that people who wonder about their future can hear" (Weisberg)—make one a bit nostalgic for the ironic clarity of "God is Dead."

Rorty, in *Contingency, Irony and Solidarity*, takes the opposite tack to discover where truth lies, locating truth in contingent language—"only sentences can be true, and . . . human beings make truths by making languages in which to phrase sentences" (9)—and grounding human rights in liberal institutions. These philosophical constructions seem to be built on equally shaky ground. Rorty tells us: "I should like to replace both religious and philosophical accounts of a suprahistorical ground or an end-of-history convergence with a historical narrative about the rise of liberal institutions and customs—the institutions and customs that were designed to diminish cruelty, make possible government by the consent of the governed, and permit as much domination-free communication as possible to take place" (68). One of the outcomes of liberal institutions has been a human rights discourse, as codified in documents such as the Universal Declaration of Human Rights and the various United Nations conventions concerning racial discrimination, discrimination against women, and the rights of children, which has itself been critiqued for its false universalism. This discourse is an extension of what was particular to the "Enlightenment, its reliance on decontextualized reason, as embodied in the language, ideas, diplomatic style, experience and rules of representation that originated in Western Europe," as Richard Falk has argued in his *Human Rights Horizons* (149). The result of this hegemonic extension of the West's social imaginary onto the rest in the human rights arena often manifests itself as a negation of other social imaginaries, a "geopolitics of exclusion":

> We are in the midst of a period in international history in which the normative architecture of international society has been increasingly expressed by reference to a human rights discourse that combines, somewhat confusingly, ethical, political, and legal perspectives; these perspec-

> tives are intertwined in various ways, but more in the form of claims, grievances, and practices than as binding rules and standards. To a large extent, this human rights discourse is unavoidably perceived, with varying degrees of justification and opportunism, as tainted by false universalism and as an expression of Western hegemony, one feature of which has been, and continues to be, the suppression of civilizational identity and difference—particularly Islam, which has historically been perceived as a threat by the West. (150)

The need for "normative adjustment" of the architecture of international society, such that human rights discourse would be reshaped to make "belated provision for intercivilizational participation on the basis of equality," and as a move "to legitimize world order by improving the procedures for intercivilizational participation by establishing better means for equitable civilizational representation in the main authority structures of the world" (such as having a permanent member of the security council from the Islamic world) is made clear by the double standards concerning human rights being practiced on the ground (153). Double standards are obvious in the wanton violation of Palestinian human rights by Israel, in reactions to human rights violations in Bosnia, Chechnya, and Kashmir "making it seem probable that if the identities of victim and perpetrator had been reversed, the international response would have been altered" (158). If we compare the level of aid given to white refugees fleeing European conflicts to that given black refugees fleeing sub-Saharan conflicts, we see the same double standards. The universalist discourse of human rights has, ironically, blocked the full recognition that those same rights must be based upon.

Recognition in this study is associated with the paradigm of reciprocal recognition that Frantz Fanon was developing based on his experience in North Africa. Critical of the shortcomings of Western theories and practices concerning human dignity, Fanon struggled to understand the social imaginaries of the Africans among whom he lived and worked. His early theorizing about lack of recognition as a form of oppression was developed in a European frame in *Black Skin, White Masks*:

> I am not merely the here-and-now, sealed into thingness. I am for somewhere else and for something else. I demand that notice be taken of my negating activity insofar as I pursue something other than life; insofar as I do battle for the creation of a human world—that is, of a world of reciprocal relations.
>
> He who is reluctant to recognize me opposes me. In a savage struggle I am willing to accept convulsions of death, invincible dissolution, but also the possibility of the impossible. (218)

Fanon seems indeed prescient as we struggle at the outset of the twenty-first century with the fact that "reciprocal recognition"—or in a larger sense what Falk referred to as the need for intercivilizational recognition—seems further away than ever before.

Falk, in fact, begins his chapter on Islam and the "geopolitics of exclusion" by noting that what is really interesting is not the lack of intercivilizational recognition, *per se*, but the astonishing vibrance of theories that feed the practice of nonrecognition: "In *Twilight of the Gods* Nietzsche insists that what makes Socrates interesting to the modern mind is not his thought or method, but the extraordinary societal significance for Athens of having taken so seriously such silly and banal ideas. Huntington's clash thesis can be regarded in a similar spirit. What is interesting about the piece is not the argument, as such, but its extraordinary resonance around the world. . . . It remains important to ask, "What is this resonance telling us?" (147).

In his assessments of Islam's grievances concerning the normative architecture of human rights institutions and practices (such as unequal participation in bodies like the U.N., double standards about human rights, a discriminatory nonproliferation regime for nuclear arms, punitive peace (Serbia vs. Iraq), policy making and participation in the world economy (e.g., no Islamic member in the Group of Eight), biased media treatment of terrorist incidents (e.g., reporting on the Oklahoma City bombing with quick attribution to Middle-Eastern suspects), undercutting of democratic elections if won by Islamic groups (Algeria 1992; Palestine 2006), Falk adds "unevenness of compassion": "media treatment of suffering in the Muslim world tends to be abstract, general, and scant, if given at all, and is dwarfed by repeated inquiry into the tactics and mentality of Islamic extremism. Little attention is given to understanding the moral and political pressures that might explain the desperation that induces such highly publicized extremist behavior" (161).

The power of Fanon's writing about Africa and about the psychology of oppression resides in his ability to bring to light the sociogenesis of suffering, and to bring to life the human voices of those caught in the violence. Analyzing Fanon's understanding of the social and historical roots of oppression and the need for intervention, psychiatrist Hussein Abdilahi Bulhan stresses the reality of suffering for Fanon. Fanon focused neither on the *whys* of oppression in an academic fashion as Hegel did in *Philosophy of Mind*, nor did he theorize in the absence of a concrete discussion of the material violence done by colonial institutions and practices as Octave Mannoni did in *Prospero and Caliban: The Psychology of Colonization*. Bulhan states:

> First and foremost, as Fanon pointed out, the problem of oppression is a problem of violence. The violence may be crude or subtle; often it is both. Yet it is this aspect of oppression that is most prone to confusion and mystification. This is so precisely because those who monopolize and benefit from violence find it convenient to obfuscate and mystify the meaning and reality of violence. They enlist the services of religion, the law, science, and the media to confound and bewilder even the oppressed who otherwise would recognize that the social order is founded on and permeated by violence. But this pervasive and structural violence is often masked and rationalized as the natural order of life. Thus there is "legitimate" and "illegitimate" violence—the former deriving legitimacy by use of superior force and convenient legal edicts, not by the actual consent of the oppressed.
>
> Those who monopolize and benefit from violence typically judge their violence as necessary, justified, for the good of all. Any exercise of self-defense to ward off the violence of the social order is viewed with alarm and considered illegitimate. The oppressed are permitted no right of self-defense, no due process of law. (120–121)

Where are we to locate the enactment of that reciprocal recognition that would shift the energies now being channeled into violence toward a more just world order? Can we, by locating the violence of empire and exploring its attendant ironies, begin to institute the practice of reciprocal recognition at the level of international relations, national politics, or personal psychology? We need to challenge the false universalism of globalization; we need to conceive of an "*intercivilizational* world order that combines the ecological and biological conditions of unity with the *civilizational* realities of difference and self-definition" (Falk 163; emphasis added). The misrecognition embodied in the "clash of civilizations" thesis is pathogenic, part of a larger destructive system. Anouar Majid argues in his recent *Freedom and Orthodoxy: Islam and Difference in the Post-Andalusian Age* that today "we are living under the dark cloud not of an ominous clash of civilizations, but of a world order racing headlong toward a global wasteland, an apocalyptic landscape that will ultimately engulf winners and losers alike" (vii):

> As the quest for freedom continues, Westerners and Muslims are called upon to make a valiant effort to resist the temptation to convert Others, to see Others as needing salvation or death. Those who blame Islam for being conservative need to understand how their own assumptions have fed that conservatism. Muslims must be lured out of their defensive orthodoxy by allowing them, as François Burgat suggested, to participate in a "consensual modernity" with truly universal dimensions, one that is not imposed in the name of false universality. (xiii)

But the presumption of equal worth is difficult to ground at a human, non-transcendent level where evidence of gross abuses of human dignity are so concrete and inequities so widespread.

Alienation and recognition are related but inverse ways of experiencing and constructing the world, and both are ironic modes. No one captured this dynamic better than Fanon who, while rejecting Hegel's transcendent dialectic, worked within the Hegelian view that "self-consciousness exists in and for itself when, and by the fact that, it so exists for another; that is, it exists only in being acknowledged" (Hegel 111). The essays in *Of Irony and Empire* analyze the dynamics of alienation and recognition among alternative social imaginaries as they have come into contact over the course of the twentieth century in Muslim Africa. Alienation, as Fanon defined it, is experienced in various modes: "(a) alienation from the *self,* (b) alienation from the *significant other*, (c) alienation from the *general other*, (d) alienation from one's *culture*, and (e) alienation from creative *social praxis*" (Bulhan 188). Reversing alienation, conceptualizing difference and sameness such that they foster empathy and respect, results in recognition: A (alienation) returns as non-A (recognition). Irony can employ as its operative goal either alienation or recognition. In his *A Grammar of Motives*, Burke puts it this way: "Irony is never Pharisaic, but there is a Pharisaic temptation in irony" (513). To illustrate the point, he quotes Allen Tate: "Mr. Tate characterizes irony as 'that arrangement of experience, either premeditated by art or accidentally appearing in the affairs of men, which permits to the spectator an insight superior to that of the actor'" (513–514). When irony works to locate the author or the reader outside of, and superior to the character he mocks, superior to the "enemy" (514), then he has given in to the Pharisaic. True irony, in Burke's view, is engendered by recognizing the other within the self:

> True irony, however, . . . is not "superior" to the enemy. . . . True irony, humble irony, is based upon a sense of fundamental kinship with the enemy, as one *needs* him, is *indebted* to him, is not merely outside him as an observer but contains him *within*, being consubstantial with him. (514)

Fanon claimed that "irony was one of the forms good conscience assumed" because irony can be both apotropaic, a "mechanism of defense against neurosis" by keeping us from taking the other or ourselves too seriously (*Toward the African Revolution* 19), and therapeutic in giving us, as Burke notes, that "sense of fundamental kinship with the enemy" (514).

CHAPTER TWO

African Conscripts/European Conflicts

Race, Memory, and the Lessons of War

> You Senegalese Soldiers, my black brothers with warm
> hands under ice and death
> Who can praise you if not your brother-in-arms, your
> brother in blood?
>
> I shall not let the words of government ministers nor
> generals,
> No! I shall not let the words of scornful praise secretly bury
> you.
> You are not empty-pocket poor men without honor
> But I will tear off the banania grins from all the walls of
> France
>
> —Senghor, "Liminary Poem"

In Henri Camus' 1917 black and white watercolor, *Tirailleur dans les barbelés* [*Tirailleur (infantryman) on barbed wire*], we see the isolated, distorted body of an African soldier hung up on a few strands of barbed wire and leaning posts (figure 1). Shot dead, his body arcs back, face toward the sky, one knee forever straddling the top wire. Behind him is the empty gray of no-man's-land, before him just the viewer. He is arrested forever in this hideous borderland. There is something uncanny about this African soldier suspended on the frontier between two cultures that are not his own, something that demands to be explained. Tracing Heidegger's idea that "a boundary is not that at which

FIGURE 1. Henri Camus, *Tirailleur dans les barbelés*, watercolor, 1917 (Musée d'Histoire Contemporaine—Bibliothèque de Documentation Internationale contemporaine: MHC-BDIC), *Images et Colonies (1880–1962)*, BDIC-ACHAC (Association Connaissance de l'Histoire de l'Afrique Contemporaine), 1993, 95.

something stops but . . . that from which something begins its presencing," Homi Bhabha notes that while "beginnings and endings may be the sustaining myths of the middle years . . . in the *fin de siècle*, we find ourselves in the moment of transit where space and time cross to produce complex figures of difference and identity, past and present, inside and outside, inclusion and exclusion" (*Location of Culture* 1). This African soldier, who would have been born at the end of the nineteenth century, and brought to die in Europe at the beginning of the twentieth century, begins his presencing as the figure of transit: Where did he come from? Who brought him to Europe? Why did he come? Whom did he leave behind? What did he experience? How was he treated? What is thc connection between this dead *tirailleur*, used as cannon fodder, and those commodified *tirailleurs* with banania grins, referred to by Senghor in the epigraph, used to advertise the French breakfast cereal *Banania*. What begins its presencing in the hideous borderland inhabited by the dead *tirailleur* is a demand that the distance between the discourse about the *tirailleur* and the reality of his dislocation and death be examined. And the beyond in this presencing is in the voice of this *tirailleur* himself.

The modern cataclysms embodied in World War I and World War II are remembered as examples of intra-European hatred that seemed, at the time, irreversible and irremediable. And yet these enemies have managed, time and again, to forgive and forget and unite with each other in order to turn on the perennial enemy: the cultural, racial other—the body on the barbed wire suspended in no-man's-land. This chapter deals with Western racial paradigms prevalent in Europe during the first half of the twentieth century, as they relate to the experience and representation of African soldiers forced to fight other people's battles in World Wars I and II. Brought in from places like Senegal, Ivory Coast, Morocco, Algeria, and Tunisia, these soldiers were conscripted into wars that were not their own, fighting for nations that extended to them the duty of defense, but denied them the rights of citizenship. These "colored" soldiers provided popular images for propaganda, and yet, like Ralph Ellison's invisible man, remained themselves largely unseen and unheard. Western writing about African involvement in these intra-European conflicts, as well as the personal narratives of Africans about conscription, combat, and demobilization, provide rich ground for the exploration of the odd hybridity of the situation of the colonized. These texts illustrate, on the one hand, how "the universalist narrative of nineteenth-century historical and political evolutionism" unraveled (Bhabha, "Signs Taken for Wonders" 172). On the other hand, they demonstrate the longevity of racial theories claimed to have disappeared with colonialism. This chapter explores the hybrid identity forced upon the colonial soldiers by the West and confronts it with these soldiers' own stories as they try to make sense of their experiences of World Wars I and II. In the first section, entitled "People without a Past are People without a Future," I draw comparisons between colonial and postcolonial epistemologies—the paradigms used to explain the dialectics of difference and identity, past and present, inclusion and exclusion—by reviewing nineteenth-century racial theories and tracing the ways they continued to operate in the twentieth century. In the next section, "The Banania Republic Needs You!" I look at the three stages of military involvement of African soldiers: conscription, combat, and demobilization. "Conscript" is used here to refer to both soldiers and workers brought to Europe during the war effort. Although some of these men were technically volunteers, the facts belie the discourse. The Africans were usually dragged into the war against their will.[1] The scope of this essay is limited to French colonial conscripts from North and West Africa, but it is clear that many other colonial peoples suffered similar circumstances during these wars. Finally, although the focus will be on the stories of the conscripts themselves, their stories suggest the tragic impact these wars had on the families and societies the conscripts were taken away from, an impact that is the boundary of yet another "presencing."

People Without a Past Are People Without a Future

The conscripted colonial soldiers were on the side of the victors, but were not among those who got the spoils: "they said nothing to us and they took everything," was the way one Ivory Coast veteran described the demobilization process run by the Allied forces at the end of World War II (Lawler 199). The veterans were supposedly among the winners, but not among those who wrote the history. As Eric Wolf describes this conspiracy of silence in his *Europe and the People Without History*, the people of sub-Saharan Africa were the "primitive contemporaries" of the colonizers, and so they were "treated as a people without a history of their own" (x) on the one hand. On the other, because the people of Muslim Africa have a history of challenging the West and could not believably be considered as "people without a history," they were seen instead as either mired in centuries of stagnation (Turner 67), or in the case of the more unruly southern bedouins, as "contemporary ancestors"—people who have not aspired to civilization and are defined by the colonial powers "by an absence of features, [they are] 'classless,' 'acephalous,' or 'stateless'" (Wolf 89).[2] For our purposes in this essay, the silences of history are threefold: the silence surrounding an indigenous past in the colonies, the misrepresentation of the historical relations between the colonizer and the colonized (centuries of contact, often brutal), and the silence of denial in the contemporary moment, as for example, in the erasure of the colonial conscripts' roles and perceptions as actors in World War I and World War II.

The danger in not exploring these silences is that the "people without a past" in the colonial era, have become the "people without a future" in the postcolonial world. In his 1992 study of the legacy of colonization in sub-Saharan Africa, *The Black Man's Burden: Africa and the Curse of the Nation-State*, Basil Davidson drew a comparison between "Balkanised" Central and Eastern Europe on the one hand, and Africa on the other, the Trojan horse of the nation-state left by the colonial powers in Africa being likened to the disastrous legacy of the Balkans. The most recent war in the Balkans, however, illuminates some of the crucial racialist paradigms that continue to structure global history and to separate Africa from Europe, Africans from Europeans. In an article in the *Los Angeles Times* (21 May 1999), "Relief Camps for Africans, Kosovars World Apart," relief workers who had traveled from war-torn places like Somalia, Eritrea, Liberia, and Rwanda to the refugee camps in Macedonia compared the treatment of African refugees to that of Balkan refugees: the U.N. High Commissioner for Refugees is "spending about 11 cents a day per refugee in Africa. In the Balkans, the figure is $1.23, more than 11 times greater" (Miller et al.). Although the largest camp in Macedonia holds 33,000 people, camps in Africa hold up to 500,000. Life isn't easy in any refugee camp, but the aid pouring into Balkan camps from Europe translates into clean water, basic sanitation, and tents for shelter. These minimal forms of aid help "to maintain the refugees' sense of dignity and stability" (Miller et al.). In Africa, up to 6,000 refugees die each day from cholera and other public health diseases, refugees often live out in the open, and scarce water can be limited to as little as a gallon or so a day for a family of up to 10 people. Some camps in Macedonia have 1 doctor/700 refugees; in Africa, some camps have as few as 1 doctor/100,000 refugees. Accounting for the disparity in resources, some officials and workers attribute it to culture—the higher standard of living in the Balkans, a CARE worker explained, translates into a need for a higher level of resources: "Life in Africa is far more simple. To maintain the dignity and lifestyle of Europeans is far more difficult"; however, and more to the point, a relief worker fresh into Macedonia from Sierra Leone explained it somewhat more simply: " What's the difference? There's white people here" (Miller et al.).[3]

Colonialism's Manichean Allegory

One of the lessons of war is that racial differences, even more than political disputes among racially homogenous first-world participants, emerge as defining the longer-term targets of hatred and enmity: race is the essential boundary between "us" and "them." The racial common denominator among those from the West matters more than other divisions like Allied versus Central Powers; Allied versus Axis Powers; liberal versus conservative; humanitarian versus exploiter. In his essay "The Economy of Manichean Allegory: The Function of Racial Difference in Colonialist Literature," Abdul R. JanMohamed defines the discursive practices of the "dominant" phase of colonialism (as opposed to the later "hegemonic" phase of neo-colonialism) as operating through the economy of the trope of the "manichean allegory," which, as noted earlier, transforms "racial difference into moral and even metaphysical difference" (80). The covert purpose of colonization—"to exploit the colony's natural resources thoroughly and ruthlessly through the various imperialist material practices" is disguised by "the overt aim, as articulated by colonialist discourse, [which] is to 'civilize' the savage, to introduce him to all the benefits of Western cultures" (81). The destruction of native legal and cultural systems as well as their traditional modes of production, combined with the European negation of the existence, let alone the value of non-European civilizations, produced pathological societies, "ones that exist in a state of perpetual crisis" (80).

The manichean allegory has at its core the "opposition between the putative superiority of the European and the supposed inferiority of the native" (82). During World War I and World War II, France distinguished itself from the other Western powers by bringing colonial conscripts onto French soil. The French reliance on African military conscripts,[4] African food production, and African conscripted labor to bail out a failing French war effort against the Germans, risked giving the lie to the discourse about "the putative superiority of the European and the supposed inferiority of the native." Efforts were made to contain these contradictions discursively. For example, references to "*nos frères musulmans*" [our Muslim brothers] suddenly started appearing in colonialist newspapers in Algeria in 1915 when settlers feared the indigenous people might well find it better to ally themselves with the Turks and Germans rather than with the French (Ageron 2: 254). Attempts to ensure the cooperation of the colonized also translated into draconian material practices (forced conscription combined with denial of French citizenship, censorship of mail sent home by conscripted African workers and soldiers, unequal pay and food).

In the early twentieth century, nothing revealed more dramatically the hideous downside of progress and development than the "Great War," which, as we recall, Paul Fussell argued, in *The Great War and Modern Memory*, highlighted the ironic disparity between Western discourse and brute reality. In time of war, there is an effort to draw clear lines between "us" and "them" and to force everyone to commit to one side or the other. There is a need to know who the enemy is. And yet this very act of demarcating boundaries also brings to the fore questions of criteria: how do we define "us" and on what grounds do we exclude those whom we label "them"?

Narratives of Evolutionism: Raced and Gendered

A detour into the racialized and gendered theories of "progress and civilization" at this point sheds some light on the extensiveness of these theories of embodied otherness, which the Enlightenment and nineteenth century bequeathed to the twentieth century. "The universalist narrative of nineteenth-century historical and political evolutionism" referred to earlier had its roots in Enlightenment thought and was exemplified during the period of the French Revolution by the 1794 declaration of the National Convention that "all men resident in the colonies, without distinction of color, are French citizens and enjoy the rights assured by the Constitution," and the further declaration in 1795 that the colonies were "integral parts of the Republic" (Lewis 134). One place where the outlines of this universalist narrative can be found is in Condorcet's *Sketch for a Historical Picture of the Progress of the Human Mind.* As Stuart Hampshire has observed, Condorcet, whose optimistic view of the progress and perfectibility of human nature within a rational scheme grounded in natural law greatly influenced Saint-Simon, Comte, and later, the French educational system itself, envisioned "universal education; universal suffrage; equality before the law; freedom of thought and expression; the right to freedom and self-determination of colonial peoples; the redistribution of wealth; a system of national insurance and pensions; equal rights for women" (Condorcet x). Condorcet traced ten stages of human progress that take us from stages one and two, where we find tribal and pastoral peoples who are benighted by superstition and barbarism, through the course of Western history to stages nine, "From Descartes to the founding of the French republic," and, lastly, ten, "the future progress of the human mind." This belief in the perfectibility of humankind would, in the nineteenth century, become linked to the view that evolution in the natural sciences found its scientifically grounded counterpart in cultural, moral, and economic progress in the human sciences. The human sciences themselves, as Edward Said points out in *Orientalism*, came into being as part and parcel of the colonial enterprise, as we see, for example, in Napoleon's *Description of Egypt* (42–43) and in the "knowledge industry" that developed around Oriental Studies as the discipline became institutionalized (190–191). Commenting on this connection between knowledge and power in the field of anthropology, Johannes Fabian writes:

> The use of Time in evolutionary anthropology, modeled on that of natural history, undoubtedly was a step beyond premodern conceptions. But it can now be argued that wholesale adoption of models (and their rhetorical expressions in anthropological discourse) from physics and

> geology was, for a science of man, sadly regressive intellectually, and quite reactionary politically. . . . Radical naturalization of Time (i.e., its radical dehistorization) was of course central to the most celebrated scientific achievement of that period, the comparative method, that omnivorous intellectual machine permitting "equal" treatment of human culture at all times in all places. (16–17)

Faith in progress and industry replaced the earlier Christian-medieval view of faith in salvation. The modern human sciences were linked to colonialism and imperialism in ways that were not just moral and ethical excuses but epistemological justifications:

> Anthropology contributed above all to the intellectual justification of the colonial enterprise. It gave to politics and economics—both concerned with human Time—a firm belief in "natural," i.e. evolutionary Time. It promoted a scheme in terms of which not only past cultures, but all living societies were irrevocably placed on a temporal slope, a stream of Time—some upstream, some downstream. Civilization, evolution, development, acculturation, modernization (and their cousins, industrialization, urbanization) are all terms whose conceptual content derives, in ways that can be specified, from evolutionary Time. They all have an epistemological dimension apart from whatever ethical, or unethical, intentions they may express. A discourse employing terms such as primitive, savage (but also tribal, traditional, Third World, or whatever euphemism is current) does not think, or observe, or critically study, the "primitive"; it thinks, observes, studies *in terms* of the primitive. *Primitive* being essentially a temporal concept, is a category, not an object, of Western thought. (17–18)

A similar epistemological point is made by Robert J. C. Young in his detailed study of hybridity, its genealogy, and its disavowal in nineteenth- and twentieth-century racialized thought. In *Colonial Desire: Hybridity in Theory, Culture and Race*, Young demonstrates that race and gender were categories tied to power and oppression rather than being specific objects of study in their own right: they were signs pointing to other concepts. Civilization itself was defined by these "marks" of race and gender. In the hierarchy of civilization,

> the cultivated white Western European male [was] at the top, and everyone else on a hierarchical scale of [evolutionary] development from a feminized state of childhood (savagery) up to full (European) manly adulthood. . . . Civilization and culture were thus the names for the standard of measurement in the hierarchy of values through which European culture defined itself by placing itself at the top of a scale against which

> all other societies, or groups within society, were judged. The principle of opposition, between civilization and barbarism or savagery, was nothing less than the ordering principle of civilization as such." (94–95)

For most colonialists in the late nineteenth and early twentieth centuries, this hierarchy, based on the idea of progress toward the apex of the pyramid, that is, European civilization, was severely threatened by the idea that those at the top might breed with those further down the evolutionary structure; especially heinous was the idea of miscegenation between white women and the colonized (Lorcin, *Imperial Identities* 210–211).

The outcome of miscegenation was argued over, producing views ranging from denial that different peoples could mix at all (despite the obvious facts "on the ground" throughout the colonial period) to the claim that maybe worn-out European civilization would find new vigor in mixing with peoples who were closer to nature (138). It goes without saying, of course, that this "new vigor" would involve the mixing of white men with indigenous women. Influential race theorists like Gobineau and Agassiz believed that a negative sort of amalgamation would result if peoples mixed; in their view miscegenation "produces a mongrel group that makes up a 'raceless chaos,' merely a corruption of the originals, degenerate and degraded, threatening to subvert the vigour and virtue of the pure races with which they had come into contact" (Young, *Colonial Desire* 18). Like the race theories of Renan and Cuvier, Arthur-Joseph de Gobineau's *Essai sur l'inégalité des races humaines* (first published in 1853–1855 in three volumes) was based on the idea that different races carried different tendencies in their blood.[5] In his scheme, the yellow race has a talent for common sense. The black race is endowed with an intensity of sensation, thus it is the source of all art. Gobineau is quick to point out, however, that even the strengths of the black race are really weaknesses, because Blacks are undiscriminating in their use of their senses, thus "the very strength of his sensations is the most striking proof of his inferiority" (*Inequality of the Human Races* 205). The white race has a talent for creating order (civilization) imbued with liberty. Gobineau's racial theory, while not particularly popular when he first published it, did gain a following after the defeat of France and the loss of Alsace-Lorraine in 1870.

We find in Gobineau's scheme that race, class, and sex are all correlated to serve as markers indicating the level of civilization one can hope to attain. Thus it is that the black race constitutes the lumpen proletariat of the world's peoples: "no negro race is seen as the initiator of a civilization" (212). The yellow race, on the other hand, are likened to a stable "middle class": "He has a love of utility and a respect for order, and knows the value of a certain amount of freedom. He is practical, in the narrowest sense of the word. He does not dream or theorize; he invents little, but can appreciate and take over what is useful to him" (206). As a result, "no spontaneous civilization is to be found among the yellow races" (212). Not surprisingly, Gobineau's hierarchy envisions the white race as the aristocracy of human kinds, gifted as they are with "reflective energy," "energetic intelligence," "a feeling for utility," "perseverance," "a greater physical power, an extraordinary instinct for order" and an "extreme love of liberty" (207).

Finally, in Gobineau's view, "every human activity, moral or intellectual, has its original source in one or the other of . . . two currents, 'male' and 'female'" (88). Nations then, belong to either male (instrumental, materialist) or female (imaginative) series. While Gobineau recognizes a certain need for racial mixing, he concludes: "The white race originally possessed the monopoly of beauty, intelligence, and strength. By its union with other varieties, hybrids were created, which were beautiful without strength, strong without intelligence, or, if intelligent, weak and ugly" (209).

Just where to rank the majority of the peoples of North Africa in this hierarchy created some difficulty. As Lorcin points out in her study of the Kabyle Myth, *Imperial Identities: Stereotyping, prejudice and race in colonial Algeria*, French colonizers spent a good deal of time and ink proving hypotheses based on the essentialist belief in "good" Berbers versus "bad" Arabs. During the nineteenth century, the connection between power and knowledge was quite literal: the military man and the scholar were one and the same.[6] For example, the prolific scholar Colonel Louis Rinn served in the Bureaux Arabes for twenty years (1865–1885) and then as governor-general of Algeria, was also vice-president of the Société Historique Algérienne and president of the Société Géographique d'Alger. Best known for his *Marabouts et khouan*, a study of Islam in Algeria, Rinn also studied the Berbers in depth, contributing a serialized piece to the *Revue africaine*. As Lorcin points out: "He concluded with the statement that 'the Berbers . . . were of the Indo-European race and language.' Using a theory derived from the Book of Genesis (Chapters 9 and 10) which attributed racial ancestry to the three sons of Noah—Japheth, Shem and Ham—Rinn claimed that the Berbers were descended from [Japheth]. According to Rinn's theory Japheth sired the white race, Shem the Asiatic and/or Semitic, and Ham the black" (qtd. In Lorcin, *Imperial Identities* 142).[7] Although many did not agree wholesale with Rinn's thesis, the ideas that the Berbers were white and had once been Christian were central to scholarship in the colony.

As for the Semites, they posed a thorny problem—they were white but not quite, as we see in the work of the influential polygenist, Ernest Renan, who turned to making discriminations among those who were Caucasian and civilized—"the civilized world only includes the Jews, Christians and Mussulmans" (*De la part des peuples sémitiques* 21). As Renan explained in a letter he wrote to Gobineau, in his view, a little miscegenation is not a bad thing—as long as it is going in the right direction: "In reality, a very small quantity of noble blood mixed into the circulation of a people is enough to ennoble it, at least as to its historical effects; thus it is that France, a country so completely fallen to a plebian level, in reality, out in the world, plays the role of the gentleman. Setting aside wholly inferior races, whose blending with the major races would only poison the human species, I foresee a future in which humanity is completely homogenous, where all the original tributaries mix into one great river" ("Letter" 204).

In Renan's view, the Aryan and the Semite are not physical races, but linguistic ones. In *L'Origine du langage*, Renan explains how the river of humanity he'd described to Gobineau would come about: "The Aryan race and the Semitic race, therefore, being destined to conquer the world and restore unity to the human species, the rest of the world only matters, alongside these races, as testing grounds, obstacles or auxiliaries" (114).

Gobineau saw the races rather as physically separate, and believed that interbreeding—even when it involved the daughters of the inferior race with the men of the superior one—would result in the degradation of the higher race. As he explained in his chapter on the "mutual repulsions of civilizations," we have historical evidence of this fact: "Civilization is not communicable, not only to savages, but also to more enlightened nations. This is shown by the efforts of French goodwill and conciliation in the ancient kingdom of Algiers at the present day, as well as by the experience of the English in India, and the Dutch in Java. There are no more striking and conclusive proofs of the unlikeness and inequality of races"(*Inequality of the Human Races* 171). We see, at this juncture, that the Enlightenment idea of the perfectibility of all humankind, has shifted to a hierarchy of races, and those at the bottom (black and yellow races) are seen as inherently incapable of progress and civilization. When Semitic races are included among the yellow race, then their barbarism is an inherent quality. When it is acknowledged that they have given rise to civilizations then they are seen as part of the white race, but a degenerate and lesser part of it: "the Aryans are to the other white races (that is, to Semites—Jews or Arabs) what the white race is to the other two races, namely the people destined to rule the world" (Todorov 149).

On a grimmer note, the first volume of Gobineau's *Essai* was translated into English in 1856 as *The Moral and Intellectual Diversity of Races* by Henry Hotze and Josiah Nott, both white supremacists of the pre–Civil War era who altered Gobineau's text to make it even more poisonous. In addition, Nott and George Gliddon, whose popular book *Types of Mankind: or, Ethnological Researches, Based upon Ancient Monuments* . . . had already seen eight editions by 1860 (Young, *Colonial Desire* 123), argued that the ancient Egyptians were Caucasian and that current inhabitants of Egypt and North Africa were of inferior races. As Nott explained his views in *Two Lectures on the History of the Caucasian and Negro Races*: "This adulteration of blood is the reason why Egypt and the Barbary States never can rise again, until the present races are exterminated, and the Caucasian substituted. Wherever in the history of the world the inferior races have conquered and mixed in with the Caucasian, the latter have sunk into barbarism" (qtd. in Young, *Colonial Desire* 129–130). To these racial hierarchies, late nineteenth-century racial theorist Gustave Le Bon added the evidence of his studies of craniology in *The Psychology of Peoples*, which supposedly proved that "white skulls were larger than black skulls—but only in men; male skulls were larger than female skulls—but only in whites" (Todorov 114). Thus, the weight of race and gender theory coming out of the nineteenth century held that embodied traits—blood and sex—dictated one's place on the evolutionary scale ranging from savagery to civilization. It is within this raced and gendered paradigm that the experience of colonial conscripts can best be understood.

The Banania Republic Needs You!

The manichean allegory that transformed racial difference into metaphysical and moral difference was reflected in the discourse of the *mission civilisatrice*. This discourse vaunted the benefits native peoples were said to enjoy thanks to their assimilation into or association with the French republic, while on the ground the brutal, material acts of colonization exploited native peoples, plundered their resources, and destroyed their cultural systems. When colonial conscripts were brought onto European soil during the period of the two World Wars, they personified the contradictions upon which this allegorical economy was founded. Popular imagery served as one way to contain the contradictions. Not welcome as full members of the French Republic, colonial conscripts were rather citizens of what I would call a Banania republic. At the very outset of World War I, the Senegalese infantryman was commodified in the advertising campaign for Banania, a drink made from banana flour, ground cereal, cacao, and sugar, "discovered" by journalist Pierre Lardet during a 1912 visit to Nicaragua ("Banania"). Lardet began producing *Banania* commercially in Paris in 1914 and quickly dumped the early advertising image of an Antillean woman for the Senegalese *tirailleur* so popular in France in 1915. Advertising copy claimed that Banania was "for our soldiers, the long-lasting nourishment they need, and which takes up the least amount of space." The product's slogan mimicked the African soldier's pidgin French, announcing "*Y'a bon*" [Sho' good eatin'].

For racial theorists like Gobineau, the realm of language mirrored the hierarchy of race: "when a language of a higher order is used by some human group which is unworthy of it, it will certainly become mutilated and die out" (Gobineau, *The Inequality of the Human Races* 204). Thus, the unremitting critique of the way colonial subjects spoke French was far from innocent fun. It rather suggested that colonial conscripts were not part of the nation, and that the nation, and its language, would degenerate if the colonized were assimilated into it. In "The Negro and Language," the first chapter of *Black Skins, White Masks*, Fanon describes the double bind of hybrid identities for the black French citizens of Martinique when they speak French, we are tempted to say, *like a native*. On the one hand, there is "mastery": "In any group of young men in the Antilles, the one who expresses himself well, who has mastered the language, is inordinately feared: keep an eye on that one, he is almost white. In France one says, 'He talks like a book.' In Martinique, 'He talks like a white man'" (20–21). On the other hand, there is speaking "pidgin-nigger" (20), which automatically invokes the "myth of the nigger-who-eats-his-R's" (21). In either case, the Martinican quite literally "betrays himself in his speech" (24), caught as he is in the bind of being either a poseur ("a white man") or a "pidgin-nigger-talker" (32). As Fanon explains a bit later, the experience of being black is the experience of nonrecognition, of wearing the racialized uniform of his skin, of being a stereotype rather than a unique human being: "I was responsible at the same time for my body, for my race, for my ancestors. I subjected myself to an objective examination, I discovered my blackness, my ethnic characteristics; and I was battered down by tom-toms, cannibalism, intellectual deficiency, fetichism, racial defects, slave-ships, and above all else, above all: 'Sho' good eatin'' [*Y'a bon*]" (112). The image of the *Grand Enfant*, or simpleton soldier, is part and parcel of French rhetoric about the mentality of the colonized in black Africa. The commodified, widely distributed, grinning Banania *tirailleur*, which appeared on everything from food products to postcards joking about the barbarism of the African soldier, to manuals used in World War II to teach Senegalese troops to distinguish good from evil, disguised the horrors of the experience of colonial recruits and the discrimination they suffered.

Depictions of black soldiers maintained much of the same iconography as found in earlier periods: on the "happier" side of this imagery, the black soldier was represented as a grinning simpleton who is really a big child; on the more grimly racist side, he was seen as a subhuman and undisciplined cannibal, as a potentially dangerous and uncivilized chaser of white women, or as a primitive, barely differentiated from the apes. As William H. Schneider points out in his study *An Empire for the Masses: The French Popular Image of Africa, 1870–1900*, popular illustrated journals had for years specialized in sensationalized accounts of military action in the colonies, accompanied by manichean imagery: "The violence, gore, and savagery which were portrayed formed a complete antithesis to the civilized, ordered existence of '*La Belle Epoque*'" (92). Illustrated newspapers like the *Petit Journal* (with a circulation of more than a million in 1890) and the *Petit Parisien* shaped the opinions of the masses about the colonies. Matching sensational stories of murder, suicide, and anarchist bombings in Europe with extravagant accounts, illustrated by full-page engravings, of military action in the colonies, these journals were copy, not history. One could say that quite literally, this "copy" created simulacra of the North African and sub-Saharan colonial territories.[8] The appearance of real colonial soldiers and workers in France itself and the recognition that they were an important part of the war effort in both World Wars, brought home the disjunction between colonial rhetoric and colonial material practice. The hybrid identity of the colonial soldier (hero and savage; conscript and unenfranchised) undercut the manichean allegory and replaced it with what looked more like a manichean oxymoron: an allegorical hybrid embodying qualities usually assumed to be mutually exclusive. Normally, the allegorical excludes the hybrid, and the hybrid excludes the allegorical.

The propaganda images and popular press at the time of the two World Wars make manifest the contours of this manichean oxymoron. White women and colonial soldiers were the suspect "Others" who combined a series of traits that made them, at base, both ambiguous and threatening because of their very hybrid instability, their potential to shift from ally to enemy. European women were not seen as participating in the battlefront; rather, they remained on the homefront, where careful regulations were needed to protect them from the enemy with whom they might consort while their own men were away at war. They are both the repository of the race (given their reproductive role) and its possible downfall. For the "colored" colonial conscripts who served as manpower or as "cannon fodder" during World War I, the interwar period, and World War II, the lines of demarcation between ally and enemy also were not so clearcut. The heightened social categorizations that tend to emerge in the us/them, homefront/battlefront mentalities of war illuminated the fact that while the enemy might be called the German, the French, the English, the American, the Australian, or the Italian, in the narrower sense of the term, the essence of the Enemy was found in those categorized as other: "coloreds" and women would remain the embodiment of this more generalized threat after the war (whichever war) was over. Both women and colonial subjects were associated with a world that was nonrational and asymbolic, the mute world of raw nature. If the gender of the "civilizing mission" was masculine,[9] the race of the civilizing mission was white. To the extent that women and colonial subjects crossed these lines (white women and indigenous males), they could partake in civil society, but they would never be full-fledged participants; to the extent that they embodied a difference from this cognitive and physical center, they were as untrustworthy as the enemy ("them").

While the French depended on the conscripted labor of non-Europeans to support the war effort, and while they praised African soldiers for their bravery, counting on them to "single-handedly, scare the *boche* all the way back to Berlin" (Balesi 99), their reputation for hard work and valor was diminished and polluted by racist European assumptions about African mentality and capability, assumptions that reflect the hierarchies evident in the earlier racial theories of Gobineau, Renan, and Le Bon. Left-wing, anti-colonialists often shared the social Darwinism of their gung ho colonialist countrymen, however much they may have differed from them in the area of politics or economics. As Allen Douglas has demonstrated in his "Between Racism and Antimilitarism: The *Canard enchaîné* and France's Colonial Wars of the 1920s," the satirical weekly newspaper started in 1915 was perfectly capable of merging nonconformist politics with conformist humor, using racist iconography to "exploit and redirect French racism towards a politically conscious anti-imperialism" (72). In its early years, it was dominated by issues concerning World War I:

> The *Canard* preached a kind of binary sociology: self-sacrificing soldiers (and later veterans) against exploitive merchants and professional patriots who had avoided combat. Correcting the paternalistic image of the devoted colonial troops was, thus, part of their antimilitarism. On more than one occasion, the satirical weekly explained how the Senegalese "volunteers" were recruited. Ropes were stretched across the two ends of a village and all those in between were considered volunteers "and presumptive heroes." When discussing the Senegalese soldiers, the *Canard* rarely failed to mention the remark attributed to General Mangin, that these were troops "to be consumed before winter." (73)

Complaints about militarist instrumentalism did not stop the paper from engaging in racist humor, however, in that it depicted black Africans as cannibals hawking dismembered white bodies and crying their wares in patois (*le petit nègre*).

European artists tended to depict North African *spahis* and *tirailleurs* as having a formidable tenacity and dignity—perhaps because of their more elegant flowing burnouses and turbans. When they were being made fun of, they were imaged as patois-speaking blacks in ragged *gandouras*. This general European view of the Africans as savages is illustrated by postcards such as "Forbidden meat" that showed a *tirailleur* eating the ear of a German officer and bore the caption: "Mohammed please forgive me if just once I eat pig" (*Images et colonies* 94). While drafted Africans were expected to die for the mother country France, the popular press depicted blacks who were lustful and primitive, who chased white nurses, fondled waitresses, and were fondled by whores, all combinations that would "blacken" the white race. The image of black conscripts that most clearly equates the African with the Enemy is found in the common joking association of Africans with apes. This comparison reveals its far more sinister side when simian images are used to represent the rape, carnage, and savagery of war itself as the real enemy of civilization.[10]

When we look at the material conditions of the colonial conscripts, their experiences during the war and its aftermath, through their own narratives, we find that they are not just "writing back at the Empire," they are rather in many ways writing beyond it and its instrumental epistemologies. The images in texts, memoirs, films, and art works created by colonial conscripts drafted into these modern debacles do not focus on Western women, and even go beyond critiques of racism, to comment on the double-edged destructiveness of Western modernity: its instrumental destruction of the natural world, and its sociopolitical disruptions of alternative forms of social and cognitive organization—in short, they focus on the blowing up of landscapes and beings, and the tearing apart of families and villages.

Conscription

> "I don't understand a thing," said the sergeant.
> "Senegalese—and a volunteer!"
> —Senghor, "The Enlisted Man's Despair"

In his essay on immigrant labor, "Colour-blind France? Colonial workers during the first world war," Tyler Stovall details the differences in pay, jobs, surveillance, ghettoization, and even food that made the experiences of colonial and Chinese laborers (223,000 workers) different from those of white European immigrant laborers (330,000 workers). While many European workers chose to emigrate to France during World War I, the non-European workers were recruited, often by force. "The largest, single [non-European] group came from Algeria (78,566); other large contingents came from Indochina, principally Annam and Tonkin (48,995), China (36,941) and Morocco (35,506), followed by Tunisia (18,249) and Madagascar (4,546). Only token numbers of conscripted workers came from France's sub-Saharan African possessions" (37). When workers did not sign up voluntarily in Algeria and Tunisia, for example, the French government backed by local powers like the Bey of Tunis, reinforced the effort with the threat of forcible conscription. To handle this labor force, the French created the "Colonial Labour Organisation Service" (known by its French acronym SOTC) to manage the workers. Once the workers arrived on French soil, they were given the most difficult jobs in the worst conditions, such as jobs in munitions factories where grueling physical labor, a cold climate, noxious gases, and risks of explosion took their toll on workers who, if they fell sick, were perceived as lazy or weak. Meanwhile, French workers used the system to avoid these bad jobs, as did the European immigrant labor. To minimize the danger of conflicts with local labor, the nonwhite workers were housed in barracks and other substandard quarters, segregated within their respective groups, prevented from freely moving around, and given inadequate and inappropriate food. Shortages of interpreters and the lack of administrators with cross-cultural experience led to misunderstanding: "Officials also used sanctions to enforce discipline. One Tunisian worker complained of being forced to spend fifteen days in prison for refusing to eat pork, while an Indochinese wrote that sending postcards depicting nude French women was punishable by a month in jail" (46). The SOTC strove to keep the nonwhite labor force from coming into contact with French society: "SOTC hoped to prevent contacts between non-white labourers and French women" (43). Claiming the nonwhite laborers were physically and morally deficient, the officials argued that "without strict supervision, . . . these people would quickly fall prey to gambling, drink and, most shocking of all, white women" (48).

Fear that the non-European workforce would contaminate French society was based on both immediate and long-term concerns: first, there was the concern that they might be carriers of disease, and second, there was the deeper fear of miscegenation should nonwhite men be allowed in the vicinity of white women (who themselves lacked judgment). Thus the miners' union in Pas-de-Calais, for example, objected to the use of North African workers on moral grounds "given the close proximity of North Africans to working class families whose heads are absent" and on grounds of hygiene, "inspired by the fear of the possible contamination of the local population" (50). The SOTC instituted prophylactic measures to guard against miscegenation: Postal censors kept a close lookout for letters from colonial workers mentioning sexual exploits and/or projected engagements to French women, as well as pornographic postcards; their monthly reports often included specific sections devoted to these issues alone" (51). When the war ended, "North Africans, in particular, were rounded up in police raids in Paris and Marseille and quickly repatriated," and French authorities felt they had "successfully purged [French society] of the most 'troublesome' elements and restored a semblance of European homogeneity" (52). When we take into account Malek Alloula's perceptive analysis of the voyeuristic postcards in *The Colonial Harem*, with their studio shots of bare-breasted odalisques openly available to settlers and soldiers alike, and their objectifying ethnographic types, it follows that the discrepancy in these regulations is not random, but rather a matter of policy, power, and arbitrary dominance.

Colonial soldiers inhabited the borderland between a disciplined, strong masculinity brought to bear in defense of civilization (the protection of the home front) and an aggressively bestial masculinity that would destroy civilization, reducing it to utter primitivity, and possibly pollute the white race through miscegenation. European civilization was endangered as well by the possibility that colonial soldiers might, one day, turn on them the technologically advanced weapons they had learned to use in the West. This concern had to be balanced against the need for more troops on the battlefront. "During the [World War I], both Britain and France had supplemented and strengthened their armies with vast amounts of African and Asian manpower. India alone had provided 800,000 soldiers and 400,000 laborers, while the French colonies had supplied more than half a million combatants and 200,000 workers" (Nelson 606). In *Colonial Conscripts: The Tirailleurs Sénégalais in French West Africa, 1857–1960*, Myron Echenberg estimates that 175,000 Africans served in France over the five years of the war (mainly from Senegal, Ivory Coast, the French Sudan, Madagascar, Tunisia, Algeria, and Morocco), and that 30,000 of them lost their lives there. As M'Barka Hamed-Touati notes in her study of North African immigration and political activism, *Immigration maghrébine et activités politiques en France*:

> The State, that directed these operations, confided the task of recruitment of Maghrebi workers to a special unit called: "*Service des Travailleurs Coloniaux*," part of the Ministry of War. It was to fill the needs of the "nation's" defense that the authorities shipped the North Africans to the Metropole. Needless to say, the early campaign to mobilize workers from the colonies was in the form of forced recruitment. More than 130,000 Maghrebi men were drafted at gunpoint and sent in military convoys to France. Among them: 78,000 Algerians, 35,000 Moroccans, and 18,000 Tunisians, conscripted against their will. (24)

Soldiers from French West Africa made up about 3 percent of the French army and, like the French, suffered a death rate of about 26 percent. But, as Suret-Canale points out in *French Colonialism in Tropical Africa 1900–1945*, the greater destructiveness of the war was being played out back in Africa: Conscription was a new exigency that "robbed [French West Africa] of its youngest and most vigorous men. It came on top of the 'customary' exigencies, which were now further intensified by war taxation, forced labour, the supply of agricultural produce, etc." (139). France purchased the entire 1917 harvest from French West Africa. This purchase, however, was done via an agreement between the colonial government and a consortium of business houses who collected the products: "[T]he products were made available, in fact, through compulsory crops and quotas which the population were forced to bring for sale, whether they liked it or not. This 'extravagant programme' took the forms of 'raids' and enforced 'famine, with no result other than the export of a few thousand tons of sorghum which could not be preserved and of paddy'" (136). In World War II, the military contribution of French West Africa in terms of "cannon" fodder was more disproportionate, considering that the ratio of Africans to French soldiers went up from 3 percent to 9 percent in 1940 (Echenberg 88). Forced requisitioning continued in World War II, and when villagers hid their farm produce, they were subject to raids and even sacking of the village by French troops (Shaka 70).

Although the British recruited more heavily in World War II than in World War I as well, the 500,000 men they recruited were mainly porters and laborers, taken from a total British colonial population of more than 100 million; the French recruited 200,000 African soldiers during World War II, from a total African population of only 18 million (Echenberg, n11 191). A second difference between French practices and those of other European colonial powers was that, dating from the early period of colonization, the French used African troops for conquest, occupation, and finally even for the defense of the mother country. The Belgians, the British, and the Germans, for example, saw the war in Europe as "a white man's war" (Balesi 2), and even felt that African troops should not be used against whites. Echenberg points out that

> France was the only colonial power to bring Africans by the thousands to the trenches of northeastern Europe in the First World War, to form a key element in the continental defense of France in the late 1930s. While it is true that Great Britain used colonial troops from the non-white tropics as well as from the European dominions overseas in both world wars, the British studiously avoided assigning non-white troops either for home defense, to oppose a European enemy, or to occupy enemy territory. In short, France did what other colonial powers dared not do: arm

> and train large numbers of potentially rebellious colonial subjects in what was euphemistically called the art of modern warfare but what could also be described as modern methods of exercising military will against their European overlords. (5)

Hamed-Touati gives concrete examples of this carry-over, pointing out that the first political movement for independence in the Maghreb, the North African Star, was founded by war veteran Hadj Ali Abdelkader: "Doubtless, the war was a terrible experience during which one learned to kill and to hate the other; that other died to defend his country, but what sense did this butchery make to the colonized? Wouldn't it have caused some questioning about the fate of his own country? And how would he understand his place in the scheme of things amid all this chaos?" (31). Even before World War I when General Mangin was arguing for the Black Army, he noted that Algerian settlers were afraid that training Arabs to fight in the army would lead to insurrection: "The Arabs, whom we would instruct and set free, would turn against us"; but Mangin goes on to deal with this fear, saying: "But our Algerian settlers would be reassured if they felt themselves protected by regiments of Senegalese infantry, most of them fetishists" (qtd. in Suret-Canale 135). Thus in line with racial hierarchies, Arab troops could be sent to Europe, while sub-Saharan African troops were used to quell rebellion in North Africa.

Studies of recruitment of West Africans by Balesi, Echenberg, and Lawler agree that the French tended to reduce the African soldier to his military qualities alone, assuming there were no complex cultures, no civilization really, to analyze in the first place. Balesi comments that throughout the invasions now called the Scramble for Africa, "the French, for the most part, overlooked or ignored the cultural environment and the psychological intricacies of their [African] adversaries" (28). This reductionist approach to African culture is evident as well in the 1911 book *Le Tirailleur soudanais* by Captain Marceau of the French army. Marceau claimed that the best soldier was not the Tukulor (who "was a born soldier but not always understanding of the virtues of discipline") but rather the Bambara who though "limited to the comprehension of simple and concrete ideas" was an excellent soldier who combined " the solidity and strength of a rock" (qtd. in Balesi 36). Captain Marceau echoes the view of earlier army recruiters, one of whom wrote at the beginning of the twentieth century: "Our recruitment goes wonderfully well; we only have too many to choose from among all these beautiful black Sudanese, all well-built and delighted to go *en colonne*. Fifteen francs a month and three meals a day, that is all that is necessary to find as many men as are needed when the recruitment is done by an officer whose name is known among them" (36). Facing a decline in birth rate in France at the turn of the twentieth century and then struggling from the loss of more than 2 million men during World War I, men who would be there neither for production nor for reproduction, the French passed colonial conscription laws both in 1912 and 1919. General Charles Mangin, author of *La Force noire*, advocated the creation of a large, colonial army (although he opposed forced conscription) and spearheaded the lobby to get the French government to allow black troops into the European theater of war—despite the fact that he had initially written, "we will keep our black soldiers in West Africa or in Algeria, [so] no mixture of blood can occur with our nationals" (319). Mangin, like his chief rival in the colonial arena, Hubert Lyautey, argued that in the army colonial soldiers would find opportunities not available to them otherwise. They made excuses for the larger system of injustice that French colonization and conscription imposed upon colonial subjects. Lyautey wrote in his essay, "The Role of the Officer in Universal Military Service" (1891), that "through universal conscription the army could cease to be only the preparation for the next war's reserves and become the nation's great school of social justice" (Balesi 32). Lyautey envisioned the military as a place where hearts and minds, as well as bodies, could be improved: "Imagine the officer called upon by his country in his role as agent of social change not so much to train youth in armed struggle but rather to discipline their minds, form their souls, strengthen their hearts" (Lyautey 454). Lyautey imagined the officer acquiring, through this active social role, a new sense of social justice and civic duty: "[what if] he were moved by a personal love of the downtrodden, passionate about these new duties given to all these social leaders, convinced of his role as an educator, resolute, but without changing an iota of his usual functions, only seeing them reborn in his sense of mission" (446).

Conscription was highly unpopular with the colonial private sector, who wanted that manpower for its labor force, and with many in the French government who regarded it as a blood tax and compared it to slavery. It was even more unpopular with the Africans who were forcibly drafted or who fled across borders or committed suicide rather than participate in the war. Universal, male military service was understood as being done in exchange for the benefits of citizenship. Most Africans, however, were not citizens, and did not enjoy even the same military benefits accorded French conscripts:

> Military service for the African subject was quite another matter. Service was for three years [rather than two years or 18 months] and often involved combat in colonial wars or garrison duty in remote and uncomfortable outposts of the empire. The pay was considerably lower than for French citizens, the food of lower quality, and the perquisites fewer. . . . Moreover, the African recruit faced indignities of a sort that French citizens would not

> have tolerated. Medical exams prior to induction took place in public with the men completely nude. Conscripts could sometimes be required to march hundreds or even thousands of miles on foot to reach their induction centers. . . .
>
> The burden of conscription reached well beyond soldiers. African families were separated or divided, thousands of men were lost forever, and opportunities for injustice and divisiveness abounded at the local level of authority. . . . [A]nxiety over the annual drafts touched millions of families in [French West Africa] during the colonial period. (Echenberg 84)

During World War II these abuses continued. In West Africa, for example, other than the members of the *Quatre Communes* in Senegal who were granted citizenship, the total number of natives holding French citizenship was 2,136 in 1936: "The overwhelming majority of the population was classified as *sujets* or subjects, who came under the harsh code of the *indigénat* or code of administrative justice whereby they could be imprisoned without trial by the administration. It also subjected them to compulsory service, obligatory forced labour, compulsory cultivation of crops and above all made any form of political activity impossible" (Crowder 269).

Ivory Coast veterans of World War II interviewed by Nancy Ellen Lawler were eloquent about the injustice they suffered. Djirigue Soro told her, "Without any warning, the French came to the village at night—they took us all away. There was no time to prepare for my absence" (32). And Laqui Kondé, who had been drafted in 1928 for three years, then discharged, then redrafted in 1939, said: "If someone called you to fight a war—fire a rifle—would you be happy? We had to go. If you wouldn't leave, they would gather all your family together and put them in prison. If you go, you may die, but it is only you. No, there were no volunteers, not even one from here" (34). Noting that African recruits would be kept in the dark as to what was being done with them, Senoufo Samongo Soro described the panic and despair that affected recruits who suddenly learned they were going to war: "In Abidjan, they told us there was war. The very day they informed us, many killed themselves. They hung themselves on trees. Many people. The governor's wife came to try to reconcile us to going" (35). In Tunisia, the brutality of conscription during World War I is remembered to this day, as was demonstrated by a spontaneous recitation by Muhammad M. . . . As a boy he'd learned about the miseries of recruits in World War I from a poem. Its refrain described the forced recruitment: "Worried but bearing my pain with patience/with tears running down my cheeks,'/"You who [seem] not to believe what I'm saying/[I tell you] I saw soldiers everywhere/I saw them gather and line up/Women lamenting bloodied their cheeks/when their menfolk had to leave/They left their children orphans . . ./They left their brides behind" (personal interview 1997).

Combat

As part of their propaganda against the use of nonwhite troops in Europe, the Germans published a document entitled *Der Völkerzirkus unserer Feinde* [*The Ethnic Circus of our Enemies*] in 1917 with a preface by Leo Frobenius, the man of whom Léopold Senghor would say, in describing the impact this man had on the students who would found *negritude*: "But suddenly, like a thunderclap—Frobenius! All the history and pre-history of Africa were illuminated, to their very depths. And we still carry the mark of the master in our minds and our spirits, like a form of tattooing carried out in the initiation ceremonies in the sacred grove" (Senghor, "Forward" vii). In the preface, Frobenius berates the use by Allied powers of colonial soldiers to fight their battles, comparing it to the display of native people at circuses and colonial expositions. Illustrated by hundreds of photographs of colonial soldiers, the book attempted to emphasize the cultural otherness of these conscripts, defending them under the aegis of respect for other cultures—but it was unfortunately part of a larger German propaganda campaign claiming that the colonial troops polluted and blackened white Europe. Speaking of the racist mythology Europeans engaged in during the war, Echenberg notes:

> The German press reduced Africans to the level of savagery. These accusations, of course, had another purpose in mind: to show the ruthlessness of enemies who were prepared to stoop so low as to employ cannibals, an accusation frequently leveled in the German press. One account of June 1918 drew particular attention to the determined resistance of *Tirailleurs* around the city of Reims as being conducted by mindless blacks drunk on reserves of brandy and all brandishing the "*coupe-coupe*, the big combat knife." Thus the image of a head-cutting barbarian who took no prisoners was cultivated by some elements on the French side, and given credence by equally doubtful sources on the German side. (33)

In his essay "Black Horror on the Rhine," Nelson points out that "German troops, for instance, were reported to be terrified of [Africans'] 'aboriginal ferocity,' and rumors were rife, even among Allied soldiers, that the Senegalese often returned from a fight with a 'pocketful of white men's ears'" (Nelson 608).[11] Thus the conscript, forcibly taken from his culture and his home and thrust into the trenches in a strange land, ironically, becomes the image of the evils of war, becomes what he always was for the West—the enemy of civilization.

Representing the enemy as an African soldier seems all the more obscene when we realize the extent to which these soldiers were victims of the terror and disorientation of war in ways that European soldiers, although they may have been next to them in the trenches, were not. In *All Quiet on the Western Front*, Erich Maria Remarque describes the panic of the soldier, caught in no-man's-land between the trenches, who waits for the cover of night to try to crawl out of the carnage and back to his own territory. In the dark, he becomes disoriented, fearing that either he is crawling parallel to the trenches and will never get back to safety, or that he has become turned around and is crawling toward the enemy. How much greater, then, must have been the fear and disorientation of African soldiers: they were conscripted into a foreign war being fought for obscure reasons; they were unable to speak the language; they were ignorant of the geography of the place (in a general sense as well as in the specific sense that Remarque focuses on); they were deprived for years from seeing their families; they were discriminated against by the white soldiers; they were clear targets unable to blend into local populations should they become prisoners and try to escape; and finally, given the mythology of barbarism attached to them by white soldiers on all sides, they were likely to be summarily executed if captured. If the colonial troops were ferocious fighters, there is little wonder why—they were trapped and terrified in a war between colonizers.

Serving in a unit of *tirailleurs* in Morocco in 1914, Bakary Diallo in his *Force-Bonté* described what Africans understood of the declaration of war: "The sergeant-major read a report. It was somewhat long and we only understood two things: Germany had declared war on France. . . . And France was calling on all her children [to defend her]" (Diallo 94). Colonial soldiers arrived in France and were immediately sent to the front where, expected to stand because of their reputation as soldiers, they were mown down by the Germans. Balesi writes of the battle in Belgium along the Yser: "The Senegalese were under constant artillery fire, their positions were dug in mud trenches, filled with water, 'as it rains in the Flanders. . . . A thin fine rain . . . implacable, which in its freezing fog, confuses sky and earth.'[12] They waited under shells day after day" (97). Balesi adds: "*There is little to write* about the attitudes of the first Senegalese troops who saw France so briefly between landing piers and shell-holes. . . . Against the endless, disciplined grey columns of the Germans, they fought with a desperate fury that the most eloquent panegyrist could hardly exaggerate. Those were the days before armies had learned to bury themselves in tunnels and trenches, before the French had learned that the courage of men charging, bayonets high, could not match the rapid fire of machine guns. The technological magnitude of the German war machine stunned the French during these first months of war: valor alone was not enough to tip the scales in their favor" (98; emphasis added). The "desperate fury" with which the conscripts fought, too often explained by their purported cultural background (barbarism, fanaticism, primitivism), was no doubt rather due to lack of other options, options that European soldiers had by virtue of their being from the place; that is, they could speak the language, blend in with the population, or find their way home.

Few records seem to have been kept of African attitudes and experiences during World War I. The fact is that military authorities didn't care to ask and assumed there was little to be told. Often, as in the description above, even apologists for the performance of African troops, simplify the cultural dislocations suffered by colonial soldiers. For example, in a similar description of the German breakthrough near Verdun in 1916, talented historian Alistair Horne acknowledges that the Algerians and Moroccans who served as *tirailleurs* in the 37th African Division were rapidly brought to the front to plug the holes in the line "like clay shoveled into the cracks of a dyke":

> Brilliant, brave to the point of *fanaticism* on the attack, the North Africans—in common with most *southern races*—were, however, strongly subject to *temperament* and *less consistent* fighters than the more dogged northerners. When [the division] reached the Verdun battle area on the 23rd, muffled to the ears like *medieval Saracens*, everything had been against the proud North African division. Split up into packets, it found itself under the command of strange officers—and the regular French Army tended to regard the Colonial troops all too frequently as mere cannon fodder. At the front, . . . [they] learned they were expected to hold a line devoid of any prepared positions. All shelters, either against the weather or bombardment, had been razed by the German shelling. The bitter cold gnawed into the bones of the wretched, unacclimatized North Africans, and a night of exposure had reduced their morale to a low ebb. Meanwhile, through their lines had flowed the steady, demoralizing debris of defeat; the aimlessly wandering wounded and shell-shocked with their staring eyes . . .
>
> Nothing like this had ever been experienced. When the German infantry had appeared like a great, grey carpet unrolling over the countryside, a section of the *tirailleurs* had lost its nerve; then a platoon, a company, and finally a whole battalion wavered and broke. [Ordered to fight to the last man, the 3rd Zouaves] had, it seems, dissolved like the early morning mist. . . . What happened to the Zouaves still remains something of a mystery; the French official history is uncommunicative. (100–101; emphasis added)

The details given to describe the reactions of the North African troops mix realism with mythology. Horne does solve the mystery of their disappearance, noting that records left suggest that a captain, thrust into a position of command and frustrated at the retreat, ordered guns to fire on his own troops: "a section of machine guns fired at the backs of the fleeing men, who fell like flies" (102).

Records from German intelligence about the behavior of prisoners taken comment as follows: "The Zouaves and Turkos particularly give one an impression of complete breakdown. The prisoners complain loudly and without moderation of their officers and senior commanders, and spit at the captured officers of other French regiments" (102). Brought into a strange land to be cannon fodder in a foreign war, the colonial troops trusted only their own officers who were known quantities; the anger shown at their treatment by both Allied and Axis powers should hardly be surprising and has little to do with cultural primitivity or fanaticism or fiery southern racial traits. Nevertheless, in a medical thesis, Doctor Lacaze, who treated Senegalese soldiers, said of the pathology of the black soldier: "Not only did he not fight sickness, but it often seemed he unconsciously encouraged it. . . . Having an undeveloped intellect, the *tirailleur* suffers from psychiatric troubles which do not exhibit the complicated manifestations that we can observe in civilized people of a superior order. The [medical] interview, difficult to begin with, with any normal *tirailleur*, does not allow for deep analysis of his mental problem. . . . Often enough we discovered during the course of the medical visit patients who were sad, indifferent to everything, silent, so we considered them melancholics" (12). One wonders in what language these interviews were conducted. In his essay on "Colonial War and Mental Disorders," Fanon analyzed how it was that ethnopsychiatrists working in North Africa, such as Porot, explained the anomalous behavior of Algerian melancholics who, rather than committing suicide, became homicidal:

> How did the Algerian school deal with such an anomaly? First, said the school of Algiers, killing oneself is a turning into and against oneself; it implies looking at oneself; it means practicing introspection. Now the Algerian is not given to an inner life. There is no inner life where the North African is concerned. On the contrary, the North African gets rid of his worries by throwing himself on people who surround him. He does not analyze. Since by definition melancholia is an illness of the moral conscience it is clear that the Algerian can only develop pseudo-melancholia. (*The Wretched of the Earth* 299)

Balesi explains that sick and wounded *tirailleurs* were sometimes cared for at hospitals especially set up for them and that at least one doctor, Chief Surgeon Maclau, tried a holistic form of medicine (106), but this was rare. Lacaze's dissertation is clinical, matter-of-fact, and focuses only on physical illness, ignoring any real sense that the pathologies he was seeing were sociogenic—exacerbated by the very Western forms of medicine being used to treat them.

Interviews done by Lawler with the "soldiers of misfortune" from the Ivory Coast who saw action in the early part of World War II in the Battle of France at the Somme have provided voices to fill in some of this silence. Laqui Kondé serving with the *tirailleurs* during the final days of battle of the Somme, between June 14–25, 1940, told Lawler:

> We took our machine guns, our cannons, our tanks and left for the bush—on foot—right away. . . . It was miserable. When we went to sleep and woke up again, we thanked God. The [firing] started. . . . It was very confused—people were running. We were trying to find a place to shoot from that would be safe. Bombs were dropping. Everyone was for himself. There was no one in charge then. . . . We were always on the move. Sometimes we were stronger—sometimes they were and we ran. . . . It was a bullet that broke off my tooth—not a peanut you know. Yes, we were with the French all the time. We were stronger than the whites. . . . That bullet which hit my tooth would have killed a white. When the shooting came, the whites ran. They knew the area and we did not—so we stayed. Our officers? They were behind us. I didn't know or think about anything except life or death. We were between the two. The officers said: "Stand. We will win." But it was the Germans who were stronger, so we forgot what they said. (80)

Other interviews reinforce the idea that the African soldiers were tenacious, partly because they saw themselves as stronger than their white counterparts (the French army was the only Western army not to segregate African units completely), and partly because they had nowhere else to go. The Africans, in the context of Hitler's policy of ethnic cleansing, were more likely than other prisoners of war to be shot. Daouda Tuo-Donatoho touched on the difference that race made for a prisoner of war:

> There was no way out. We were all taken—the French, Malagaches, Tunisians, everyone. We were the first there at the front. It was very hard. A woman from the Red Cross saved us. The Germans wanted to kill the prisoners—the Africans. The woman said no—you cannot do this—if you capture someone you must keep him. The Germans said they had to kill us and then bury us deeply in a hole for they had heard from the French that when you kill an African soldier, he rises up again. The woman said that was not true. Then the Germans asked her why the

> Africans were here—why they were fighting. She said we were forced to come. She asked them if they had seen any black women? Any black children? No—they were forced to come. So we were taken prisoner. (97)

One of the most famous African prisoners of war was Senegalese poet and president, Léopold Sedar Senghor who spent 1940–1942 in German camps. Talking forbidden, Senghor began writing poetry about his experiences, analyzing the social inequalities and forms of nonrecognition and misrecognition that European society fed upon.

Demobilization

> They put flowers on tombs and warm the Unknown Soldier.
> But you, my dark brothers, no one calls your names.
> They promise five hundred thousand of your children the
> glory
> Of future deaths and thank them in advance, future dark
> dead.
> *Die Schwarze Schande!*
>
> —Senghor, "To the Senegalese Soldiers Who Died for France"

Die Schwarze Schande, the black shame, refers to the German press campaign objecting to the use of nonwhite colonial troops as occupation forces in the Rhineland following the armistice of 1918. "From January 1919, to June 1920, the average number of black troops in the French Army of the Rhine was 5,200, and of colored races, ranging from Moroccans to Malagaches, 20,000. In June, 1920, the black regiments were withdrawn," the *Nation* noted ("Black Troops on the Rhine" 365). The withdrawal of the troops was, as we shall see, largely in response to "colored" soldiers policing white people and coming into possible contact with white women. This was an attitude that could be shared, apparently, by all Europeans—both the fascist and the confirmed liberal humanitarian. In reference to the outrageous treatment of Africans who served in the war, René Maran writes in his 1937 preface to *Batouala* (1921): "The Negro question is relevant. Who willed it so? Why, the Americans. The campaigns of the Outer Rhine newspapers" (9). Maran was a French-identified, black colonial official who was born in Martinique, grew up in France, and served in the French colonial system in Central Africa (Ubangi-Shari). In *Nationalists and Nomads*, Christopher Miller notes that

> Maran appears as a prime example of the theory that the French—for lack of a significant white settler population to occupy sub-Saharan

> Africa—got blacks to colonize each other in the name of France. The contents of *Batouala* seem to flow directly from the subject position of a collaborator: in the preface, the narrator sympathizes with the Africans in front of him, but only from the comfort of his easy chair ("On moonlit nights, stretched out on my chaise longue on my veranda, I would listen to the conversations of these poor people. Their jokes proved their resignation. They suffered and laughed about suffering"). (Miller 124)

However, as Miller notes, the book was seen as a subversive threat. *Batouala*, subtitled a "*véritable roman nègre*" (true black novel) by the publishers, won the Prix Goncourt in 1922. It also caused a scandal because of the way Maran called on France to uphold its Enlightenment promises of equality:

> After all, if [the Africans] break down from hunger by the thousands, like flies, it is because their country is being 'developed.' Only those who don't adapt to civilization disappear.
>
> Civilization, civilization, pride of the Europeans, and their burying-ground for innocents . . .
>
> You build your kingdom on corpses. Whatever you may want, whatever you may do, you act with deceit. At your sight, gushing tears and screaming pain. You are the might which exceeds right. You aren't a torch, but an inferno. Everything you touch, you consume . . . (*Batouala* 8–9)

Maran called on "his brothers of France" to defend equality, a "right and noble idea" (9). He was "rewarded" with the banning of his novel in the colonies, and eventually he was forced to resign from his job in the colonial service (Coundouriotis 31). Miller points out that it is Senghor who identifies Maran as "the first man in the Francophone world to be called upon to choose between being "French writer" and "black man" (*Nationalists and Nomads* 127).

Maran's reference in his preface to campaigns in the Outer Rhine points to his identification with the black colonial soldiers. In July 1921, the *Nation*, in a section entitled "Is the Black Horror on the Rhine Fact or Propaganda?" used readers' letters about a German propaganda film, *The Black Horror*, "in which each white woman and each growing girl is forcibly seized by Negroes in French pay and violently enticed [sic] into a brothel" to document the reaction of its readers to black soldiers ("Is the Black Horror" 44). This film was being shown in towns around Germany. Germany maintained that the use of nonwhite colonial troops by the French was a deliberate attempt by the French to humiliate the Germans. Between the time of the negotiations concerning the 1918 armistice and those concerning the Treaty of Versailles (1920), the Germans, partly through Swiss intermediaries, specified that "colored troops should not be made part of the army of occupation" (Nelson 609).

In January 1919 U.S. President Woodrow Wilson asked Clemenceau if the French really planned to use Senegalese to occupy the Rhineland, and Clemenceau replied that while one battalion was currently there, "I believe as you do that it would be a grave error to occupy the left bank with black troops." And along these same lines, the American liaison to the French chief of staff warned: "Do you not think that in having black troops in your army of occupation, . . . you run some danger . . . ? One or two cases of rape, committed by your blacks on the German women, well advertised in the southern states of America, where there are very definite views with regard to the black man, would likely greatly reduce the esteem in which the French are held" (Nelson 610).

The French did finally decide to use colonial troops for occupation, and the German propaganda campaign began circulating inflammatory stories, in bilingual format, especially in the United States. The overseas *Hamburger Nachrichten* ran "The Blackest Crime in the World's History"; Americans were told that the sadistic excesses of the French exceed those of Nero:

> Everything which the morbid brain of that scoundrel ever concocted must pale before the deeds which a whole nation—to wit "La Grande Nation"—is allowed to perpetrate with impunity on the whole white race. The "Black Disgrace in the Rhineland" will henceforth be in history the signal example of abysmal depth of human depravity. The blackest crime in history!
>
> We do not exaggerate when we speak of a whole nation of sadists. For it is the French nation, which appoints and delegates the emissaries who flood according to a well-devised devilish plan the Rhineland with Niggers and Moroccans; and what these brutes perpetrate on the white race is sanctioned and excused by the functionaries of the French nation. ("Is the Black Horror" 45)

The article then cites an American woman living in Munich who called on men to "take justice in your own hands: Your weapons have been taken away from you, but there still remains a rope and a tree. Take up the natural arms which our men in the South resort to: lynch! Hang every black who assaults a white person" (45).

In England, E. D. Morel, a British radical who had fought against the exploitation of the African natives in the "Scramble for Africa," none the less wrote to the *Nation* (London) on March 27, 1920, that one should beware of those who "thrust barbarians—barbarians belonging to a race inspired by Nature . . . with tremendous sexual instincts—into the heart of Europe" (qtd. in Nelson 615). In response to articles Morel published in England about "colored outrages," fifty thousand Swedish women signed a statement supporting his views, as did women in Norway, Italy, and France, while in the U.S. a protest rally against the "horror on the Rhine" brought 12,000 people to Madison Square Garden (28 February 1921). In the Senate, the minority leader, Gilbert Hitchcock (D-NE), responded to the fact that the black Africans had been withdrawn from the Rhine by saying: "there is no need to make a distinction [between the Senegalese and the Algerian and the Moroccan]. They are all men of an inferior, half-civilized race. They are brutes when stationed among white people, as the evidence shows" [Actually, the evidence didn't show great abuses] (Nelson, 616–623). While it is no surprise that racism would be so virulent among various groups in the United States, it is sobering that a life-long campaigner for human rights like E. D. Morel supported vicious racial stereotypes. Even humanitarian Bertrand Russell, writing also at the time of World War I, thought of the Africans as oppressed, exploited . . . and savage.[13]

If *Die Schwarze Schande* is emblematic of the racism colonial conscripts suffered in the aftermath of World War I, then the massacre at Thiaroye, commemorated in Ousmane Sembène's film *Camp de Thiaroye*, is the icon for shame in the aftermath of World War II. Arbitrarily, Africans were conscripted to fight for the French against the Germans in 1939, then forced to fight for the Vichy government against the British in the early 1940s, then conscripted to fight for de Gaulle's Free French Army in the colonies. At the same time, Nazi propaganda portrayed the "French" soldier "as a hideous African molesting blonde Aryan women" (Nelson 626). In the same mode of racialized injustice, de Gaulle himself, in 1944, gave the order to "whiten" the French forces by withdrawing black African troops:

> Chadians and French West Africans had formed the rank and file for Leclerc's raids against the Italians in North Africa in 1940 and 1941. They were part of the Free French Army which was included in the Allied invasion of Italy in 1943. To [the 6th regiment of the Senegalese *Tirailleurs*] went the privilege of liberating Elba in the late Spring of 1944. In the landings in Provence in August 1944, black Africans had seen considerable combat, especially in the taking of Toulon. Just as these 20,000 battle-hardened men were preparing to share in de Lattre's anticipated triumphs in France, de Gaulle ordered their replacement with young Frenchmen of the class of 1943, and by the elements of various Partisan groups. For de Gaulle the reasons were clear. It was essential that young Frenchmen be given a taste of victory, a share in the Allied success in ridding France of its shame and humiliation. (Echenberg 98–99)

These young Frenchmen would be de Gaulle's political support. And the arbitrary abuse and degradation of black soldiers did not stop there. Lacking adequate transport to get them back to Africa, and lacking material and equipment for his replacement French troops, de Gaulle left the black troops in limbo, in inadequate quarters in southern France waiting for transport home and suffering from shortages of food, clothing, and firewood.

The indignities continued, as *tirailleurs* from the Ivory Coast explained to Lawler. Panafolo Tuo remembered listening to de Gaulle on VE Day in 1945: "He told us to be calm—the ship will come one day and we will pay you. All of you will get money and those who were in prison will have a great deal of money. He said they couldn't give it to us now, but that we would get it in Africa, but I got nothing" (195). Nonpayment of back wages, promised bonuses that never came through, worsening exchange rates between France and West Africa, and contradictory information were added to the degradation of being stripped of their uniforms. Colonial authorities, who had no funds to make good on these confused promises, dealt harshly with unhappy returning veterans. Ehouman Adou, an ex-POW, said, "It was in Abidjan that they hurt us. They collected everything we had with us—all the gifts the whites had given us. They left us only one black uniform. At Port Bouet, they took all our suitcases. . . . We spent two months trying to get our things back. They gave us money for the train—that's all" (199). For Sekongo Yenibiyofine, another ex-POW, it was worse: "No one came to welcome us when we got to Abidjan. They gave us new papers, because the Germans had taken ours. Then they took everything away from us except one shirt and one pair of shorts. We came back to our villages with nothing. They said nothing to us and they took everything" (199).

At Thiaroye, the transit camp at Dakar, African veterans lost even their lives when they rose up against this mistreatment. While Echenberg reports that there were at least fifteen recorded incidents like the one at Thiaroye, and "the spark that set off the trouble was most often a physical attack on African soldiers by French military personnel or else a racial slight," the most serious confrontation was at Thiaroye, December 1, 1944: "The uprising involved some 1,280 African ex-POWs in the first contingents to be repatriated from Europe in 1944. The affair drew the label of mutiny because the men were still partially armed, uniformed, and under military discipline. They not only refused to obey their officers but for a brief time actually held hostage the [Commander-in-Chief] of French Forces in [French West Africa]" (101). Denied their pay, having their French francs confiscated, being treated in an authoritarian manner, all these things were "a bitter reminder that they were returning home to an unchanged colonial system, unappreciative of the great sacrifices they and their fallen comrades had made" (101). Their protest was a living example of the self-fulfilling prophecy the French most feared, the ally had turned enemy, now armed and dangerous. Fired on by French troops, thirty-five colonial soldiers were killed, an equal number seriously injured and hundreds more wounded. On the French side, no lives were lost, one African policeman was wounded, and three French officers suffered lacerations. Thirty-four POWs were charged, tried, and put in prison.

In Thierno Faty Sow and Ousmane Sembène's 1987 film *Camp de Thiaroye*, the demobilized African characters arrive home to learn of Pétain's massacre of villagers at Effok for refusing to surrender their farm produce to the French; their own massacre at Thiaroye would be sanctioned by de Gaulle's government. As Sembène explains on an earlier occasion in a 1976 interview, the demobilized soldiers don't see the point of drawing distinctions between the acts of the collaborator of Vichy and those of the leader of the Free French: "For us, who were then the colonized, Pétain and de Gaulle were the same thing. . . . The story of the soldiers killed in Senegal is de Gaulle; the story of Algeria in 1945 is de Gaulle; the story of Madagascar is de Gaulle: why do people want de Gaulle presented as a hero or super-hero? . . . Where I come from, he was a colonialist and he behaved as such" (Shaka 70). In Sembène and Sow's historical re-creation of the events at Thiaroye, we see the world through the eyes of Pays, a POW tortured at Buchenwald who has lost his power of speech. His identity is confused. In the film, he wears a German uniform; he believes the French demobilization camp in Senegal is the same as the prison camp in Germany. In a central scene, soldiers who are going to hang their wet clothes on some barbed wire to dry are blocked by Pays who holds his arms out crucifix-like. A black-and-white flashback cuts to a lone German soldier in the same pose: "Next there is a cut to a man hanging on a barbed wire fence accompanied by a burst of gunfire. This is followed by a cut to a side view of the man hanging on the fence with the fence stretching out into a vanishing point" (72). German or French, Pétain or de Gaulle, death camp or demobilization camp—it doesn't really matter: these *tirailleurs* suspended in no-man's-land seem to be the prisoners of a different war that is continuing on into the twenty-first century.

CHAPTER THREE

Ambiguous Adventure

Reading Cheikh Hamidou Kane

> Cheikh Hamidou tells the story of how, at an art exibition, he was astounded by a canvas by Paul Klee "who painted extremely mechanized figures, beings almost reduced to the state of machines." The anguish expressed in the painting, and so intensely felt by Kane, he extends to any African, leaving his native land, his world of trees, and animals and men, whose longest journey is limited to about thirty kilometers, to quick footsteps along brushy paths. Transplant this same African to the Place de la Concorde, he'll testify that living flesh has been supplanted by a hallucinatory mechanical horizon.
>
> While this "dehumanization" happened gradually for most Europeans, such that they barely even register a tentative revolt against it except in occasional verbal violence, the terror that inundates the African in the face of this mechanization of the human body amounts to a protest, to a condemnation of this technological era.
>
> —Mercier et Battestini, *Cheikh Hamidou Kane*

The traumatic experience of colonization and of conscription suffered by Africans had the ironic effect of both strengthening and weakening their social imaginaries. Local people acknowledged the physical might of the European powers and their impressively instrumental ways of dealing with matters of this world: their technologies of war, communication, and commerce (cannons, telegraph lines, steel boats that could be disassembled and portaged); their scientific domination of the natural world; their cultural domination through colonial languages and institutions. The protagonist of Tayeb Salih's *Season of Migration to the North* sums up the experience of colonization for many Africans this way: "The ships at first sailed down the Nile carrying guns not bread, and the railways were originally set up to transport troops; the schools were started so as to teach us how to say 'Yes' in their language. They imported to us the germ of the greatest European violence, as seen on the Somme and at Verdun, the like of which the world has never previously known, the germ of a deadly disease that struck them more than a thousand years ago" (95).[1] Africans tended to fault the West for lacking the relational abilities needed to build community. When African colonies were asked in 1958 if they wished to join the French Community, Guinée was the only former colony to choose complete independence instead. President Sekou Touré explained to Charles de Gaulle that indeed Guinée wanted there to be a relationship between France and Guinée—just not that of rider and horse. Africans also criticized the West for the limited, analytical epistemological lens through which they viewed reality. Ironically, scientific progress became synonymous with social regress. In the early 1700s Vico had criticized Cartesian rationalism, which reduced eloquence to logic, wisdom to science, and culture to reason (Mooney 102–105); he called Cartesian analysis a "barbarism of reflection" because in both its logical and mathematical forms, it destroyed the imaginative ground of moral and civic public life and was a sign of "humanity tending to decay," of the "dark underside of cultural maturity" (233). In essence, Vico faulted Cartesianism for its elimination of both imagination and context from its method. Entering the inter-European North–South debate of his time, Vico distinguished between a metonymic scientific method that mechanically reduced life to numbers, and a metaphoric praxis that provided the intellectual spark of understanding in both natural and civic life:

> We must recognize that the French are the only people who, thanks to the subtlety of their language, were able to invent the new philosophical criticism which seems so thoroughly intellectualistic, and analytical geometry, by which the subject matter of mathematics is, as far as possible, *stripped of all concrete figural elements, and reduced to pure rationality.* The French are in the habit of praising the kind of eloquence which characterizes their language, i.e., an eloquence characterized by great fidelity to truth and subtlety, as well as by its *notable deductive order.* We Italians, instead, are endowed with a language which *constantly evokes images.* We stand far above other nations by our achievements in the fields of painting, sculpture, architecture, and music. Our language, thanks to its perpetual dynamism, forces the attention of the listeners by

> means of *metaphorical expressions*, and *prompts it to move back and forth between ideas which are far apart*. (Vico, "On the Study Methods" 40–41; emphasis added)

Michel Foucault also noted that "up to the end of the sixteenth century, resemblance played a constructive role in the knowledge of Western culture" (*The Order of Things* 17). In natural history, the movement from Renaissance resemblances to Cartesian classifying is a shift from "theater" to "catalogue": "the natural history room and the garden, as created in the Classical period, replace the circular procession of the 'show' [Renaissance fairs, tournaments, legends, bestiaries, fables] with the arrangement of things in a 'table'"; while Renaissance natural history included, for example, the virtues, uses, and legends associated with a particular plant or animal, Enlightenment classifying of information to fit it into gridded tables, removed the plants and animals from their ecological contexts; it "squared and spatialized" the world (131–132).[2] This mindset leads to the dehumanization that Cheikh Hamidou Kane experienced in the West, the "hallucinatory mechanical horizon" that has set grim limits to Western epistemology in African eyes. Through a close reading of Cheikh Hamidou Kane's novel *Ambiguous Adventure*, I trace in this chapter the elements of a Muslim social imaginary from which Kane drew in creating his work (orality, religious and political history, mystical Sufism), and the elements of the Western social imaginary (individualism, notions of progress in literary narratives, existentialism) that distort the reception of this non-Western text by Western audiences. The ambiguous adventure, of course, for both characters in the novel and readers of the novel, involves envisioning how these differing social imaginaries, shaped by separation in the past, will participate in a shared future.

In Cheikh Hamidou Kane's novel, two villagers have had the "ambiguous adventure" of traveling to the West and then back to Africa. One is Samba Diallo who has been educated at Qur'anic school—"What purity! What a miracle! Truly, this child was a gift from God" (5)[3]—before studying Western philosophy at the Sorbonne. The other is the Fool who disappeared from the village one day, fought in the "white men's war" (*AA* 86), and returned to the village with his wounds and his traumatic memories of the West: "[His] features were immobile and impassive, except for the eyes, which were never quiet for an instant. One might have said that the man knew a secret which was baleful to the world, and which he was forcing himself by a constant effort to keep from springing to his lips" (*AA* 86). In an interview, Kane explains how he imagined the background that shaped this fictional character:

> He was someone who had been a soldier, who had been conscripted into the *Tirailleurs Sénégalais*, who had in fact never been to school, but they took him just as he was, they extracted him from his village, and after a brief military training, sent him to Europe into the kinds of European conflicts the *Tirailleur Sénégalais* participated in, and this fellow, who was thus plunged into one of the most violent crises ever known in the history of the West, crises of a proportion so much greater than the local conflicts that the Diallobé could have experience of, so this fellow having suffered this traumatizing experience, returned saying to himself if that was the West, it would be better not to take the path of Western society. (Little, "Origins of Samba Diallo" 113–114)

The Fool protects himself from the physical violence of war and the encroachment of Western ways by embracing Islam, literally, in the person of the Qur'anic teacher, Thierno. Samba Diallo, Thierno's young protégé, is sent to France to learn about "the [Western] art of conquering without being in the right"; of all the Diallobé, he is chosen to cope with the risks the West presents because he is among those "most firmly attached to what they are" (*AA* 37). Upon his return, Samba struggles to find the path he will need to take to serve as a mediator between the symbolic violence of the Western social imaginary and the alternative social imaginary of the village with its rootedness in Sufi Islam and traditional African religion.

Both the Fool and Samba, although different in their understandings and reactions, are secure in the knowledge that Islam with its transcendent framing of reality is the right path. The Fool's embrace of religion is largely apotropaic: he wants to be protected from the West. Samba's, on the other hand, is both apotropaic and therapeutic: he wants to understand how to save the West from itself before it destroys everything in its path. From Samba's perspective, the Western soldier shares a social imaginary with the missionaries and the Marxists of the novel: they all perceive the West as ahead of the rest of the world in terms of social evolution. An examination of the reception of this novel in the West indicates that Western readers, quite often, share in this perception, especially in terms of seeing Islam as either a distorted frame of reality or a frame that is simply outmoded. These readers interpret the novel as ending in failure. Unable to protect believers from the depredation of Western instrumentality or to offer an anchor in the face of modernization, Islam is seen as no longer providing a viable alternative social imaginary. Ella Brown, for example, writes: "The madman asks the hero to lead the prayers, but, torn by his education in two cultures, Samba is unable to do so, and the madman kills him. It is almost as if, in his despair, the hero had invited his own destruction. The killing is the response to Samba's spiritual desolation; it seems merely to complete what had begun with his exposure to the West. The madman's voice is clear enough. Sickened by his experience of the West, he rejects it completely. Samba attempts to absorb Western culture without losing his mystical sense of the presence of Allah, but he fails. The question has become not one of willingness to accept but the possibility of acceptance. The author's answer is that it is impossible" (217). Had the novel ended with its penultimate chapter and the death of Samba Diallo at the Fool's hand, this reading would be more persuasive. But the novel ends on a fully transcendent note. Applying the standard Western literary critical paradigms does not lead to adequate readings of the novel. Thus, Western readers are left with an ambiguous adventure: either they start learning about the alternative modernities that have shaped this novel, or they assume the power of critiquing without being in the right, and see the novelist and his characters as failed because they don't reflect a Western social imaginary.

In an interview given in 1997, Cheikh Hamidou Kane explained that a desire to document his own experience with Western education inspired him to begin writing what would eventually become his novel *Ambiguous Adventure*:

> [It was the] desire to put down in black and white what was happening to me in the passage . . . from a traditional society belonging to an oral culture, to a modern society whose principal medium was writing. It's this passage which was so extraordinary that, as I followed this path, I was led to note down impressions, important moments, questionings, answers to these questionings . . . it's that which provided the material for a document . . . which was a sort of personal diary. (Little, "Autofiction 73)[4]

Kane's writing began as a form of witnessing, and he explains that he had no intention, at first, of writing in "one of the literary forms practiced in Europe" (73). As Kane's fellow novelist Chinua Achebe once noted in speaking of the experience of many African writers during the 1950s and 1960s: "This form [the novel], we were told, was designed to explore individual rather than social predicaments" (54). Yet it is precisely the social predicament of a society under colonization that Kane wished to explore, both for the benefit of Western readers and for the benefit of Africans of his generation who were living this alternative modernity. Kane says of his protagonist: "Samba Diallo is more representative of a whole group and a whole generation than of my own personal story" (Little, "Autofiction" 75). Typically, Africans writing at the time of independence ended up writing in the colonizers' language, the colonizers' literary forms, with the former colonizers as the audience. They have, consequently, been read and judged by the colonizers' standards anchored in the colonizers' social imaginary—and usually have been found wanting. This negative or condescending reception is not necessarily simply a conscious wielding of hegemonic power. The practices and perceptions shaping ideas of literary competence and scientific method are sometimes so naturalized and embedded in the Western academy that their symbolic violence becomes invisible: "Being 'natural' and 'ineffable,' such forms seem to be beyond human agency, notwithstanding the fact that the interests they serve may be all too human. This kind of *nonagentive* power saturates such things as aesthetics and ethics, built form and bodily representation, medical knowledge and material production. And its effects are internalised—in their negative guise, as constraints; in their neutral guise, as conventions; in their positive guise, as values" (Comaroff and Comaroff, *Ethnography* 28). Kane, who considered Enlightenment thought to be a sort of ontological accident, created in *Ambiguous Adventure* a work that is ambiguous precisely because it employs a Western genre and invokes the attendant literary competencies in Western readers. At the same time, however, it merges Islamic subject matter syncretically with traditional African perspectives to tell a story that challenges the conventions of the bourgeois novel, thereby exposing the limitations of a Cartesian social imaginary.

One way we readers make sense of authors and their characters has to do with our most basic, agreed-upon understanding of what comprises the self. In the contemporary Western social imaginary, this self is a detached individual who is autonomous and who experiences the world from the inside out, we might say. Thus authors are seen as independent originators of their stories, and the characters they create move through a world seen largely as an external environment. Chinua Achebe argues that Western literature

> played a central role in promoting the ideal of individual autonomy. . . . It promoted a view of society and of culture as a prisonhouse from which the individual must escape in order to find space and fulfilment.
>
> But fulfilment is not, as people often think, uncluttered space or an absence of controls, obligations, painstaking exertion. No! It is actually a presence—a powerful demanding presence limiting the space in which the self can roam uninhibited; it is an aspiration by the self to achieve spiritual congruence with the other.
>
> When people speak glibly of fulfilment they often mean self-gratification, which is easy, short-lived and self-centered. . . .
>
> Fulfilment is other-centered, a giving or a subduing of the self, perhaps to somebody, perhaps to a cause; in any event to something external to it. (52–53)

In Western *bildungsroman* and Western autobiographies contemporary with Kane's novel, we find autonomous protagonists whose individual trajectories lead them to success or failure, depending upon their personal character and their strength of will. John Galt, hero of Ayn Rand's 1957 *Atlas Shrugged*, put it this way: "I swear by my life and my love of it that I will never live for the sake of another man, nor ask another man to live for mine"; *Atlas Shrugged*, we are told, "is the 'second most influential book for Americans today' after the Bible, according to a joint survey conducted by the Library of Congress and the Book of the Month Club. One of the most acclaimed and influential works of the twentieth century, *Atlas Shrugged* portrays the murder and rebirth of the human spirit" ("Atlas Shrugged: A Novel by Ayn Rand"). The human spirit, murdered by the fictional John Galt, is now reincarnated in the body of mass market commodity fiction. And, in real life, the cult groupie whom Ayn Rand dubbed "the undertaker" was Alan Greenspan—"the world's most powerful banker," according to biographer Jerome Tuccille in *Alan Shrugged* (xiv). Chinua Achebe argues that while the oral story has no physical solidity, the book does. Books become commodities and that can be handled and moved about and individually owned. However this alone does not account for the kind of individualist proprietorship found in Western literature, rather it "facilitates the will to ownership which is already present" in the Western social imaginary; "this will is rooted in the praxis of individualism in its social and economic dimensions" (48).

African oral stories, on the other hand, do not belong to their composers but are communal property. The self is understood to be relational, built and rebuilt through the interaction with others. The basic unit through which we make sense of the self is the community.[5] In a similar way, Islamic practice, through oral recitation, joins the speaker into the larger *umma* or nation of believers. Kane, interestingly enough, crossed the boundaries of these genres with his *Ambiguous Adventure*, and the result has been that his Western readers often try to force the tale into Western paradigms, while the tale itself quite ironically challenges that process. But the irony does not dwell in the advent of unsatisfactory readings or in the sudden revelation, for example, that the bourgeois subject has surfaced in the body of the postcolonial reader. Kane's purpose is clearly not Pharisiac, in Burke's sense of the word: that is, Kane does not take a position "outside and superior" to his readers but rather recognizes a fundamental kinship between himself and his readers, between Samba and the Westerners he meets. Kane reaches out to readers who are limited by their dependency on the written word and on the scientific method; this effort is at once apotropaic—he seeks to protect his own culture, and therapeutic—he seeks to protect Western culture from itself given that all cultures are now sharing a mutual global future. In speaking of his decision to publish his journal in the form a novel in 1958, Kane points to a constraint in Western culture (dependency on print culture) that has been naturalized by most Western readers as a virtue: "At the time of writing [the first edition of *Ambiguous Adventure* in 1958] it was to some extent to bear witness to Westerners of the existence of a black culture, a black civilization, a black sensibility, because Westerners could have access to that culture only through the medium of writing and books . . . we ourselves were already committed to the demonstration of the existence of values and culture through the oral tradition, values and culture which were universal and which we could share with others" (Little, "Autofiction" 74). Like his character Samba, Kane sees Westerners as brothers—"The world belongs as much to them as it does to us" (*AA* 105)—but as brothers who have lost the way because they are too focused on material things.

Samba must bridge the gap between a world that gives a central role to illumination and a world largely limited to so-called "scientific" evidence. The juxtaposition of these two "paths" to knowledge reveals a difference of sensibility anchored deep in the social imaginaries of the two cultures. In each, we see that the hidden shall become manifest—in the first case by the rememoration of the Word, that is, by the oral recitation of the Qur'an; and in the second case, by the scrutiny of scientific evidence that discloses the laws of nature hidden beneath the seemingly random behaviors of surface events. In the first case, the exoteric becomes esoteric through the act of speech—prayer is a straight path the Sufi worshipper follows to become one with the ineffable. In the second case, the chaos of nature is brought to order by laying bare (or perhaps rather imposing) the abstract systems of natural law that are seen to underpin it. When Samba leaves Senegal for Paris to study Western philosophy, he is expected to bridge the chasm between "the straight path" and a path defined by Western notions of progress. While in Paris, he is never really seduced by Western ways, nor does he lose his faith (the straight path), but living with the colonizer, he does grow to doubt his own worth and his own ability to know the "straight path." Intuiting Samba's spiritual struggle, his father calls him back to his village, and once there, Samba is shot by the Fool who has misunderstood this spiritual struggle and thinks he has turned away from religion.

In her *African Literature in French*, Dorothy Blair categorizes the plot of *Ambiguous Adventure* in the following way: "It is a variation on the 'cross-roads' theme, that is a young black man, representative of his generation, finding himself at the cross-roads, where two civilizations meet; he abandons or compromises his African origins and traditions, precipitated into, rather than choosing, Western civilization by his educational or professional ambitions, by economic necessity or political expediency. . . . But on the second level, Samba Diallo typifies the more general conflict between Afro-Islamic values and the demands and expediencies of modern times which bedeviled the generation coming to maturity with Kane in the forties and fifties" (261). To present the protagonist as arriving at a "cross-roads" where two cultures meet imposes a binary set of options by suggesting that one must take a path leading toward one or the other of those cultures in a mutually exclusive world. Blair is forced by this paradigm to say that Samba Diallo abandoned or compromised his origins, a reading that sits very uncomfortably with the respectful tone and religious tenor of the novel. Likewise, to juxtapose "Afro-Islamic values" to "demands and expediencies of modern times" suggests the typical Western evolutionary model in which African values are somehow out of touch with contemporary life, archaic. Many Western readers have seen Kane's novel in these terms: that is, seen the protagonist as a failure who can neither embrace the West nor go back to his traditional ways. In our view, Samba Diallo's struggle has rather to do with his feeling that, having witnessed the symbolic violence of the Western social imaginary, he has lost his intuitive sense of the straight path. The end of the novel, however, indicates that he has found the straight path again. In this reading, it is not failure but final resolution that Kane depicts in the closing chapter of the novel.

It is a curious fact that many Western readings of the novel omit discussion of the final chapter, and choose rather to analyze the narrative as if the penultimate chapter in which Samba Diallo is shot by the Fool were the conclusion of the narrative. For example, J. P. Little writes: "Samba Diallo's death is . . . in some ways a symbolic death of part of Cheikh Hamidou Kane himself, that part of him that was backward looking and could not handle the transition to the new. To take a psychoanalytical approach, one could even go so far as to say that it is the symbolic putting to death of his father's dream for him of a religious career. . . . Whichever way one interprets Samba Diallo's death, it would seem to highlight the dangers of his particular itinerary" ("Autofiction" 86). Considering Diallo a sort of "contemporary ancestor" or reading his death in the framework of Western psychoanalysis as the death of the father['s dream] not only frames it in terms of a Western social imaginary, it seems to conflict with the interpretations Kane himself clearly expressed in a 1997 interview with Little:

> [W]e are touching on the problem of explaining the meaning that we agree to attribute to the death of Samba Diallo. Many people have thought that Samba Diallo had somehow provoked his murder by the Fool, because he had reached an impasse, because he wanted to commit suicide. Others have thought and said that Samba Diallo had lost his faith. I don't share either of these opinions. Samba Diallo all the way to the end never had the impression at all that he was cut off from his roots. ("Origins of Samba Diallo" 113)

Kane, in a much earlier 1964 interview with Fabien Eboussi, also stresses the idea that death is not really considered an ending in Sufi practice: "In my view this is not a hopeless ending. The death of Samba Diallo is only the proof that there is a real conflict. You understand, if there had not been the initial civilization in which Samba was rooted, there would have been no problem when he was introduced to Western civilization; he would have thrived in it. On the contrary he dies because of it? Why? His death leads to reflection" (Qtd. in Mortimer 64). In a more Western reading, Dorothy Blair sees Samba Diallo's dilemma as an existential one: "How to reconcile his training for sanctity with his responsibilities as a temporal leader of the Diallobé; how to continue his search for the absolute, faced with the conflicting teachings of Western philosophies and the Word of the Prophet. At the root of the novel is a fundamental, existentialist, universal dilemma and, as often in an existentialist situation, the final solution comes in the form of a tragic symbol of the absurd" (263). Blair seems to collapse the tension between two ways of knowing (one quite earth-bound, the other transcendental) into one, the "existentialist," "universal" explanation. Kane himself maintains the tensions between two ways of conceiving of human experience. His novel can, of course, be read according to Western paradigms concerning reason vs. faith, the progress of the hero on a journey toward success or failure, the conceptualization of death as a final solution for those who fail. But Kane's novel sets out two paths that he never collapses; rather, as he says, the conflicting paradigms should "lead to reflection." Although one reading of these paths requires us to see a sort of existential journey that ends in failure, the other reading focuses on an Islamic path that leads to reintegration into "the heart of things" (*AA* 160). It is this latter reading that is anchored in Kane's social imaginary.

At a 1963 Dakar conference (Proceedings entitled *African Literature and the Universities*), Kane commented on the unspoken social imaginary in which his protagonist, Samba Diallo, operates:

> You know how it is; you write without always knowing why, or where your material comes from, or how you came to do it. But on thinking it over . . . I must agree that Samba Diallo's life does contain some elements drawn from the great Moslem mystic Sufi. It may be because of the traditional background against which he was brought up, as a native of one of the earliest parts of Africa to accept Islam. He comes from the valley of Senegal which was converted to Islam in the 11th century. It is an area in which Islam has always been lived and studied, almost as though in a hothouse, and I think this has genuinely left its mark on the inhabitants. (40)

Kane's focus on the spiritual, and on the therapeutic, means that his protagonist does not get drawn down the path of obsessive self-concern: the "why do they hate us" path that has limited Western thought and led to so much damage at the beginning of the twenty-first century.

Kane creates a scene that illustrates the dissonance (rather than "conflict") between the two social imaginaries about midway through the novel, just after the young Samba Diallo has been withdrawn from the Qur'anic school and sent to the French school. There he has as a classmate, Jean, the son of the French colonial administrator with whom Samba's father (the Knight) works. It is a scene set in the Sahara, an environment stripped bare, where the differing understandings of the desert in the social imaginaries of Samba and Jean manifest themselves. Samba and Jean demonstrate, in fledgling fashion, the cognitive differences that separate their fathers. Jean's confusion over Samba's worldview mirrors his father's perplexity and discomfort with the mystical philosophy of Samba's father. The disorientation of both father and son mirrors the larger confusion of the West in the face of Sufi Islam in Africa. As Jean, newly arrived in Africa, listens to his schoolmate Samba Diallo, scion of the Diallobé people, recite his prayers at twilight in the desert, he senses and obscurely fears the power of this language and system of belief that he cannot fathom: "Nothing in him was alive except his voice, speaking in the twilight a language which Jean did not understand" (*AA* 60). Looking out into the desert, Jean is fascinated by Samba's voice, "this voice that was no longer his," this "voice turned to a sob," and Jean loses track of time and place, until the arrival of Samba's father, the Knight:

> Samba Diallo was crouched on the ground, his head lowered, his body still trembling. The Knight knelt down, took his son by the shoulders, set him on his feet, and smiled at him. Through his tears Samba Diallo smiled back, a bright smile. With a fold of his boubou the Knight wiped the boy's face, very tenderly. . . .
>
> That night, thinking of Samba Diallo, [Jean] was overcome with fear. But that happened very late, when everyone had retired and Jean was alone, in his bed. That twilight's violence and splendor were not the cause of Samba Diallo's tears. Why had he wept?
>
> For a long time the little boy was haunted by the two faces of the father and the son. They continued to obsess him, until the moment when he sank into sleep. (*AA* 60–61)

Why should the child of the West be haunted, obsessed, and filled with fear at the fall of night, when it is the child of Africa who is conquered, whose traditions are being challenged, whose choices all seem to lead to defeat?

In this meeting, children of two cultures, who are without animosity and who share a future, experience the same space and the same moment in vastly different ways. The voice that fills with meaning when Samba recites his prayers in Arabic, becomes a meaningless series of sounds to the French boy listening to "this voice that was no longer his." The act of recitation, which grounds Samba and reestablishes him as a part of a community, isolates Jean, leaving him outside "the language which he did not understand." Jean stares off into the red sand of the desert not "conscious of his surroundings" while Samba, a tremor shaking his entire body, his "voice turned to a sob" witnesses the moment of twilight, turned toward Mecca: "to the east the sky was like an immense lilac-colored crystal." Jean, seeing only the surface spectacle of the "twilight's violence and splendor," its threatening and inhuman grandeur, puzzles over the presence of an understanding that completes Samba, that fills both Samba and his father with tenderness and joy. Just as Jean cannot read what is beneath the two faces because he is not versed in Sufi understandings, Western readers seem largely unaware of the Islamic narratives underpinning *Ambiguous Adventure.* The novel tells two different stories, depending upon the readers' cultural competencies: one involves the straight path or *tariqa* (an internal journey) and spiritual *jihad* (interior struggle), which Samba follows to final illumination; the other is limited to the external journey—his journey to Paris and back home to die, a "migration to the north,"[6] a negative and despairing narrative suggesting that it is impossible for Africans like Samba to survive the colonial moment.

Three key conventions operating in Kane's *Ambiguous Adventure* help to give readers some insight into the "traditional background" to which Kane refers when he says that Matam was a sort of "hothouse" of Sufi mysticism: oral recitation; travel in Muslim societies; and finally the Sufi belief that death involves a submersion of the self in God with goal of attaining *fana'* (extinction) and *baqa'* (eternality). The way Kane has composed the novel highlights these conventions. Part One of *Ambiguous Adventure* begins with a scene of recitation at Qur'anic school and ends with the recitation of the Suras on the "Night of the Qur'an." The second part of the novel mainly concerns the actual journey to Paris and back, and the examination of competing philosophical systems that Samba experiences. The final chapter of the novel concerns Samba's death, a death that has been prepared for from early on in the novel. Each of these conventions provokes competing standard Western interpretations: first, recitation brings up the paradigm of the oral/written divide interpreted as a separation between the primitive and the civilized, or alternatively as the presence/absence dialectic associated with Derrida's deconstructive philosophy; second, the journey gives rise to the paradigm of the hero's progress in the bildungsroman—a sort of quest theme; and third, the demise of the protagonist gives rise to the existentialist interpretations of death as an endpoint, a reading incompatible with both Sufism and traditional African religion. Kane's novel both encourages and undercuts these Western styles of thinking. Kane engages these competing readings. In this way, Kane shifts the focus of the "ambiguous adventure" from the narrative being told to the reception of that narrative by readers as they interpret the meaning of recitation, spiritual struggle, and mystical resolution.

Oral Recitation: The Architecture of the Word

> Paradise was built with the Words that he used to recite . . .
> —Kane, *Ambiguous Adventure*

The opening scene of *Ambiguous Adventure* shows the Qur'anic teacher, Thierno (marabout in Pulaar) punishing the young Samba Diallo severely for reciting the Qur'an incorrectly. The cruelty of this scene is such that a reader might wonder how this child could ever come to maintain "Paradise was built with the Words that he used to recite" (*AA* 43):

> The child's ear, already white with scarcely healed scars, was bleeding anew. Samba Diallo's whole body was trembling, and he was trying his hardest to recite his verse correctly, and to restrain the whimpering that pain was wresting from him. . . .
>
> The child succeeded in mastering his suffering, completely. He repeated the sentence without stumbling, calmly, steadily, as if his body were not throbbing with pain.
>
> The teacher released the bleeding ear. Not one tear had coursed down the child's delicate face. His voice was tranquil and his delivery restrained. The Word of God flowed pure and limpid from his fervent lips. There was a murmur in his aching head. He contained within himself the totality of the world, the visible and the invisible, its past and its future. This word which he was bringing forth in pain was the architecture of the world—it was the world itself. (*AA* 4–5)

Dorothy Blair sees in this scene a denigration of the body that is the necessary counterpart to privileging the spiritual; Debra Boyd-Buggs sees it as part of a larger social problem having to do with the backwardness of rural religious schools; Mildred Mortimer discusses the issue of rote learning. The role assigned recitation, in each case, makes it a challenge for the reader to understand how the "architecture of the world" Kane speaks of in this passage could flow from the child's lips. The role of recitation in Western literature is often a limited and negative one: it suggests being part of the chorus rather than being the protagonist, being a follower who repeats rather than an author who creates, being a speaker who produces physical speech without accompanying mental content. Yet Kane makes recitation a key to Samba Diallo's spiritual growth and social integration, encouraging readers to take a closer look at the role recitation plays in Diallobé as opposed to Western society.

In *African Literature in French*, Blair comments: "By the inhumanity of his treatment the Master deliberately aims at instilling contempt for the flesh, an absolute exaltation, a sole passion for the mystery and beauty of the Word of God, of which he feels his young disciple is capable" (263). One could argue, however, that it is not contempt for the flesh that Thierno tries to instill but rather discipline and concentration on the Word, the straight path. The idea of instilling "contempt for the flesh" is connected with some Jewish and Christian interpretations of God's will, as a way of warning sinful humankind of its nature, but it is not typical of Islamic belief. The Islamic concept of sin is not rooted in the corruptness of humankind, and the flesh is not evil. Humans are God's viceregents on earth, as explained in the Qur'an: "It is He who hath made you His agents, inheritors of the earth: He hath raised you in ranks, some above others: that He may try you in the gifts He hath given you: for thy Lord is quick in punishment: yet He is indeed Oft-Forgiving, Most Merciful" (6: 165). Because of this trust, and given that humans have free will, a premium is placed on submission to God's plan. To sin is to follow one's lower instincts (*nafs*/self)—seen not so much as fleshly corruption but rather willfulness such as pride or arrogance. While the Fall brought a life of shame, disgrace and hardship for Adam and Eve in the Bible, "in sharp contrast, the Qur'an teaches that after Adam disobeys God but repents, God extends to Adam his mercy and his guidance. . . . Repentance is simply remembering or returning to God's path, the straight path of Islam [which is the Qur'an]" (Esposito, *Straight Path* 28). So although we find fear of God, we do not find hatred of the flesh in Islam.

Boyd-Buggs maintains that the Grand Royale, Samba Diallo's aunt, in arguing that Samba should be sent to the French school is also arguing that Thierno's "ideology, based on death values, is impractical, and she fears that it is sapping the life out of her nephew. . . . The question that arises from this conflict involves the possibility that Thierno's teaching really did not deal with the whole man" ("Marabout-Masters" 209). Yet in this same scene Thierno explains to Samba Diallo's aunt, when she observes that Thierno's sternness focuses on death rather than life, "after this deep wounding from a hand that is fatherly, I promise you that this child will never wound himself. You will see from what stature he too will dominate life, and death" (*AA* 28). And Thierno tells the Chief of the Diallobé who is being asked by the masses for advice about how to respond to the invasion of Western ways: "Tell them they are gourds." He continues: "When young, [the gourd] has no other vocation than to achieve weight, no other desire than to attach itself lovingly to the earth. It finds the perfect realization of itself in weight. Then one day everything changes. The gourd wants to take flight. It reabsorbs itself, hollows itself out, as much as it can. Its happiness is a function of its vacuity, of the sonority of its response when a breath stirs it. The gourd is right in both instances" (*AA* 33–34). Samba must learn both to attend to the material facts of the historical changes he is living through and must grow in that environment, and later when it is time, he must make himself that vessel that is stirred by the breath of God. Boyd-Buggs, whose essay on maraboutic schools includes sections on the "physical abuse of the *Talibés* [students]," the "pedagogical incompetency" of rural teachers, "parental abdication," and "youth labor exploitation," explains Kane's novel as a sort of idealization and sees it as an aberration when compared to some other fiction concerning maraboutic teaching. She notes: "The pedagogy of the marabout generally consists of teaching the young *talibé* by means of rote memorization and a recitation of the Qur'an. This method ignores the critical spirit, and no effort is made to have the child rationally understand what he or she is reciting. . . . According to a study in 1917 [Paul Marty, *Etudes sur l'Islam au Sénégal—les doctrines et les institutions*, Paris: Ernest Leroux], 95 percent of the children who had completed the Qur'anic school could neither read, nor write, nor understand Arabic, and the situation has not changed appreciably since then" (193). Obviously a colonial study needs closer examination before it is cited as the autoritative source; claiming that things are exactly the same, almost one hundred years later and with no evidence cited, is problematic.

Mildred Mortimer points us much more usefully toward the idea that initiation and Western definitions of education need to be looked at. In describing Samba's experience at Qur'anic school, Mortimer brings up what is often a key issue concerning the memorization of the Qur'an: the extent to which the reciter understands the words spoken. Thierno is described as Samba's spiritual guide and initiator. Mortimer continues:

> I have used the verb "initiate" rather than "educate" because of the specific nature of Samba Diallo's early Quranic schooling. "Educate" is comprehensive and implies a wide area of learning, achieved by experience or formal schooling. Samba is taught to memorize verses of the Quran faultlessly. Only after he has mastered the mechanics will he begin to study the meanings of the words. As a Pulaar speaker, Samba finds the

> classical Arabic verses are all the more mysterious. Kane is careful to show that Samba as a child is caught up in the mystery: "This sentence—which he did not understand, for which he was suffering martyrdom—he loved it for its mystery and somber beauty." . . . As an adult, Samba is aware that his Quranic education was incomplete because he had never learned more that the skill of recitation: "I had interrupted my studies with the teacher of the Diallobé at the very moment when he was about to initiate me at last into the rational understanding of what up to then I had done no more than recite—with wonder, to be sure." . . . (55–56)

The context of the last part of this passage is particularly important. Samba is explaining to Adele, a French Marxist he meets while studying philosophy in Paris, why he hates the French, because as a child he had "loved them too soon, unwisely, without knowing them well enough" (*AA* 158). His French education gave him a new language and what was more, a new tool: writing. "As soon as I knew *how to write*, I began to flood my father with letters that I wrote him and delivered to him with my own hand. This was to demonstrate my new knowledge and also, by keeping my gaze fixed on him while he was reading, to establish the fact that with my new tool I should be able to transmit my thought to him *without opening my mouth*" (*AA* 159; emphasis added). It is at this point that he then says he had interrupted his studies with Thierno too soon. The French had interposed themselves, transforming Samba into their image: "Progressively, they brought me out from the heart of things, and accustomed me to live at a distance from the world" (*AA* 160). When Adele asks Samba to teach her "to penetrate the heart of the world," he replies: "I don't know whether one can ever find that road again, once one has lost it" (*AA* 160). Clearly Samba has learned from recitation something beyond what is called rote learning in the West and has been educated into a community. "Education" in a Western sense includes the ability to separate and distance the scholar from the material being studied, a process that has come under much scrutiny in recent years. Samba points to the destructiveness of thinking one lives "at a distance from the world."

Reading through the paradigms associated with Qur'anic learning is central to Kane's novel because he is, as the passage above suggests, critical of the Western paradigms of the detached observer. As William Graham points out in a discussion of the purpose of the Qur'anic school, "the [Qur'anic school] has thus been traditionally a major part of the formative experience of Muslims. Whatever its shortcomings, it has been a key influence in the early stages of 'islamization' of the Muslim individual. In Islamic societies, 'the Muslim does not put a child in a Qur'anic school in order to teach him, but in order to form him according to the immutable tradition that was that of his own parents and that of theirs'" (105). Because of the emphasis on formation and on obedience to God's will in one's life, Esposito comments that whereas for Christianity the appropriate question is "What do Christians believe?" for Islam it is "What do Muslims do?" (*Straight Path* 68). It is a difference between orthodoxy, or correct belief, and orthopraxy, or correct action. The very first words of *Ambiguous Adventure* illustrate both the seriousness of this formation in praxis for Thierno, and Samba's lack of understanding of the importance of reciting correctly: "That day, Thierno had beaten him again. And yet Samba Diallo knew his sacred verse. It was *only* that he had made a *slip of the tongue*. Thierno had jumped up as if he had stepped on one of the white-hot paving stones of the gehenna promised to evil-doers" (*AA* 3; emphasis added). Thierno gets even angrier when Samba recites the verse correctly, saying "Ah! So, you can keep from making mistakes? Then why do you make them? Eh? Why?" (*AA* 3). One way to understand the teacher's increased fury is to recognize that he sees in Samba not incapacity but rather inattention. On the subject of obedience and free will, Rumi wrote: "One does not beat an ox because he does not sprout wings,/but beats him because he refuses to carry the yoke" (qtd. in Schimmel, *Deciphering the Signs of God* 247). Schimmel explains this saying by noting that in the commentaries of some Muslim thinkers, free will and predestination have to do with the capacities God gives us: "Predestination could thus be explained as the development of one's innate talents: one cannot change them but can work to develop them as beautifully as possible until the *nafs*, which once was "inciting to evil" (Sura 12: 53), is finally tamed and, strengthened by its steady struggle against adversities and temptations, reaches inner peace so that it can return to the Lord (Sura 89: 27–28)" (247).

Thierno's anxiety over Samba's future is based not on any individual desire for Samba to succeed him but rather on his recognition of the great capacity in this child—and thus the greater distance this child could fall. For this reason, Thierno prays fervently for God to help Samba stay on the straight path:

> So closely would he live with God, this child, and the man he would become, that he could aspire—the teacher was convinced of this—to the most exalted levels of human grandeur. Yet, conversely, the least eclipse—but God forbid! The teacher was driving this eventuality from his mind with all the force of his faith. Still looking closely at the child, he made, mentally, a short prayer: "Lord, never forsake the man that is awakening in this child. May the smallest measure of Thy sovereign authority not leave him, for the smallest instant of time. (*AA* 5–6)

Thierno's aspiration for Samba—that he reach the heights of human grandeur, is not based in pride, rather it is evidence of God's goodness, the delight in His creation. Because the Qur'an is divine in its meanings and language, there really is no such thing as "only a slip of the tongue."

The rules about and importance of ritual speech are something that Kane's background would have taught him, and they have their basis in centuries of theological debate and commentary on the act of prayer. In the eleventh century, the Sufi mystic al-Ghazali (1058–1111) explained in his *Revival of the Religious Sciences*, his theory of the meaning of Qur'an reading and the rules that apply to the rememoration of God's Word. Al-Ghazali notes that there are external and internal rules that apply to recitation; the external rules have to do with observing the appropriate ritual ablutions, with attending to the amount read, the division of reading, the writing of the Qur'an, the enunciation, etc. When Samba has a "slip of the tongue," he has broken the rule of enunciation. But what is more important is that he has also committed an error insofar as internal rules or mental tasks are concerned. Al-Ghazali lists among the interior rules for the recitation of the Qur'an, first, the understanding in man that the Qur'an is God's Divine Essence (Abul Qasem 56). Next, that "only those who are clean can touch it" (60). And while cleanliness may refer to ablutions in the external rules, in the internal rules it refers to a purity of mind in the reciter, a readiness for illumination by God. Thus, one should not recite the Qur'an if one is not mentally prepared. To be prepared, one must abandon the *nafs*, the inner utterances of the self (61), and pay attention to the Word. One must also ponder the Sura recited (62). One must strive to understand what the Word means (65). To do so, one must get rid of obstacles or "veils" that block understanding.

Satan, who is man's enemy, gets quite clever at creating intellectual and sensory obstacles to understanding. Because the devil hovers around the mind of man, man cannot see the invisible world. The Qur'an reveals the invisible world, which is beyond both the senses and reason. Satan tries to fool Qur'an readers by imposing veils between man and his rememoration of God's word (69). He may preoccupy the readers with matters of pronunciation and thus turn their minds from appropriate attention to meaning (69–70). Another veil consists of dogmatic following of religious authorities rather than the opening of oneself to mystical vision in recitation (71). A third veil is caused by the desires of man; they are rust spots on the mirror of his soul so that the meanings of the Qur'an are veiled and partial (71). Recitation of the Qur'an and remembrance of death are two ways one polishes the rust off one's soul. Schimmel comments that a favorite theme among Sufis was that the "mirror of the heart [could become] covered by the blameworthy actions, and thus no longer capable of reflecting the Divine light . . . [Sufis] tried (and continue to try) to instruct the disciple in how to polish this mirror by constant recollection of God lest any dust, rust or verdigris of evil actions or thoughts be collected on it" (*Deciphering Signs of God* 31). The Qur'an teaches us "to check the external," to take a phrase from *Ambiguous Adventure* (*AA* 79), and shows us the straight path. Finally, the Qur'an reader rises to a state of rememoration where he hears the voice of God, not his own voice, and extinguishes personal attributes in the greater expanse of God.

God protects man by sending his divine inspiration in the Qur'an: "And thus have We, by our command, sent Inspiration to thee: Thou knewest not (before) what was Revelation, and what was Faith; but We guide such of Our servants as We will; and verily Thou dost guide (men) to the Straight Way" (42: 54). To find the Straight Path, humankind need only recite the Qur'an with sincerity of heart: "Recite what is sent of the Book by inspiration to thee, and establish regular prayer" (29: 45). In his commentary on this Sura, 'Abdullah Yusuf 'Ali notes:

> The *tilawat* [recitation] of the Qur'an implies: (1) rehearsing or reciting it, and publishing it abroad to the world; (2) reading it to ourselves; (3) studying it to understand it as it should be studied and understood (2: 121); (4) meditating on it so as to accord our knowledge and life and desires with it. When this is done, it merges into real Prayer, and Prayer purges us of anything (act, plan, motive, words) of which we should be ashamed or which would work injustice to others. Such Prayer passes into our inmost life and being, for then we realise the Presence of Allah, and that is true dhikr (or remembrance), for remembrance is the bringing to mind of things as present to us which might otherwise be absent to us. And that is the greatest thing in life. It is subjective to us: it fills our consciousness with Allah. For Allah is in any case always present and knows all. (998)

When Samba suffers a "slip of the tongue," he shows an inattention that discipline must correct. If, like Thierno, he is the chosen one to lead the Diallobé in understanding and interpreting the word of God, there must be no lapse of attention through which Iblis (Satan) could enter the architecture of the Word.

Thierno knows that Iblis has been from the beginning the arch-enemy of man and will try to trick him by making him stumble in his recitation of God's word. From the beginning, Iblis was the model of the scientific spirit who judged by external fact alone and who misunderstood the power of the Word, the rememoration of the word as it was breathed into man by God at the appropriate time. At the moment of the creation of man, God said to the angels: "I am about to create man, from sounding clay/From mud molded into shape; When I have fashioned him (in due proportion) and breathed into him of My spirit, Fall ye down in obeisance Unto him" (15:28–29). Iblis out of jealousy and arrogance refused to bow down. Seeing man only as a creature of dust, Iblis paid no attention to Adam's being a vessel for the divine spirit. In his commentary on this Sura, the early Islamic historian Muhammad ibn Jarir al-Tabari (d. 923) says in his *Jami' al-Bayan 'an Ta'wil Ay al-Qur'an* that God formed Adam so that Iblis would not be proud: "Adam remained on the ground a dry body for forty years. The angels used to pass by him and be frightened when they saw him, but Iblis was more frightened than all of them. He would strike the body and it would make a sound like the ringing of a clay pot. Then Iblis would enter Adam's mouth, come out from his anus, and say to the angels, 'Do not be afraid of this, for your Lord is solid but this body is hollow. If I shall be given authority over him, I will surely destroy him'" (al-Tabari 459–460; qtd. in Ayoub, vol.1 75). Thoroughly Western in his focus on "the evidence of the surface" rather than hidden substance, and unable to see the "presence" in potentiality, Iblis announces that absence is primary and suggests that he, Iblis, should be in charge of it. Thus he becomes the archenemy, not of God, but rather of man. According to Annemarie Schimmel, "Most mystics . . . have, of course, seen Satan as the one-eyed representative of intellect and false analogy, who did not recognize the divine spark in Adam and the divine breath that had been infused into the figure of clay" ("Creation and Judgment" 159). When God curses Iblis for his rebellion, Iblis begs respite from the Day of Judgment, which God in his mercy grants. He allows man free will—and thus the capacity to be misguided by Iblis, but also gives him the Qur'an as the straight path that leads to salvation. Iblis, ever the hair-splitting intellectual, reasons that God, who knows all, has "put him in the wrong" (15: 39) and thus he is justified in leading humankind down the path that will "put them all in the wrong" (15: 39).

One of the first issues that arises, then, is the purpose of Qur'an memorization and its status as "initiation" rather than "education." This way of looking at the acquisition of knowledge by dividing it into two dichotomous realms—rote learning and reasoning—is problematic. Moreover, the Western idea that we learn and move on is quite different from the Qur'anic idea that we memorize, and thus contain the Word—to which we continually return (rememoration of the Word) for guidance and completion. In his study of oral scripture, Graham quotes a story ascribed to Ahmad Ibn Hanbal (d. 855) who argued that the Qur'an was indeed the Uncreated [that is, unmediated and eternal] Word of God: "I saw God in my sleep and I asked, 'Lord, what is the best way by which those close to You draw [so] close?' God answered,

'Through My word [*kalam*], Ahmad.' Then I asked, 'O Lord, with or without understanding?' He said, 'With and without understanding'" (Graham 110). What kind of learning is this, then, that may involve reason, but seems more centered on an approach through the heart? A *hadith* of the Prophet says: "Whenever a group gathers in a house of God to recite God's scripture and to teach it to one another, there descends upon them the divine presence, mercy covers them, angels spread their wings over them, and God mentions them to those who are near him" (96). So, part of this learning has to do with participating in ritual, and part of it has to do with *baraka* or blessing that is borne on the sound of the religious chant. This blessing extends "with and without understanding" because it is based on faith. Each will understand according to his or her capacity. That one is simple or unschooled does not matter, rather it is faith demonstrated through appreciation of the sacred nature of the Qur'an that matters. Samba wishes that Thierno had had the opportunity to teach him to meet the West on its own terms—through reason, which is only one of several paths to understanding—but it is really faith that is at issue in the novel, and it is faith that saves Samba at the end.

Later, when Samba is taken from the Qur'anic school, the Glowing Hearth, to be sent to the French school in order to learn how to "check the external" (*AA* 79), he reflects upon the fact that his beloved Thierno "the teacher of the Diallobé would not leave him, even after his death" (*AA* 62) because although Thierno is frail and sickly, "he has the Word, which is made of nothing corporeal, but which endures . . . which endures. He has the fire which runs like flame through the disciples and sets the hearth aglow" (*AA* 63). The "Night of the Qur'an" is the culminating scene of Part One of the novel and occurs at the center of the book. On this night, Samba recites the holy book from memory throughout the night to honor his parents. It is most assuredly the poetic high point of the novel:

> Samba Diallo was repeating for his father what the knight himself had repeated for his own father, what from generation to generation through centuries the sons of the Diallobé had repeated for their fathers, . . . knowing that he had not failed in this respect and that he was about to prove to all who were listening that the Diallobé would not die in him. . . . Insensibly, rising from profundities which he did not suspect, phantoms were assailing him through and through and were substituting themselves for him. It seemed to him that in his voice had become muffled innumerable voices, like the voice of the river on certain nights. . . . With them, he wept their death; but also, in long cadence, they sang his birth. (*AA* 71–73)

Samba feels this night marks an end. He is filled with refusal at the path he must take into European civilization and with nostalgia at leaving the world of his childhood, but Kane's overriding message seems to be that Samba, despite his isolation in the night, will never really be alone. Samba's night differs from those of his forefathers because he is caught at the historical moment when some melding of European and African systems will happen. Samba's generation will have to find a way to cope with Western science and metaphysics without being coopted. If we remember the earlier scene when the French boy, Jean, is alone at night and "overcome with fear," we see that in contrast, Samba now carries with him the architecture of the Word, learned by heart and recited on the "Night of the Qur'an."

INTERNAL JOURNEYS: THE GREATER HIJRA/THE GREATER JIHAD

> Evidence is a quality of the surface. Your science is the triumph of evidence, a proliferation of the surface. It makes you the masters of the external, but at the same time it exiles you there, more and more.
>
> —The Knight to the Colonial Official (*AA* 78)

In their collection *Muslim Travellers: Pilgrimage, Migration, and the Religious Imagination*, Eickelman and Piscatori stress the idea that travel is an act of the imagination. When Samba Diallo's father prepares him to go to the West for his education, he does not focus on the external details of the journey, but rather on the philosophical distance Samba will need to travel. He speaks to him of the metaphysical dangers of the journey: the limitations of Descartes, and the seductions of Pascal. Thierno's teaching at the "glowing hearth" provides the background for these discussions between Samba and his father. The Qur'anic school teaches a form of mystical revelation, knowledge that exists beyond the realm of reason. The path Samba will follow is not a linear one that takes the believer to a distant point, rather it is both an outward journey and an inward meditation. Western narrative conventions—the bildungsroman, the hero's progress, the journey from innocence to experience—do not suffice to explain an experience that involves religious struggle rather than progress, community rather than individuation, and revelation rather than development through time.

Islamic culture includes many paradigms of the "journey" that structure the social imaginary for Samba. These forms—*hajj* (pilgrimage), *hijra* (emigration), *rihla* (travel for learning and other purposes), *ziyara* (visit to a shrine)—are figurative and constitutive structures. For example, the *hijra*, while it is a literal emigration, may also refer to the movement of the soul from corruption to purity (one might think of it as a journey from experience to innocence). In classical times, the *hijra* represented the movement from non-Muslim lands (*dar al-kufr*) to Muslim ones (*dar al-Islam*). In a postcolonial world, literal emigration to non-Muslim lands for educational or economic purposes may coexist with (an even be the impetus for) an emotional and spiritual migration back toward *dar al-Islam* (Eickelman and Piscatori 11). *Ambiguous Adventure* follows this pattern of both external and internal *hijra*. Samba Diallo's external *hijra*, travel to the West, is actually paralleled by an internal *hijra*, travel from a state of corruption to a rediscovery of purity attained at the close of the novel.

Muslim perspectives challenge Western paradigms that assume that development is dependent upon secularization, that the notions of center and periphery are unidirectional, that "written texts are more central than oral traditions or other cultural forms of authority" (11–14).[7] For example, *Ambiguous Adventure* begins by questioning whether the faithful of Senegal have ruled according to God's law: "I have learned that in the country of the white man, the revolt against poverty and misery is not distinguished from the revolt against God," the Qur'anic teacher Thierno observes. "They say that the movement is spreading, and that soon, in the world, that same great cry against poverty will drown out the voice of the *muezzins*. What must have been the misbehavior of those who believe in God if, at the end of their reign over the world, the name of God should arouse the resentment of the starving?" (*AA* 11). The assumption Thierno makes is that if Europeans know how to "conquer without being in the right," they do so as part of the will of God (as a scourge or punishment) to warn Muslims to examine their behavior. The Diallobé send Samba to the French school and then later to Paris to study in an effort to understand the will of God in bringing the French into Senegal.

In the context of Saharan Africa, the meaning of *hijra* and of *jihad*, "a general injunction to strive in the way of God," which was a community obligation (Hourani 66) had special imaginative and individual dimensions. "The only *hijra* that could be performed individually was withdrawal in the heart. Such interiorization of *hijra* in the esoteric sense was popularized by the Sufis" (Masud 35). Between 1500 and 1800, approximately 60 to 80 percent of all Muslims in Egypt, North Africa, and the Muslim portions of East and West Africa belonged to some Sufi order (B.G. Martin 1). Among the followers of the Prophet, there were always those who believed that sincerity of intention was the path that led to oneness with God, and that external observances meant nothing without this purity of desire for union, based on the greatness of God and the obedience of the believer: "There was a gradual articulation of the idea of a path by which the true believer could draw nearer to God; those who accepted this idea and tried to put it into practice came to be known generally as Sufis" (Hourani 152). Those who followed the same spiritual leader (*Cheikh*) and who followed the same path (*tariqa*) made up the various Sufi brotherhoods. Thus, from early on Saharan cultures include important narratives of the "journey"—in imitation of Mohammad's *hijra*. This close connection between language, literature, the rhythm of travel, and the centrality of community to individual identity finds its paradigmatic form in the narrative concerning Mohammed's establishment of Islam. As John Esposito notes in *Islam: The Straight Path*:

> Migration (*hijra*) marked a turning point in Mohammed's fortunes and a new stage in the history of the Islamic movement. Islam took on a political form with the establishment of an Islamic community-state at Medina. The importance of the *hijra* is reflected in its adoption as the beginning of the Islamic calendar. Muslims chose to date their history from neither Mohammed's birth nor his reception of the first revelation in 610, but from the creation of the Islamic community (*umma*). The community, as much as the individual, was to be the vehicle for realizing God's will on earth. (8)

Hijra bears a doubleness at its root as it means both "to abandon," "to break ties with someone"—such as ties of kinship or other personal association—and it means "to migrate."[8] This migration, as Hourani points out, is not simply negative in meaning (as in flight from Mecca) but positive as well in the sense of seeking protection by settling in a place other than one's own (Hourani 17). Travel takes students of Islamic culture to centers of learning, and in doing so, "unites them with the wider community of the faithful (*umma*) . . . [but travel] is ambivalent: through it the traveler becomes more linked to the idea of the Muslim community as a whole, but at the same time learns what is specific to his own people and culture" (El Moudden 69). Samba Diallo's travel seen from the perspective of this social imaginary cannot be understood as simply leaving Africa to go West. Kane noted, as was pointed out earlier, that his own particular geographic area was a "hothouse" of Sufi mysticism. J.P. Little traces some of the characteristics of Kane's social roots: He and his family are of Toukolor origin, or Haalpulaaren, "speakers of Pulaar," as they prefer to be known. The designation of Tukolor is a French corruption of "Tekrur," the old Arabic term dating from the tenth century for the area, corresponding to the modern Futa Toro, which extends over the Senegalese and Mauritanian banks of the Senegal River ("Autofiction" 76).

The traditions of the Islamic mystical brotherhoods provide the conventions and practices found in Saharan narratives. Leaders of these brotherhoods followed the path of the *talab al-'ilm* (seeking of knowledge) and engaged in *hijra* and *jihad*, each of which has both metaphysical and literal dimensions. Kane's own family were among the religious leaders of the area. According to Little, the social, political, and religious structures of Futa Toro were so resistant to "direct control by the French, that the colonizer simply used the structures in place, and political organization in the Futa resembled the 'indirect rule' of the British colonial regime" ("Autofiction" 76). Kane's family were both marabouts and school teachers:

> It was by no means a selling-out to the conqueror, however. Kane is emphatic that compromise was necessary for survival, but underlines constantly the role played by his family in maintaining the traditional, largely Islamic culture. . . . Cheikh Hamidou [Kane's grandfather[9]] did not receive a Western-style education, but became a leading Muslim teacher (*thierno* or marabout), in Matam, as well as a Muslim judge, or *qaadi*. He in fact had a reputation for being somewhat anti-French. . . . A noted sufi mystic, he had a great influence on Cheikh Hamidou, the novelist, as a child. ("Autofiction" 79)

The Sufi orders were the nexus of power in the Sahara. Historian David Robinson identifies five major *jihads* that took place in and around what Kane calls the land of the Diallobé. A reform movement in Futa Toro in the late eighteenth century under Almamy Abdul Kader, assassinated in 1807, did not create a strong central regime adhering to an Islamic code of conduct, "however, many of the changes he and his generation instituted, especially the mosques and schools at the village level remained and nurtured a strong Islamic identity throughout the middle valley of the Senegal River. It is this Islamic culture, and the nostalgia for an earlier day, which we see reflected in Kane's story of Thierno and Samba Diallo" (113).

The particular Islamic social imaginary reflected in *Ambiguous Adventure* has other connections to the region in which Kane grew up. For example, the reform movement, which occurred from approximately 1804 to 1812 in Hausaland led by the *Qadriya* Sufi leader Usuman dan Fodio, provides a strong paradigm of the journey as both imaginative act and literal displacement. Usuman dan Fodio, born in Hausaland in 1754, led a Muslim *jihad* (personal struggle in a spiritual sense; holy war in a political sense) along with his brother, Abdallahi and his son Muhammad Bello. Usuman dan Fodio's history ties him in several ways to the larger narrative patterns of a work like Kane's *Ambiguous Adventure*. Usuman Dan Fodio learned the Qur'an by heart, mastered Arabic grammar, and learned Arabic poetic traditions. In 1789, and again in 1794, he experienced mystical visions that pushed him to take action. He decided to carry out a *hijra* based on the model of the

Prophet, emigrating with the faithful. Then, from 1804 to 1808, he carried out a literal *jihad* against the Hausa armies to instill a more orthodox Islam in areas where syncretism and accommodation of fetishist traditions prevailed. A caliphate was created in 1808 and installed in Sokoto in 1815 (B. G. Martin 16–21; Mantran 178–79).

Kane's novel has ties to two other historical examples of the Islamic social imaginary of the region along the southern rim of the Sahara: the Timbuktu chronicles (the *Ta'rikh al-Sudan* and the *Ta'rikh al-Fettach*) written in the seventeenth century, and the fifth *jihad* led by Al-Hajj 'Umar. In *Ambiguous Adventure*, the old, black magistrate whom Samba Diallo meets on a Paris street explains how he came to be named Pierre-Louis by referring to the Timbuktu chronicles: "My great-grandfather was called Mohammed Kati—yes, Kati, like the author of the *Tarikh El Fettach*—and he was from the same region as his great namesake, the very heart of the old empire of Mali. My great-grandfather was made a slave, and sent to the [Caribbean] Islands, where he was rebaptised Pierre-Louis Kati. He dropped the name Kati so as not to dishonor it" (*AA* 130).

Al-Hajj 'Umar, who led the fifth *jihad*, which took place in Futa Toro, followed the same cultural patterns as Usuman dan Fodio. Born near Podor, Senegal in 1794, he had memorized the Qur'an by age 15. In 1825, he began a long journey as *talib al-'ilm*, heading to Mecca. When he reached Cairo, he was interrogated from early morning until the noon prayers about "the oddities of tradition, unintelligible passages in the Qur'an, and details of law, grammar, logic and rhetoric" (B. G. Martin 71). After reaching Mecca, he traveled to Medina where he stayed three years to study with the Moroccan Muhammad al-Ghali who had been a close associate of al-Tijani and was an initiate of the *Tijaniya* brotherhood, which 'Umar also joined.

He returned to Futa Toro and became the leader of the resistance to the Bambara, on the one hand,[10] and to the French who were moving upstream on the Senegal river from Saint Louis, on the other. In the early 1850s, al-Hajj 'Umar, who controlled most of the eastern part of Senegambia, opposed the French expansion into the interior. A scholar first and military commander second, 'Umar drew distinctions, in his book the *Rimah*, between the major and minor *jihads*:

> The former was defined as the struggle for self-control; the latter (and lesser *jihad*) was a military matter. In 'Umar's opinion, self-control was logically prior to military concerns. He says: "Every person must make an effort to purify his soul. He should make a serious attempt, and genuinely strive to serve His Lord: Nothing should hinder him from it. He should not be diverted by any family claim, his father or his son, his native coun-

> try, a friend, his house, his clan, his money, or other things which hinder him from nearness to God . . . even if this should lead him to absence from his native place." (B. G. Martin 82)

This narrative of the major *jihad* is one that closely resembles the interior struggle of Samba Diallo in Kane's *Ambiguous Adventure.* Among the traits that define Samba Diallo's character as he experiences this dislocation to the West is his confusion over his own strength of will, but never resentment toward others, and anguish about his ability to live up to Thierno's Islamic teachings, but never rebellion against them or doubt concerning their rightness.

Al-Hajj 'Umar's scholarly work also included an emphasis on the *hijra.* Wanting to establish Islamic rule in the eastern part of Futa Toro and the Bambara states, which remained fetishist, 'Umar wanted French weapons and also an agreement that would assure that the French would not attack him from the rear. Meeting with them in 1847, 'Umar was willing to protect French trading rights on the upper Senegal river as long as they paid the *coutume*, a tax he considered equivalent to the *jizya* paid by subordinate non-Muslims in Muslim territory. He is reported to have said: "I am the friend of the whites. I want peace and detest injustice. When a Christian had paid the *coutume*, he may trade with safety. When I become Imam of Futa [Toro], you must build me a fort. I shall discipline the country, and friendly relations will exist between you and me" (88). The French did not take this offer of a subordinate position seriously, and relations worsened. By 1854, 'Umar had decided to move his population away from "'oppressive non-Muslim rulers'—African or French" (88). Between 1857 and 1859 he moved 50,000 of his people to the east in a *hijra* (emigration) (Mantran 179). His *Rimah*, used as a text by his students, devoted an entire chapter to the *hijra*: "migration is now necessary for every person living in a town where disobedience to God is openly practiced without any concern over it, where the situation cannot be altered. Migration is imperative from the land of the unbelievers. . . . *Hijra* is of two kinds, the greater and the lesser" (B. G. Martin 89). As with the *jihad*, the greater *hijra* is a personal, internal "migration" in which one separates oneself from worldly things and concerns; the lesser *hijra* is a result of a political situation. Thus among Sufi brotherhoods, the concepts of the *jihad* and of the *hijra* involved personal, metaphysical obligations as well as the more commonly recognized communal ones. Interior struggles for self-control and distancing from worldly concerns replicate exterior displacements caused by migration, exile, and travel engaged in while seeking knowledge.

Samba Diallo's Greater Jihad

> Descartes . . . would probably become an American citizen if he should return. He had rejected the traditional contemplative ideal of philosophy and put in its place a new experimental rationalism and a mechanistic view of the physical world. He regarded science as a means of acquiring mastery over nature for the benefit of mankind and led the way himself with experiments in optics and physiology. But—and this perhaps more than all else makes him a true modern, Western man—he made the foundation of his philosophical edifice including the existence of God contingent on his own first person singular! *Cogito ergo sum. I think therefore I am.*
>
> —Chinua Achebe, "The Writer and His Community"

Toward the end of Part One of *Ambiguous Adventure*, Samba Diallo contemplates his father who is reading the Qur'an. Samba is struggling with unspoken thoughts about the instrumentality of the West, and wondering if it is their focus on work, especially science, that makes Westerners forget God. Noticing his struggle, the Knight comments on what Samba is reading:

> "*Les Pensées*. . . . Hmm . . . Pascal. Of the men of the West, he is certainly the most reassuring. But be distrustful even of him. He had doubted. Exile had known him too. It is true that he came back running. He wept, sobbing, over having gone astray, and he called upon the 'God of Abraham, Isaac, and Jacob' against that of the 'philosophers and scholars.' The road of his return began like a miracle and ended like an act of grace. The men of the West know less and less of the miracle and the act of grace. . . ."
>
> Samba did not dare to reveal to his father the whole tenor of his thought. . . . He tempered his words, therefore:
>
> "You have spoken of Pascal's exile, thinking no doubt of that part of his life which preceded the *Mémorial*. . . . Now this period of dereliction was also a period of intense scientific toil. . . ."

For Western readers, this particular discussion of Pascal's "Memorial"[11] and of the value of work has suggested the model of the Socratic dialogue; Samba's father asks the crucial questions to lead Samba to discover that for the believer, work and all other human activity can be likened to prayer. Thus one is not neglecting prayer and religious duty if one is working in the field, for example. For the unbeliever, however, work is turned toward secular ends such as the accumulation of material wealth. Commenting on the style of Kane's philosophical exchanges, Bernadette Cailler notes: "Certain passages follow a Cartesian pattern; the discourse is sober, without flourishes; the characters exchange ideas. Emotion, mysticism, are absent here, or almost (see for example the discussion between the Knight and Samba in Chapter Nine concerning work and the West)" (748–749). Muslim readers, on the other hand, might see that the discourse here is done in the fashion of al-Ghazali or the *mutakallimun* (speculative theologians), carried out both through witnessing God's greatness in prayer (revelation of the Word) and through reasoning:

> The Knight regarded his son in silence for several seconds. Then, instead of answering his implied question [about the value of Pascal's intense scientific work during his period of dereliction before his 1654 revelation], he asked,
>
> "Why, in your opinion, does one work?"
>
> "In order to live."
>
> "Your answer pleases me. But in your place I should have been less categorical. My reply would have been enumerative, in the following form, for example: 'One can work to live, one can work to outlive. . . . My enumeration is not restrictive. Do you admit that I am more in the way of truth than you are, and that my enumeration is just?"
>
> "Yes" . . .
>
> "Even while he thinks, he has the air of one praying," Samba Diallo said to himself. "Perhaps he is really praying? God has indeed entered into his entire being."
>
> "Therefore," the Knight went on, "one may work from necessity, for the cessation of the great pain of need which wells up from the body and from the earth—to impose silence on all those voices which harass us with their demands. Then, too, one works to maintain oneself, to preserve the species. But one can also work from greed . . .
>
> "Would you like us now to enlarge upon and examine these ideas in relation to God? (*AA* 97–98)

The Knight demonstrates here, as al-Ghazali did in his *Ihya 'ulum ad-din* (Revival of the Religious Sciences), that the conduct of one's life, such that one is conscious of God's presence at each moment, is central to religion: "This feeling of God's presence is valid even while one is busy with most nonreligious actions, and for this reason [al-Ghazali's text] contains in its first three parts injunctions about correct behavior in every moment, be it marriage or prayer, commerce or travel. Only the fourth part is devoted to more clearly religious and mystical issues" (Schimmel, *Islam* 109–110).

Chapter Nine of *Ambiguous Adventure* is, as was noted, the pivotal chapter between Samba's training in his native Senegal (first at the Qur'anic school with the stern master Thierno and then at the French school) and his journey to the metropole to study Western philosophy at the university. He realizes, with his father's guidance, that the "death of God," which Nietzsche envisioned is not necessary to bring about the birth of modern, technological society. Nonetheless, he remains confused about his responsibility: The West has conquered "without being in the right" (*AA* 37); they have denied God in order to serve man. Samba's father suggests to him that "the history of the West . . . [reveals] the insufficiency of the guarantee that man offers to man. For man's welfare and happiness we must have the presence and the guarantee of God. . . . Perhaps Pascal had caught a glimpse of this" (*AA* 101–102). Samba is, at this point, secure in his knowledge that he is following the straight path (thus he is at one with the universe), but confused about how he should act toward those unbelievers with whom he will necessarily share a common future:

> Samba Diallo was not seeing the shining firmament, for the same peace reigned in the heavens and in his heart. Samba was not existing. There were innumerable stars, there was the earth chilled anew by the coming of night, there was the shade, there was their simultaneous presence.
>
> "It is at the very heart of this presence that thought is born," he reflected, "as on the water a succession of waves is set off around a spot where something has fallen. But there are those who do not believe . . ."
>
> Samba Diallo suddenly saw the sky. In a flash he realized its serene beauty.
>
> "There are those who do not believe. . . . We who believe—we cannot abandon our brothers who do not believe. The world belongs as much to them as it does to us. Labor is a law for them as much as it is for us. They are our brothers. Often their ignorance of God will have come to them as an accident of their labor, in the workyards where our common dwelling is being put up. Can we forsake them? (*AA* 104–105)

Samba Diallo's journey to Paris involves not just a journey to the West, but a journey into Western philosophy. Samba Diallo struggles to understand the philosophical rift that separates Descartes from Pascal. At the same time, however, he is seeking to understand what separates the West philosophically from the Sufi ways of knowing that he has grown up with. The obligation he feels is a tremendous one: he is being sent to the West not only to save the Diallobé by finding a way for them to survive interaction with the West, but also he is concerned for the West, itself: "We who believe—we cannot abandon our brothers who do not believe" (*AA* 105). At this moment, Samba remembers a page from Descartes saying "The rapport between God and man is first of all a rapport of will to will; can there be a rapport more intimate?" (*AA* 104). Samba assumes, at this point in his education, that a merging of philosophical traditions is possible: "'the masters are in agreement. Descartes, as well as [Thierno] the teacher of the Diallobé, as well as my father—they have all experienced the irreducible inflexibility of this idea.' Samba Diallo's joy increased with the realization of this convergence" (*AA* 104). This belief in convergence is undone by Samba Diallo's experience in the West where "will to will" suggests a contract rather than the submission integral to Sufi practice as Samba defines it: "To believe: that is to recognize one's own will as a small fragment of the divine will" (*AA* 103).

Part Two of *Ambiguous Adventure*, Samba's stay in Paris, is largely depicted through the philosophical debates he has with his Marxist classmate Lucienne Martial and her protestant family, and with the family of the Cameroonian immigrant Pierre-Louis, especially his daughter, Adèle. The section opens with the protestant pastor Paul Martial asking Samba: "From what you have been able to grasp of the history of our thought, has it seemed to you radically foreign, or have you indeed recognized yourself a little, just the same?" (*AA* 113). Samba replies:

> It seems to me that this history has undergone an accident which has shifted it and, finally, drawn it away from its plan. Do you understand me? Socrates' scheme of thinking does not seem to me, at bottom, different than that of Saint Augustine, though there was Christ between them. *The plan is the same, as far as Pascal. It is still the plan of all the thought that is not occidental.*
>
> What is it? Pierre [the pastors's son] asked.
>
> I do not know. But don't you feel *as if the philosophical plan were already no longer the same with Descartes as with Pascal*? It is not that they were preoccupied with different problems, but that they occupied themselves with them in different ways. It is not the mystery which has changed, but the questions which are asked of it, and the revelations which are expected from it. Descartes is more niggardly in his quest; if, thanks to this and also to his method, he obtains a greater number of responses, what he reports also concerns us less, and is of little help to us. (*AA* 113–114; emphasis added)

Samba recognizes in the philosophy of Pascal an emphasis on the "heart" as the way to knowledge of God; in Sufi belief, the heart is the locus of Spirit and through it the individual knows God. The Cartesian approach to knowledge is rejected by Pascal, in the very terms Samba has mentioned, in *Les Pensées* # 84: "*Descartes.* In general terms one must say: 'That is the result of figure and motion,' because it is true, but to name them and assemble the machine is quite ridiculous. It is pointless, uncertain, and arduous. Even if it were true we do not think that the whole of philosophy would be worth an hour's effort" (52). Descartes' philosophy sets itself at a distance from the world it examines, making the world the distant object of its scrutiny. Samba assumes, as did Pascal, that if man is indeed separated from the world in such a way "the whole of philosophy would not be worth an hour's effort."

But Samba did not learn this way of approaching the world from Pascal, rather it is part of his own social imaginary. The Qur'an says of unbelievers "Truly it is not their eyes/That are blind, but their/Hearts" (22: 46). As in most mystic traditions, the Sufi way locates the heart as the gateway by which the spirit travels to unity with God:

> In the macrocosm, the Garden of Eden is both centre and summit of the earthly state. Analogously the Heart, which in the microcosm corresponds to the Garden, is both centre and summit of the human individuality. More precisely, the Heart corresponds to the centre of the Garden, the point where grows the Tree of Life and where flows the Fountain of Life. The Heart is in fact nothing other than this Fountain, and their identity is implicit in the Arabic word *'Ayn* which has the meaning of both 'eye' and 'spring.' . . . The Heart is the isthmus (*barzakh*) which is so often mentioned in the Qur'an as separating the two seas which represent Heaven and earth the sweet fresh-water sea being the domain of the Spirit whereas the brackish salt sea is the domain of the soul and body. (Lings 50)

The soul, *nafs*, exists in three forms in the Qur'an—as a lower willfulness that is evil, as a mediate form of conscience, and as the self at peace when reconciled to God. Unlike the organs of knowledge we call the senses and the intellect, the heart is the seat of belief, of true knowledge.

Pascal also sees humankind as having three ways of knowing: through the senses, through reason, and by way of the heart; while the first two paths involve the use of evidence to lead to knowledge, the latter rather depends on faith. As he writes in *Les Pensées* #7: "Faith is different from proof. One is human and the other a gift of God. *The just shall live by faith* [1.Rom. 1.17]. This is the faith that God himself puts into our hearts, often using proof as the instrument. *Faith cometh by hearing* [2.Rom.x.17]. But this faith is in our hearts, and makes us say not 'I know' but 'I believe'" (34). In his study of Pascal's life and thought, A. J. Krailsheimer points out that "authority," for Pascal in his later life, stemmed not from external rulings but rather from an inner order, which he called heart. Divine truths are given by God alone:

> "He wants them to enter the mind from the heart, and not the heart from the mind, to humiliate that arrogant power of reasoning."[12] . . . At all times, Pascal recognised three ways to truth and knowledge. Whether in a scientific or explicitly religious context he added a third term to the usual reason and senses (or mind and body), and variously defined it as the will that submits to authority, instinct, intuition, or heart. The continuity of this triple division, so radically different from Descartes' dualism of mind and matter and the unchallenged supremacy of reason, is unmistakable and basic to an understanding of Pascal's life and thought. (25–26)

Pascal writes in *Les Pensées* # 887 "Descartes useless and uncertain" (300). Because of his emphasis on knowledge through the heart, Pascal seems to Samba to reflect a Western Christian social imaginary that, before the advent of Cartesian dualism, had been much closer to Sufi belief and practice.

Following his discussion with the Martials about the split between Western philosophy and Sufi thought, Samba suffers his own disorientation, brought about by a letter from the chief of the Diallobé telling him that Thierno has given up teaching and that a former classmate of Samba's, a secularized village dolt, will become the new Qur'anic teacher since Samba has gone away. Confused about his own responsibility and by his experience of the West, Samba asks God to remember him: "I am that soul whom thou hast made to weep in filling him with Thy grace. I beg Thee, do not allow me to become the utensil which I feel to be emptying itself already. . . . Thou wouldst not know how to forget me like that. I would not agree, alone with us two, to suffer from Thy absence. . . . Remember, Lord, how Thou hast nourished my existence from Thine. So time is nourished by duration. I felt Thee to be the deep sea from which spreads out my thought and, at the same time, everything. Through Thee, I was the same wave as the whole" (*AA* 126–127). This plea, filled with Sufi images of the sea as the "domain of the Spirit" (Lings 50), encourages Samba to write to his father for guidance.

After this night of anguish, he feels alienated by the Cartesian dualism of the streets of Paris, as was Rilke's Malte Laurids Brigge: "These streets are bare. . . . No, they are not empty. One meets objects of flesh in them, as well as objects of metal. Apart from that they are empty. Ah! One encounters events. Their succession congests time, as the objects congest the street. Time is obstructed by their mechanical jumble. One does not perceive the background of time, and its slow current . . . their street is empty, their time is encumbered, their soul is silted up" (*AA* 128–129). Samba's discomfort is caused by precisely what gave Descartes great satisfaction in the city—its mechanical anonymity. Descartes writes of Amsterdam in his *Discourse on Method*: "Living here, amidst this great mass of busy people who are more concerned with their own affairs than curious about those of others, I have been able to lead a life as solitary and withdrawn as if I were in the most remote desert, while lacking none of the comforts found in the most populous cities" (126).[13] Samba's sense of well-being only returns when he runs into an "obstacle" who introduces himself as Pierre-Louis. This black magistrate had served, after he retired, as an advocate before the bar in Geneva for the "natural rights" of the poor folk of Gabon and Cameroon who had lost their land to the rapacity of the French State and French settlers. Pierre-Louis, the "old black lion," by the example of his passion for justice despite the odds, brings Samba back in touch with the natural world and his stewardship of it (*AA* 134).

A short while later, when he meets with Lucienne, the Marxist, Samba is able to explain clearly the unadulterated value he places on his Afro-Islamic roots:

> You have not only raised yourself above Nature. You have even turned the sword of your thought against her: you are fighting for her subjection—that is your combat, isn't it? As for me, I have not yet cut the umbilical cord which makes me one with her. The supreme dignity to which, still today, I aspire is to be the most sensitive and the most filial part of her. Being Nature herself, I do not dare to fight against her. I never open up the bosom of the earth, in search of my food, without demanding pardon, trembling beforehand. I never strike a tree, coveting its body, without making fraternal supplication to it. I am only that end of being where thought comes to flower. (*AA* 139–140)

Lucienne tries to attribute Samba's feeling to "negroness" (*AA* 141), but Samba rejects this racialist, essentialist interpretation: "I confess that I do not like the word, and I don't always understand what it would be meant to cover" (*AA* 142). Samba's Qur'anic schooling has taught him that humans are God's stewards of nature and are not separate from it. His worry is that, having been acculturated to the West, he "can no longer find the world's pathway" (*AA* 144).

Visiting with Pierre-Louis' family, Samba follows up on this train of thought: "It might be said that I see less fully here [in the West] than in the country of the Diallobé, I no longer feel anything directly. . . . It seems to me, for example, that in the country of the Diallobé man is closer to death. He lives on more familiar terms with it. His existence acquires from it something like an aftermath of authenticity" (*AA* 148–149). Rememoration immerses believers in God; it makes of the human body, in Thierno's image, a gourd resonating with God's word. This social imaginary no longer surrounds Samba in the West: "Here, now, the world is silent, and there is no longer any resonance from myself. I am like a broken balafong, like a musical instrument that has gone dead. I have the impression that nothing touches me any more" (*AA* 150).

Pierre-Louis' Westernized son, Captain Hubert, assumes that the West has its technological know-how to give and that it does not matter if there is no reverse transfer of knowledge. Samba recognizes that having been asked to learn Western ways has led to a deeper confusion, with two social imaginaries shaping his reactions at an unconscious level: "I am not a distinct country of the Diallobé facing a distinct Occident, and appreciating with a cool head what I must take from it and what I must leave with it by way of counterbalance. I have become the two. There is not a clear mind deciding between the two factors of a choice. There is a strange nature, in distress over not being two" (*AA* 150–151). Migration for the purpose of knowledge may well not be simply a mission to acquire technical know-how. Its purpose might also be learning to read God's signs, to see in the French way of life not an exemplar but a warning. For this reason Samba says to Captain Hubert, who suggests that Africans must adopt Western ways if they are to be realistic: "If we accept [Western instrumentality] and accomodate ourselves to it, we shall never have the mastery of the object. For we shall have no more dignity than it has. We shall not dominate it. Have you noticed that? It's the same gesture as that of the West, which masters the object and colonizes us at the same time. If we do not awake the West to the difference which separates us from the object, we shall be worth no more than it is, and we shall never master it. Our defeat will be the end of the last human being on this earth" (*AA* 153–154). In this discussion, Samba Diallo takes the same stance as his father had in Part One with Jean's father, the colonial administrator, Paul Lacroix.

As Paul Lacroix watched the sun set through his closed window, he thought: "They are right. . . . The world is about to come to an end. The moment is fragile. . . . No!" (*AA* 74). When he asks Samba's father if he is not disturbed by the twilight, by the thought of the end of the world, the Knight responds: "On the contrary, I even hope for it, firmly. . . . Our most simple-minded peasant does not believe in such an end as that, episodic and accidental. His universe does not admit of accident. In spite of appearances, his concept is more reassuring than yours" (*AA* 75). Paul Lacroix sees this response as mere superstition on the one hand—a sort of primitivism—and as a psychological dodge on the other—"the truth which they do not now possess, which they are incapable of conquering, they hope for in the end" (*AA* 76). Later in Paris, his mentor Pierre-Louis tells Samba Diallo: "The West passes you by, you are ignored, you are useless—and that at a time when you yourself can no longer pass by the West. Then you succumb to the complex of the Unloved. You feel your position is precarious" (*AA* 150). Samba will need to discover the same truth that his father expresses to Paul Lacroix in the earlier scene:

> "From the bottom of my heart I wish for you to rediscover the feeling of anguish in the face of the dying sun. I ardently wish that for the West. When the sun dies, no scientific certainty should keep us from weeping for it, no rational evidence should keep us from asking that it be reborn. You are slowly dying under the weight of evidence. I wish you that anguish—like a resurrection."

> "To what shall we be born?"
>
> "To a more profound truth. Evidence is a quality of the surface. Your science is the triumph of evidence, a proliferation of the surface. It makes you masters of the external, but at the same time it exiles you there, more and more." (*AA* 77–78)

The diametrical opposition between this Western social imaginary and that of the Diallobé must be reconciled because they share a future. As Samba's father suggests, it is not death that is the problem, but rather a lack of appreciation of the fullness of life, including the need for a certain flexibility of mind and humility of spirit, on the part of the West that is problematic. Samba's death, seen in this light, is not a failure as we shall see. To think so is to stick to the evidence of the surface. He reconciles his experience with the West with his beliefs at the end of the novel. The problem is rather how to get the West to foreground this need for reconciliation in their social imaginary.

"The place where there is no ambiguity"

Shortly after his discussion with Pierre-Louis' family, Samba receives an answer to the letter he had written his father. His father tells him to return home: "It is high time that you should come back, to learn that God is not commensurable with anything, and especially not with history, whose vicissitudes are powerless in relation to His Attributes" (*AA* 162). The Islamic context in which Kane places Samba's story makes of *Ambiguous Adventure* a literary masterpiece, joining as it does historical ambiguity with spiritual clarity. Critics who read *Ambiguous Adventure* as Samba Diallo's "journey of initiation," which ends in tragedy and despair are approaching the novel from the perspective of Western instrumentality. For example, A. C. Brench writes: "The tragic outcome of the encounter between Samba and European philosophy is never in doubt. It underlines the precarious nature of the logic which supports the Diallobé's faith and the futility of their struggle" (102). Christophe Dailly says, in comparing Samba to the protagonist, Okonkwo, in Achebe's *Things Fall Apart*: "The disarray of these people is total. Okonkwo and Samba Diallo die of alienation. . . . They appear as losers. They have not succeeded in adapting themselves to their actual social conditions" (207). Other critics—Victor Aire, Kenneth Harrow, and Mildred Mortimer[14]—discuss the double ending of this novel in which Samba seems to fail on the mundane level but succeed on the spiritual one. Mortimer's nuanced reading deals with the issue of why Kane did not reintegrate Samba Diallo into the community rather than having him die unexpectedly; she offers the insightful observation that we must "view the fool as a catalyst rather than as a guide"

(65). The fool is a catalyst who forces readers to recognize that there are a number of ways of practicing Islam, even within a small village. Kane in his interviews with J. P. Little sees the Fool as representing the kind of intolerant Islam associated with fundamentalism today. In focusing on a tolerant, mystical Islam, Harrow gives an especially significant weight to a non-Western understanding of Kane's ending.[15] He emphasizes Samba's attainment of sufi *fana'*—the extinction or death "of the created in the Uncreated, of the temporal in the Eternal, of the finite in the Infinite" (Lings 25), but does not go further to discuss the philosophical roots of Sufism and its representations of *baqa'*—remaining, substance, eternality (Lings 78). Kane, when asked about the meaning of Samba's death, replied:

> Did it strengthen the vital force, or some other force, that existed in Samba Diallo before he died? I think it did, because it is only his death that may have enabled him to overcome the "ambiguity," to overcome his dual nature. That, I think, is why the last chapter should probably be read with this in mind. It is really a kind of opening or liberation, and hence, to some extent, a strengthening of the being of Samba Diallo who is torn between his position as a black man and the beginning of this metamorphosis or identification of himself with the white world, with the white man whose culture has attracted him. He is torn also between the mystical believer that education and nature have made him, and the atheist and disciple of materialism that his Western education has to some extent made of him as well. (*African Literature* 39–40)

In other interviews, Kane has explained that the meaning of "ambiguous" in his title is not "equivocal" but rather "obscure" (Kotchy 479–486). By this, I believe he intends for readers to understand that Samba is not equivocal about the value of Islam, but rather that he is uncertain that the world belongs to all and the future will be shared. The West has material power; it conquered its colonial possessions "without being in the right" (*AA* 37); it dehumanized the world while claiming the opposite. This imbalance of physical power makes the way forward obscure. As Anouar Majid points out in *Unveiling Traditions: Postcolonial Islam in a Polycentric World*, Kane succeeds in presenting a Muslim social imaginary that can hold its own against the forces of dehumanization: "Inspired by 'conventional Muslim views,' the novel brings into sharp relief, and perhaps prophetically anticipates, the growing impasse between the cultures of Islam and Western secularism in the contemporary period. Indeed, because it insists on privileging indigenous traditions, *Ambiguous Adventure* may still be—although it was originally published in the early 1960s—the most 'committed' African novel to propose a 'radical alternative'" (94).[16]

If Samba's death is a sign of hope, it is because he dies at peace with God and enters a place "where there is no ambiguity" (*AA* 177) where he experiences *baqa'*: "The moment is the bed of the river of my thought. The pulsations of the moments have the pulsations of thought; the breath of thought glides into the blowpipe of the moment. At the heart of the moment, behold man as immortal, for the moment is infinite, when it is. The purity of the moment is made from the absence of time. . . . The sea! Here is the sea!" (*AA* 177–178). The divine word allows Samba to reconcile the world of fact and spirit:

> The world is a multiplicity which disperses and divides; the Qur'an is a multiplicity which draws together and leads to Unity. The multiplicity of the Holy Book—the diversity of its words, sentences, pictures and stories—fills the soul and then absorbs it and imperceptibly transposes it into the climate of serenity and immutability by a sort of "divine ruse." The soul, which is accustomed to the flux of phenomena, yields to this flux without resistance; it lives in phenomena and is by them divided and dispersed—even more than that, it actually becomes what it thinks and does. The revealed Discourse has the virtue that it accepts this tendency while reversing its movement thanks to the celestial nature of the content and the language, so that the fishes of the soul swim without distrust with their habitual rhythm into the divine net. (Schuon 47–48)

Samba's redemption and merging with the Divine Spirit bring up some difficult questions if we are trying to read the novel through Western literary paradigms. What progress has Samba made in the course of the novel? On what grounds is Samba redeemed? What kind of journey can take place, what form of historical thought do we have, in a culture that speaks of the "absence of time"? Samba has already pointed to the philosophical rift that has taken place between Islam and the contemporary West: "The plan is the same, as far as Pascal. It is still the plan of all the thought that is not occidental"(*AA* 114). This same rift is spoken of by Islamic philosophers and Sufi thinkers. In his introduction to *The Sufi Path of Knowledge: Ibn al-'Arabi's Metaphysics of Imagination*, William C. Chittick discusses the differing structures of imagination that have emerged in the East and West:

> Somewhere along the line, the Western intellectual tradition took a wrong turn. Arguments arise over when and why this happened. Many important thinkers have turned to the Oriental traditions in hope of finding resources which may help revive what has been lost and correct the deep psychic and spiritual imbalances of our civilization.
>
> One result of this on-going search for a lost intellectual heritage has been the rediscovery of the importance of imagination. In putting complete faith in reason, the West forgot that imagination opens up the

> soul to certain possibilities of perceiving and understanding, not available to the rational mind. . . . As [Henry] Corbin has explained in his works [cf. *Creative Imagination in the Sufism of Ibn 'Arabi*], the "imaginal world" or *mundus imaginalis* possesses an independent ontological status and must be clearly differentiated from the "imaginary" world, which is no more than our individual fantasies." (ix)

At some point, Kane would argue, Western tradition lost touch with this "imaginal" category so central to Sufi thought and oral culture. In *Ambiguous Adventure* Samba says to Pierre-Louis' technocratic son,

> "It is not in a difference of nature between the West and what is not the West that I should see the explanation of the opposition in their destinies. . . . I believe that [the difference] is artificial, accidental. Only, the artifice has grown stronger with time, covering up what is of nature. What we miss so much in the West, those of us who come from the outlying regions, is perhaps that: that original nature where our identity bursts forth with theirs. . . . This feeling of exile, which weighs upon us does not mean that we should be useless, but, on the contrary, establishes the necessity for us, and indicates our most urgent task, which is that of clearing the ground around nature. This task is ennobling" (*AA* 151–153).

The task is to bring the imaginal realm where God and humankind meet, back into the world.

Contemporary Islamic philosopher, Mehdi Ha'iri Yazdi in his *Principles of Epistemology in Islamic Philosophy: Knowledge by Presence* writes: "the notion of knowledge by presence not only possesses a historical legacy but has itself acted as the agent of history in bringing about the separation of Islamic and Western philosophies, both of which had emerged from the bosom of the Hellenic philosophical tradition" (6). What Yazdi calls "knowledge by presence" and Corbin calls the "imaginal world" is associated with ideas of emanation, apprehension by presence and illumination. Philosophers such as Ibn Sina (Avicenna, d. 1037) and Al-Ghazali (d. 1111) associated presence with the Qur'anic verse on Light, which begins "Allah is the Light." Ibn Sina called this emanating light a transcendent "Active Intellect" (Yazdi 14) that illuminates the mind of humankind. Al-Ghazali claimed "the human mind is like the niche of a light which, due to conjunction with an external transcendent fire, obtains illumination and reflects in itself whatever is given to it, and depending on the degree [to which] it can approximate the fire, it becomes closer to the source of light that is intellectual knowledge" (16). As Samba Diallo travels further from his Qur'anic school, the "Glowing Hearth," he feels himself exiled from divine light and its resonance in Qur'anic rememoration. Early in

Ambiguous Adventure, Samba says of Thierno: "he has the Word, which is made of nothing corporeal, but which endures . . . which endures. He has the fire which runs like flame through the disciples and sets the hearth aglow" (*AA* 63).

The split between the West and Islam is also attributed to the West's dependence on written texts. In his *Beyond the Written Word*, William Graham maintains that "the biases and presuppositions of modern Western book and print culture have diminished our capacity to grasp the meaning of scripture as an active vocal presence in the lives of individuals and communities everywhere. . . . The contemporary Western conception of books as silent written documents has skewed our perception of the special kind of book that we call 'scripture,' especially as regards its important oral functions" (8). Samba Diallo confesses that his French education gave him "a new language and a new tool," which allowed him to transmit his thoughts to his father "without opening his mouth" (*AA* 159), and thus before he knows it he discovers this education has brought him "out from the heart of things, and accustomed [him] to live at a distance from the world" (*AA* 160). Graham sees recitation of the Qur'an as that self-presence, that illumination that Samba refers to as living at the heart of things. "The Qur'an as the verbatim speech of God given once and for all through a single chosen prophet sets it apart from the Bible in either of the other two traditions" (87). To demonstrate the meaning of the Qur'an—as both a scripture and the act of reciting that scripture—Graham makes a comparison among Judaism, Christianity, and Islam:

> For Jews, the prime medium of divine-human encounter is the Torah (literally "law," "teaching")—but Torah understood not simply as scriptural text but as divine will, cosmic order, and human responsibility, to which the scriptural Torah is the guide. For Christians the encounter comes first and foremost through the person and life of Christ (which are accessible, but not exclusively so, through scripture). In Islam, on the other hand, it is in the concrete text, the very words of the Qur'an, that Muslims most directly experience God. Scripture for Muslims is itself the divine presence as well as the mediator of divine will and divine grace. In the Qur'an, God speaks with his own voice, not through inspired human writers. Thus it is not an exaggeration to compare Qur'an recitation with the Christian Eucharist, nor to say in chanting the words of the Qur'an, one "chants not words about God, but of Him, and indeed, as those words are His essence, chants God himself." (87)

In memorizing the Qur'an, Samba has learned this imagery and participated in this imaginal realm. He does not express this understanding in the discursive fashion of the West, rather he meditates on death, which the Sufis see as a return to the One. This is the death of self, or negation, that Samba's father told Paul Lacroix he heartily wished for in embracing the thought of the end of the world: "From the bottom of my heart I wish for you to rediscover the feeling of anguish in the face of the dying sun" (*AA* 77).

From the time he is at Qur'anic school, Samba is death's familiar. As a small boy, he goes to the cemetery to the grave of the woman Old Rella to discover what death means: "For a long time, near his dead friend, the child reflected on the eternal mystery of death, and, on his own count, rebuilt Paradise in a thousand ways. When sleep came to him he had grown entirely serene again, for he had found the answer: Paradise was built with the Words that he used to recite, the same glowing lights, the same deep and mysterious shadows, the same enchantment, the same power" (*AA* 42–43).

Samba Diallo had gone to Paris at the wish of his aunt, the Most Royal Lady, who told Thierno at one point: "I am disturbed. This child speaks of death in terms which do not belong to his years" (*AA* 25). She continues, "I believe the time has come to teach our sons to live. I foresee that they will have to do with a world of the living, in which the values of death will be scoffed at and bankrupt" (*AA* 27). Samba Diallo's *jihad* is a personal coming to terms with the conflict between a system of values in which death is a familiar reminder that a larger system exists, and a new, Western context where death is the end, thus one turns one's thought toward more immediate, material realities. Annemarie Schimmel ends her essay on "Creation and Judgment in the Koran"[17] with a verse from the modern Indian Sufi scholar and poet Iqbal, written shortly before his own death, which suggests that death is not an end but part of the straight path bringing the believer into God's unity: "In the hem of his night there is dawn,/From his star the radiance of the world shines forth./How else could I describe the faithful believer?/He smiles when death approaches him" (177). While Samba's father has explained that God in his greatness is not a relative of humankind, he has also inculcated in Samba's social imaginary the images of God's mercy. Samba's Qur'anic recitations are peopled with angels:

> Humans are surrounded and protected by angels during their whole lifetime, and the pious believe in the presence of two, sometimes four, or sometimes even a whole [host] of protecting angels. Two recording angels are placed on one's shoulders: the angel on the right shoulder notes down the believer's good actions, while the one on the left takes notes of his evil actions. However, the angel on the left hesitates a while before completing his work, and if the sinner repents during a certain span of time, his mistakes and sins are not entered in the record. (Schimmel, *Islam* 82–83)

The descriptions of the Day of Judgment are frightening, as Samba reminds the villagers early in the novel when he and the other boys are asking for alms—"Men of God, reflect upon your approaching death. Awake, Oh, awake! Azrael, Angel of death, is already breaking the earth for you. It is about to rise up at your feet" (*AA* 13). The Sufis, however, believe that God is merciful and will save even the sinners. Azrael, cosmic in size, has 4,000 wings all covered with tongues and eyes; he rips the souls of unbelievers from their breasts, but gently removes those of believers (Schimmel, *Islam* 82). A bridge, thinner than a hair and sharper than a sword, leads across Hell's back and all must cross it to get to Paradise; unbelievers slide off and fall into Hell, while believers cross easily into Heaven (84). God interrogates all as he pleases, but his mercy is such that even sinners, if their hearts contain a single grain of faith, will be saved if a believer acts as intercessor and pleads for them. And even if there is no intercessor, but there is a seed of faith, God's grace will save the sinner after he has been punished. God's mercy is found in the *hadith* that says "there will be a day when the floor of Hell is humid and cress will grow out of it"; God made seven gates into Hell, but eight doors to Paradise to "show that His mercy is greater than His wrath" (Schimmel, *Deciphering the Signs of God* 237). Samba's journey and his death cannot be explained by a Western existentialist narrative that sees the protagonist as the sum of his actions. In this existentialist story, death is the end point from which to judge whether the protagonist has been a success or a failure. The social imaginary of *Ambiguous Adventure* compels us rather to ask whether, at his death, Samba has become one with God.

The end of the novel is specifically focused on the recitation of prayer. Samba is often seen by critics as "refusing to pray," and thus he is killed by the Fool who, like Sembène's Pays in *Camp de Thiaroye*, has been thoroughly terrorized by his Western experience. The Fool attaches himself to Thierno during his last days. After fighting for the French in the war, he has returned to the village to tell about his journey into *Dar al-Kufr*, also known as *Dar al-Harb* (Land of Disbelief; Land of War). Upon hearing his description of the West and its implicit social imaginary, the other villagers have decided he must be mad. The Fool thinks that Samba has refused to pray because he misunderstands Samba's comment, "No, I do not agree," as being a response to his own request, rather than being part of a mystical dialogue taking place in Samba's imagination. Samba is not mentally prepared to pray in this scene and to do so would be a profanation of the Qur'an. The scene with the Fool is the counterpart to the opening scene with Thierno when Samba, as a small boy, is punished for reciting the Qur'an with inattention. Sitting at Thierno's grave, Samba is also carrying on a mental conversation with Thierno who is in the grave (a traditional ritual act close to prayer). He then shifts to talking to God, just as he did in his evening prayers in Paris when he feared for his faith and said: "Thou wouldst not know how to forget me like that. I would not agree, alone of us two, to suffer from Thy absence" (*AA* 126–127); he repeats in this later scene: "Thou wouldst not know how to forget me like that. I would not agree, alone of us two, to suffer from Thy withdrawal" (*AA* 174). When he repeats again, "No—I do not agree," he is not refusing the Fool's importuning but refusing to be left in exile from the Word. Misunderstanding, the Fool kills him, but that too may be evidence of God's will.

The final mystical chapter returns Samba to the ocean of unity that is God and that is so central to Sufi imagery. Samba says he will constrain God to make a choice between returning to his heart, and his death in the name of God's glory. The choice is one and the same. Samba Diallo, having struggled with his split self and recognizing "I no longer burn at the heart of people and things" (*AA* 161) is saved at the end of the novel—without historical "progress" and without "rational" explanation. His father's letter, asking him to return home, began by stating that God is outside historical time and sequential or causal relationships:

> It is high time that you should come back, to learn that God is not commensurable with anything, and especially not with history, whose vicissitudes are powerless in relation to his attributes. I know that the Occident, to which I have been so wrong as to send you, has a different faith on that score—a faith of which I recognize the utility, but which we do not share. Between God and man there exists not the slightest consanguinity, nor do I know what historic relationship. If there were, our recriminations would have been admissible. We should have been entitled to harbor resentment against Him for our tragedies. . . . God is not our parent. He is entirely outside the stream of flesh, blood, and history which links us together. We are free! (*AA* 162)

The idea of sequential time, which is the necessary basis for science and history in the West is not found in the Qur'an, according to Abdoldjavad Falaturi: "The Koran affords no place for it. This does not mean that Mohammed was not able to construct and mediate such a conception of history and its basis, that is, time. His concerns transcended time and history, as his community has understood up to the present" (70). Revelation is the advent of the eternal moment. As Schimmel explains the Qur'anic notion of time, "before creation lies *azal*, eternity without beginning; after Judgment, *abad*, eternity without end" ("Creation and Judgment" 150). Samba's father reminds him of his responsibility for his distance from God: "the traitor might be yourself . . . do you give God the entire place that is due Him, in your thoughts and your actions?" (*AA* 163).

The final two chapters of the novel concern Samba's bringing his thought into conformity with God's law. In the final chapter, when Samba is still caught in sequential, historical time, he says "I am tired of the closed circle. My thought always returns upon myself, reflected by appearance, when, seized by disquiet, I have thrown it out like a tentacle" (*AA* 175). Living in historical time, Samba Diallo is trapped, just as his country was trapped by the West: "Those who had shown fight and those who had surrendered, those who had come to terms and those who had been obstinate—they all found themselves, when the day came, checked by the census, divided up, classified, labeled, conscripted, administrated" (*AA* 49). It is only when Samba Diallo collapses time and history into the moment of revelation that he is redeemed and escapes the circle of self-reflexivity. "Feel how thought no longer returns to you like a wounded bird, but is unfurled infinitely" (*AA* 176).

Noting that the "problem of whether Muslims have thought or think historically" has often been discussed by scholars from both East and West, Falaturi goes on to examine the "Experience of Time and History in Islam." He points out that Mohammed's primary concern was to spread Islam (surrender to God) and that this goal is the content of every revelation: "What is proclaimed as revealed may not be accomplished gradually or in steps: Surrender to God (Islam) is not something which can be gradually realized only in the course of time, through generations and races, and in response to several revelations. One either surrenders himself to God or not" (65). Falaturi notes, in this context, that the intensity of belief is a personal matter, a state of the soul, and has nothing to do with historicity or lack of it in the content of a revelation (73). Unlike Christianity, Islam is not based on a history of salvation: "For the [Qur'an] recognizes no original sin and no corresponding redemption, so that the [Qur'an] presents no salvation history comparable to the Christian tradition. But if salvation is understood, as it is in the prophetic religions, as 'the individual's encounter through faith and grace with a personal God,' then salvation is contained precisely in that human surrender to God (Islam) and that divine guidance (*huda*) which according to the [Qur'an] remains or should remain forever unaltered by time or history. Accordingly, there is no reason to conceive of revelation as something temporal or historical. It is not something that is realized gradually, either in regard to its ultimate fulfillment or its content" (65).

At the end of the novel, we are beyond all Western paradigms of progress, history, journey, or time: "At the heart of the moment, behold man as immortal, for the moment is infinite, when it is. The purity of the moment is made from the absence of time. Life of the moment, life without age of the moment which reigns, in the luminous arena of your duration man unfurls himself to infinity" (*AA* 177–178). Samba Diallo's death in *Ambiguous Adventure* should be understood not as the culmination of a series of ever more ambiguous contacts with the West, but rather as the eternal moment of revelation Kane describes at the end of the novel. Samba Diallo comes to self-presence when he loses himself in the riverbed of his thought and begins to lose the split voice of his conversation with God: "I am two simultaneous voices. One draws back and the other increases. I am alone. The river is rising. I am in its overflow. . . . Where are you? Who are you?" And God's voice answers, "You are entering the place where there is no ambiguity. Be attentive" (*AA* 177).

CHAPTER FOUR

Heimlich un-Heimlich

Of Home as Heterotopia in Salih, Tlili, and Mokeddem

This chapter begins with a discussion of Foucault's theories of heterotopia, which he began developing when he was an expatriate in Tunisia, and Freud's comments on the uncanny (*unheimlich*) as the unhomelike. Using their insights into the connections between the "non-place" of language and our feeling of being at-home or not at-home in the world, I look at how Tayeb Salih (Sudan), Mustapha Tlili (Tunisia), and Malika Mokeddem (Algeria) each negotiate the particulars of their postcolonial identities as expatriate authors working in transnational contexts. Salih's work focuses on the effects of colonialism on identity, Tlili's on the effect of post-independence nationalism on traditional identity, and Mokeddem's on contemporary identity politics and transnational feminism. This study of "home as heterotopia" in the postcolonial novel investigates the uncanny ways falsehood and truth, the *heimlich* (at-homeness) and the *unheimlich* (exile at home), cohabit in these aesthetic and political transcultural inventions of Muslim Africa.

We recall that Foucault was fascinated by Borges' Chinese Encyclopedia because of its ironic properties. He opens *The Order of Things* with the observation:

> This book first arose out of a passage in Borges, out of the laughter that shattered, as I read the passage, all the familiar landmarks of my thought—*our* thought, the thought that bears the stamp of our age and our geography—breaking up all the ordered surfaces and all the planes

> with which we are accustomed to tame the wild profusion of things, and continuing long after to disturb and threaten with collapse our age-old distinction between the Same and the Other. (xv)

As we saw earlier, in this alien taxonomy, "animals are divided into: (a) belonging to the Emperor, (b) embalmed, (c) tame, (d) sucking pigs, (e) sirens, (f) fabulous, (g) stray dogs, (h) included in the present classification, (i) frenzied, (j) innumerable, (k) drawn with a very fine camelhair brush, (l) et cetera, (m) having just broken the water pitcher, (n) that from a long way off look like flies" (xv). Foucault works through his fascination with this site, deciding that the laughter and a certain attendant anxiety that the passage arouses cannot be explained by its fabulous contents (sirens), nor by the charm of its exotic references (Emperors, camelhair brushes), nor even the oddity of its juxtapositions (sirens and stray dogs). Rather it is the site itself that arouses fear: not the contents of the alphabetized table, but rather what has "insinuated itself into the empty space, the interstitial blanks separating all these entities from one another" (xvi). The laughter aroused, at first, by difference—"the stark impossibility of thinking *that*"—has been displaced by what Foucault refers to as uneasiness and what Freud had earlier thought about as the *unheimlich* (the uncanny). Both link this anxiety to "the non-place of language," which is capable of juxtaposing entities that share no common ground—for example, the inclusion of a subset "(h) included in the present classification," which would logically also be co-extensive with the table itself. The anxiety, aroused in Foucault by the Chinese Encyclopedia, is aroused in Freud by the dictionaries he is using to define the *unheimlich*. Freud begins with the assumption that the *unheimlich* will be the opposite of the *heimlich*, "belonging to the house, not strange, familiar, tame, intimate, friendly, etc."("The Uncanny"). What causes the frisson of anxiety is discovering the ironic fact that the Same and its Opposite may inhabit the same site:

> What interests us most . . . is to find that among its different shades of meaning the word "*heimlich*" exhibits one which is identical with its opposite, "*unheimlich*." What is *heimlich* thus comes to be *unheimlich*. . . . In general we are reminded that the word "*heimlich*" is not unambiguous, but belongs to two sets of ideas, which, without being contradictory, are yet very different: on the one hand it means what is familiar and agreeable, and on the other, what is concealed and kept out of sight. ("The Uncanny")

A site or place that is *unheimlich* is defined in the Latin dictionary as a *locus suspectus*, and from various linguistic clues, Freud concludes that "the *unheimlich* is what was once *heimisch*, familiar [and] the prefix '*un*' . . . is the token of repression" ("The Uncanny"). As Foucault also sensed, it is *not the strangeness* of the Chinese Encyclopedia that frightens us, but rather the sense that *the familiar has suddenly become strange.* We tend to repress or ignore the fact that language mediates between ourselves and the larger world. We repress the fact that all the sites of the social imaginary, through which we process that larger world, are shaky scaffolds upon which we support our truths. When our familiar systems suddenly feel alien to us, we are rudely unhoused and left to deal with a world of unstable ironies.

We are no longer comfortably at home in the world. The familiar is hiding something—not a hidden meaning, but rather a repressed slippage of meaning. We have come full circle to the notions of irony laid out in the introduction to *Of Irony and Empire.* As Wayne Booth noted, irony is the rhetorical figure that "say[s] one thing and mean[s] the opposite" (34). The world of stable irony built on two platforms, such that we '[go] beneath the surface' to something solider or more profound; we rip up a rotten platform and probe to a solid one" (34–35), has rather become the world of unstable irony. In this world, as Paul de Man pointed out: "Curiously enough, it seems to be only in describing a mode of language which does not mean what it says that one can actually say what one means" (211). Irony is a kind of mirror space whose value lies in reflection.

It was while teaching at the University of Tunis between 1966 and 1968 that Foucault developed his concept of *des espaces autres.* In his early set of lecture notes written in 1967 and published after his death as "Of Other Spaces," Foucault notes that some sites are semiotically significant because they serve as reflectors: that is, they have the "curious property of being in relation with all the other sites, but in such a way as to . . . neutralize, or invert the set of relations that they happen to designate, mirror, or reflect" ("Of Other Spaces" 24).[1] These reflector sites, which challenge all other sites, are of two main types: utopias and heterotopias. We might think of the Chinese Encyclopedia as a heterotopia because it begins to reverberate with all those kinds of academic and scientific sites that purport to capture true knowledge—flow charts, tables, genealogical trees, archives, card catalogs. It exposes the repressed knowledge we have that these sites don't reveal truth, they rather reveal a particular mode of packaging the stuff of the world. Language and other symbolic systems don't just reflect reality, they select and deflect it as well. Foucault's run-in with the Chinese Encyclopedia caused him to think about utopias and heterotopias, to question their relation to language itself. Utopias, he posited in "Of Other Spaces," are "sites with no real place. . . . [They have] a general relation of direct or inverted analogy with the real space of Society. They present society itself in a perfected form. . . . [U]topias are fundamentally unreal spaces" (24). Utopias, then, are a form of allegory, so by definition, half of it (the better half we might say) is unreachably transcendent. Heterotopias, on the other hand, are found in every culture, and they are literal places. They reflect other concrete sites, which they echo in disturbing ways: for example, the cemetery or city of the dead as memento mori for the living; or, the bordello as mirror of the sexuo-economic politics of bourgeois society. Thus, in relation to the larger society, they serve as counter-sites that represent, contest, and invert normalized cultural sites. They tend to make us aware of the social imaginary that underpins the normalized site and the semiotic forces that have shaped the site.

In his "Preface" to *The Order of Things*, Foucault's ruminations over the Chinese Encyclopedia led him to observe that language inhabits utopias and heterotopias in opposing ways. Given that utopias are allegories in which the imperfect real world is replaced by a perfect ideal one, "utopias afford consolation: although they have no real locality there is nevertheless a fantastic, untroubled region in which they are able to unfold; they open up cities with vast avenues, superbly planted gardens, countries where life is easy, even though the road to them is chimerical" (xviii). Utopias are the result of a fabulation that weaves together a magically harmonious world disguising the essential rift between words and things; utopias "run with the very grain of language" (xviii). Heterotopias, on the other hand, focus our attention on the distance between reality and representation. Our modeling of these ideas is always mediated—always the representation of a representation:

> Heterotopias are disturbing probably because they secretly undermine language, because they make it impossible to name this *and* that, because they shatter or tangle common names, because they destroy "syntax" in advance, and not only the syntax with which we construct sentences but also that less apparent syntax which causes words and things (next to and also opposite one another) to "hold together." . . . Heterotopias . . . dessicate speech, stop words in their tracks, contest the very possibility of grammar at it source; they dissolve our myths and sterilize the lyricism of our sentences. (xviii)

Heterotopias do not mean the end of fabulation but rather suggest simply that the luxury of being unselfconscious about this figuration has come to an end. The destabilizing force of the heterotopia rests in its ability to foreground our representational construction of reality. It shifts our attention from "reality" itself (never accessible directly) to the power of representation to manage, manipulate, and distort reality.

Of special interest, perhaps, are those rare sites that are both utopias and heterotopias. One is the mirror and, we will argue here, the other is home.

Foucault noted in "Of Other Spaces" that the mirror is a very special site because it's constitutionally ironic; it is where what goes forth as A returns as non-A:

> The mirror is, after all, a *utopia*, since it is a placeless place. In the mirror I see myself there where I am not, in *an unreal, virtual space* that opens up behind the surface . . . such is the utopia of the mirror. But it is also a heterotopia in so far as the mirror does exist in reality, where it exerts a sort of counteraction on the position I occupy. From the standpoint of the mirror I discover my absence from the place where I am since I see myself over there. . . . The mirror functions as a *heterotopia* in this respect: it makes this place that I occupy at the moment when I look at myself in the glass at once *absolutely real,* connected with all the space that surrounds it, *and absolutely unreal,* since in order to be perceived it has to pass through this virtual point which is over there. (24)

It is tempting to speculate that the colonies in Africa were sites that, like the mirror, contained both utopias and heterotopias. The colony was a sort of utopia for the colonizer who was raised high by the trope of the manichean allegory built on the "opposition between the putative superiority of the European and the supposed inferiority of the native" (JanMohamed 80); this allegorical worldview "uses [the native] as a mirror that reflects the colonialist's self-image" (84). This idealized self plays the leading role in the story of the colonizing mission; however, the rift between the word and the world, between the rhetorical claims of the colonizers and the material abuses of colonization, turn utopia into heterotopia causing us to reflect upon the pathogenic effects of the idealized society.

Foucault ends his lecture "Of Other Spaces" by pointing out how it is that heterotopias unfold as the ironic reflection of all other "real" spaces:

> Either their role is to create a space of illusion that exposes every real space, all the sites inside of which human life is partitioned, as still more illusory [e.g., asylums can cause us to reflect on the madness of a normalized medical profession]. . . . Or else, on the contrary, their role is to create a space that is other, another real space, as perfect, as meticulous, as well arranged as ours is messy, ill constructed, and jumbled [e.g., archives, laboratories, experimental farms, those synthetic environments where messy realities are squared and spatialized]. (27)

Interestingly enough, Foucault calls this second type of heterotopia a space of compensation rather than simple illusion, commenting: "I wonder if certain colonies have not functioned somewhat in this manner" (27).

Postcolonial texts are ironic, and postcolonial environments heterotopic, because their meanings have had to accommodate different social imaginaries. Our social imaginaries are constructed around practices and assumptions that happen unconsciously, at the level of doxa. We become aware of our social imaginary when we look in the mirror of another social imaginary that does the same things, but differently. For example, the list of animals in Borges' *Chinese Encyclopedia* serves as a mirror of Western thought because, as Foucault comments, he becomes aware of the limits of his own imaginary by recognizing "the stark impossibility of thinking *that*" (*The Order of Things* xv). Likewise, Bourdieu's "*Docta ignorantia*" claims that our "tactics" seem to be analyzable only indirectly, through another society, because it is through this detour that they become visible to us (Certeau 50).

As writers from the more rebellious rural regions of Muslim Africa where a particularly strong sense of community identification served as a buttress against the predations of colonialism and the invasive politics of state formation at the time of independence, Tayeb Salih (Sudan), Mustapha Tlili (Tunisia), and Malika Mokeddem (Algeria) have witnessed the struggle over the transcultural invention of Africa from positions of potential strength. At the same time, as expatriate authors, they are aware of a situational irony: abroad they are representatives of their "homes"; at home they become outsiders by going abroad. Home, it has been argued, is what anchors us in the world early on in life. It is the nest woven by the invisible threads of the social imaginary that gives us a perch from which to look out on the landscape surrounding us. We are born into a "poetics of space," according to Gaston Bachelard:

> We should therefore have to say how we inhabit our vital space, in accord with all the dialectics of life, how we take root, day after day, in a "corner of the world."
>
> For our house is our corner of the world. As has often been said, it is our first universe, a real cosmos in every sense of the word. (4)

Home becomes a heterotopia, however, when we realize how contingent the birth facts that assign us a home are, and how central this home is to our conception of ourselves. The postcolonial writers whose work will be looked at more closely here all write about home from the detour of having lived abroad. While these writers, like so many other African writers, have migrated to the West for education and work, their social imaginaries remain deeply tied to traditional rural villages and desert landscapes rather than to metropolitan environments. The works examined here reflect the enormous emotional range these authors associate with the natural ecologies of their natal landscapes.

Salih's *Season of Migration to the North* (1969 [1980], Tlili's *Lion Mountain* (1990), and Mokeddem's *The Forbidden Woman* (1998) and memoir *La Transe des Insoumis* (2003) are texts that bring the narrators back home where they experience the dislocation of the *heimlich* becoming *unheimlich*, of home becoming heterotopia. Like Cheikh Hamidou Kane, Salih and Tlili are males who trace their ancestry to a stable, and sometimes illustrious, past, which has been rudely disrupted first by colonialism and then by the neocolonial complicity of their own leaders. Given this situating of their postcoloniality, one possible pitfall in any examination of identity is nostalgia. For Malika Mokeddem, a female from a traditional Saharan village, the feeling of lost wholeness is not there because she suffered the effects of gender bias early on and experienced feelings of exile long before leaving home. So in her case nostalgia is not likely to be a pitfall, but perhaps its mirror image, wishful thinking, is. These three authors have been chosen for closer examination because of the differing ways they manage the transcultural invention of their own identities. Heterotopia in this discussion is understood to be operating at the level of personal alienation and estrangement (there's no settling into a comfortable, normalized identity for these authors and their characters), but it is also looked at as a form of irony operating at the level of literary composition, sometimes with therapeutic results, sometimes not. Salih's challenge is how to keep his story about heterotopic worlds from collapsing back into the familiar; he works as hard to keep his narrative strange as his narrator and some of his readers do to explain the narrative in orthodox ways. Tlili struggles with how to keep his heterotopic narrative from being displaced into the utopic past associated with Horia, an older woman who embodies the best of tradition, on the one hand, or being reduced to the dystopic postindependence nationalism that threatens Horia and her family and friends, on the other. In Mokeddem's case, heterotopia emerges as an issue of the relationship between the production and reception of the self. Having cut many ties—familial, national, marital—she devotes herself to writing, writing about herself. She situates herself and her writing project toward the end of her recent memoir *Mes Hommes*:

> I felt my being going back to the stubborn solitude of my childhood and adolescence, to their exclusions, their uprooted dreams, disembodied.
>
> I love solitude so much. . . . Solitude was space and time for reading, for dreaming, for inventing lives. Now, it is the space of writing. I constitute myself from it—against the dissolution of the clan, against the perversions of nationalism. . . . This perfected solitude is perhaps at last loving myself. That is, a love of life that lucidity keeps from being too egocentric, but a love strong enough and stubborn enough to keep me from scattering myself, dispersing myself into various simulacra. . . .

> There are so many forms of solitude built into my life: being without family despite having parents and numerous siblings; being without a child by choice. Alone between two countries where I often am summoned to explain myself, to explain my fundamentally intimate choices, and to justify my being. (286–287)

This focus on her own life and the production of a free-floating, liberated individual self seems to be quite unironic for Mokeddem. Yet the historical circumstances shaping the reception of her literary production—stereotypical ideas about Muslim women and about Arabs, stereotypical ideas about feminism and the West—beg for ironic distance. What follows here is an exploration of the effects of heterotopia embedded in the postcolonial writer's very circumstances, and of the therapeutic mirth and the attendant anxiety that this uncanny displacement of self can cause.

Mirror, Mirror/Identity, Alterity—Home as Heterotopia Tayeb Salih's *Season of Migration to the North*

In the ironic, colonial/postcolonial world of Tayeb Salih's *Season of Migration to the North*, there are two main protagonists. One is Mustafa Sa'eed, a Sudanese Muslim who was born in 1898, the year of Kitchener's conquest of Sudan when the Mahdi was defeated. When the novel opens, Mustafa Sa'eed has taken up life in a small Sudanese village after spending years in England studying and teaching economics at Oxford and seducing British women. Having moved to England in 1913 at age 15, Mustafa Sa'eed grows up in the Britain of the Sykes-Picot agreement, the Balfour declaration and the British Mandate. Appointed a lecturer in economics at London University at age 24, Sa'eed simultaneously wrote anti-colonial books, was President of the "Society for the Struggle for African Freedom," and spent his spare time getting even with the British by seducing Britain's daughters, most of whom fell victim to the exotic charm their social imaginary had taught to look for in someone like Sa'eed. Having been found guilty of the murder of Jean Morris, his wife and nemesis, Sa'eed is imprisoned from 1928 to 1935 in Britain. Following his release from prison, he settles in rural Wad Hamid in the Sudan in 1948. The second protagonist is an unnamed narrator whose name in the later novel *Bandarshah* is given as Meheimeed. He, too, has studied in England, and after spending seven years to get a degree in English literature, has returned to the village in 1953, the year that Mustafa Sa'eed disappears without a trace into the Nile. The novel ends in 1956 just when Sudan has become an independent state. Mustafa is 55 years old when the novel opens, and

Meheimeed is 25.[2] Meheimeed is determined to find out who Mustafa Sa'eed is; Mustafa Sa'eed is willing enough to tell Meheimed his life story in fragments. Mustafa is a liar who knows he is a lie; Meheimeed is a narrator who is intent on finding the truth.

Season of Migration to the North is a heterotopic composition. In the novel, the two protagonists become mirrors for one another, just as England and Sudan become reflector sites, and the novel itself mirrors Joseph Conrad's *Heart of Darkness*, in which two doppelgänger protagonists, Marlow and Kurtz, journeyed to the South. The ironist Salih envisioned Mustafa as a liar because only by means of refraction can a storyteller hint at the truth. Speaking of the composition process of the novel, Salih explained:

> I was pondering . . . [the] illusory relationship between our Arab Islamic world and Western European civilization specifically. This relationship seems to me, from my readings and studies, to be based on illusions [*awham*] on our side and on theirs. Illusion relates to our conception of ourselves first of all, then to what we think of our relationship to them, and then to their outlook on us as well. Western Europe imposed itself and its civilization on us . . . for a long time and became part of our cultural and psychological makeup whether we like it or not. (Qtd. in Hassan 88)[3]

In creating his character Mustafa Sa'eed, Salih did not aim to counter the lies of colonialism with the truths of postcolonial experience. Rather, he says, "[I] knew the chances are the English reader of the novel will say, 'This man from the Sudan, an Arab and a Muslim, says that we oppressed and misjudged them.' No, I didn't want to do that. I accepted all of the misconceptions of Europeans" (91). So, Salih's protagonist, Mustafa Sa'eed, self-consciously embodies all the lies the English have told about him. He gives them what they wanted to see, and in doing so, he becomes a mirror exposing their lies. At the same time, however, Sa'eed comments that as a schoolboy in Sudan at a British boarding school his intellect was Cartesian in the extreme:

> My mind was like a sharp knife, cutting with cold effectiveness. . . . I was cold as a field of ice. . . . In the intermediate school I discovered other mysteries, amongst which was the English language. My brain continued on, biting and cutting like the teeth of a plough. Words and sentences formed themselves before me as though they were mathematical equations; algebra and geometry as though they were verses of poetry. I viewed the vast world in the geography lessons as though it were a chess board. (*SMN* 22)

The British thus see a Mustafa Sa'eed who is a projection of their exotic fantasies, while Mustafa Sa'eed holds the mirror up to Europe by claiming that he was from childhood the model of the detached European scientist.

Arab readers also find themselves caught in the mirror of this dialogic, transcultural invention. As Waïl Hassan notes in his book *Tayeb Salih*, Salih's *Season of Migration to the North* involves a form of narration Bakhtin called parody (which is a type of irony, often because of its mirroring qualities) because "the author . . . speaks in someone else's discourse . . . but introduces into that discourse a semantic intention that is directly opposed to the original one. The second voice, once having made its home in the other's discourse, clashes hostilely with its primordial host and forces him to serve directly opposing aims" (193; qtd. in Hassan 83).[4] We recall Fanon performed this sort of transcultural, ironic inhabiting of the dominant discourse through verbal mimicry: for example, "The colonized is elevated above his jungle status in proportion to his adoption of the mother country's cultural standards" (*Black Skin, White Masks* 18), or "The Negro loves to jabber, and from this theory it is not a long road that leads to a new proposition: The Negro is just a child. The psychoanalysts have a fine start here, and the term orality is soon heard" (26–27). The difficulty quickly becomes not the inhabiting of the other's discursive space, but of finding a discursive space of one's own. We see this nonspace of identity when Mustafa Sa'eed is on trial for the murder of Jean Morris. He says that he sat for weeks in the courtroom "listening to the lawyers talk about me—as though they were talking about some person who was no concern of mine" (*SMN* 31) and comments later that "the lawyers were fighting over my body. It was not I who was important but the case" (*SMN* 93). His defense is taken up by Maxwell Foster-Keen, one of his former professors at Oxford (a Mason and a member of the Supreme Committee for the Protestant Missionary Societies in Africa) who disliked him as a student and who would say to him "with undisguised irritation":

> "You, Mr. Sa'eed, are the best example of the fact that our civilizing mission in Africa is of no avail. After all the efforts we've made to educate you, it's as if you'd come out of the jungle for the first time." (*SMN* 93–94)

Another former professor, the dissolute, left-wing public prosecutor, Sir Arthur Higgins, is trying to send him to the gallows, ironically enough, as a "scoundrel" while Foster-Keen is trying to save him by presenting him as a "genius" (*SMN* 94) driven to murder by "mad passion" (*SMN* 32). Foster-Keen argues Mustafa Sa'eed is a victim, "a noble person whose mind was able to absorb Western civilization but it broke his heart" (*SMN* 33). Sa'eed's identity is purloined in this way and trapped between the dueling discourses of gallows literature and Shakespearean drama. Sa'eed reports to the narrator that he felt he "should stand up and shout at the court": "This Mustafa Sa'eed does not exist. He is an illusion, a lie" (*SMN* 32). He felt he should declaim: "I am no Othello. I am a lie" (*SMN* 33). As with irony, finding a discursive space of one's own can only be accomplished through refraction; one has to go by way of the mirror of the other's space, picking one's way through the ruins of colonial relations. And like irony, this obligation to proceed by means of the other can lead to productive practices, to the therapeutic benefits of reflective thought and empathetic identifications. Meheimeed, and the older and wiser Mustafa Sa'eed, are still caught in the manichean discursive spaces of colonialism in the novel, but this is not the case for the author, Tayeb Salih, who proceeds by refraction, reflecting the image of truth by way of the lie.

Salih makes autobiography itself a sort of foil for the reader in his *Season of Migration*: "Basically, the reader looks for the writer in a work. When the narration begins in the first person, the reader quickly settles down to the view that, here is an autobiography. He comfortably claims no responsibility whatsoever. I created therefore a conflicting world in which nothing is certain, and, formalistically, two voices force the reader to make up his/her own mind" (Lecture 16). Implicating the reader in the work of creating the meaning of a text is not simply a formal exercise or an aesthetic game. As Edward Said explained in a series of lectures entitled *Humanism and Democratic Criticism*, reading in an engaged way (which he associates with humanism) is a practice that opens out onto the world:

> Thus a close reading of a literary text . . . in effect will gradually locate the text in its time as part of a whole network of relationships whose outlines and influence play an informing role *in* the text. And I think it is important to say that for the humanist, the act of reading is the act therefore of first putting oneself in the position of the author, for whom writing is a series of decisions and choices expressed in words. It need hardly be said that no author is completely sovereign or above the time, place, and circumstances of his or her life, so that these, too, must be understood if one is to put oneself in the author's position sympathetically. (62)

Texts, like the people who write them, exist *in* the world, and so Said insists that texts are subject to the conditions of material existence, to the contamination of and involvement in the heterogeneous realities of location: "The key word here is 'worldly,' a notion I have always used to denote the real historical world from whose circumstances none of us can in fact ever be separated, not even in theory . . . all representations . . . are intimately tied up with worldliness, that is, with power, position, and interests" (48).

Tayeb Salih would agree. He comments in his lecture at the American University in Beirut, “the foundation of my work, for what it is worth, lies in what I am: a Sudanese Muslim Arab who was born at a certain time, in a certain place”:

> I grew up in a biggish village in the North of the Sudan, halfway between Wadi Hafa and Khartoum. It is almost in the middle between the land of the Shaigiya Arabs and the Nubians. It is also an extension of Diyar al-Kababish, which is an Arab Bedouin nomadic tribe numbering over two million, and I believe it represents the greatest concentration of Bedouins anywhere in the Arab world. . . .
>
> When I was born there were about a hundred people who knew the Koran by heart. I, myself, went to the *khalwa* as a child or to what is called in Egypt the *kuttab* to learn some Koran. I also worked in the fields with my people. The Nile was the center, a focal point and I suppose something of this rubs into one. I should mention here the special ethnic construction of the Sudan, Arab, Nubian and Negro. When the Arabs came to the Sudan, they did not take it by force, it fell to them peacefully, on the whole. Before the Arab conquest, the country had been Christian for over a thousand years, which explains why the type of Islam in the Sudan, even now, is not ideological, is not fanatical. It is a mystical, spiritual type of religion. Well, you may say, how about the Mahdist revolution? We think it was not a religious uprising but a nationalistic one. (15–16)

Transcultural interaction need not only be conceived of under the aegis of a “clash of civilizations.” In fact, as both Edward Said and Richard Falk have argued, that is one of the least useful or productive ways of thinking about differing social imaginaries or alternative modernities.[5] First, one needs to be receptive to differences, and then one can resist or critique or refine one’s insights.

Perspective becomes the key focus of Salih’s postcolonial work. In *Season of Migration to the North*, he illustrates this idea by making “home” a heterotopia. Mustafa Sa‘eed is an odd kind of protagonist who is “homeless” in that he seems to have never really had a home in the sense of putting down roots. He is the son of a nomad who died several months before Sa‘eed’s birth; his father was from the Abada tribe whose migratory circuit crosses the borders between the Sudan and Egypt, and his mother, a slave woman from the south from the tribes of Zandi or Baria (*SMN* 54). He has no emotional relationship with anyone as a small child and seems to come from nowhere. Yet he spends much of his life, in Britain and in the Sudan, building “model” homes. As for the young narrator Meheimeed, he thinks he will reintegrate seamlessly back into home at the novel's start. He is rudely dislodged from this perspective upon his return from abroad by the village interloper, Mustafa Sa'eed, who is in many ways Meheimeed's double. Because the narrator is telling Mustafa's story in retrospect to an unseen audience,[6] and because Mustafa has told his story to this young narrator who is actually never named in the novel, readers also find themselves uncomfortably dislodged from their nests and cannot remain passive receptors of the story.

Meheimeed's longing for rootedness takes on material form when he wakes on the morning after his arrival in his traditional village on a bend of the Nile, in the room where he slept as a child:

> I looked through the window at the palm tree standing in the courtyard of our house and I knew that all was still well with life. I looked at its strong straight trunk, at its roots that strike down into the ground, at the green branches hanging down loosely over its top, and I experienced a feeling of assurance. I felt not like a storm-swept feather but like that palm tree, a being with a background, with roots, with a purpose. (*SMN* 2)[7]

This rootedness is disrupted when he finds that a stranger, Mustafa Sa'eed, has established himself there. Like the narrator, Sa'eed embodies an unsettling mixture of local knowledge and the occidental ways he picked up living for years in England. He represents the sort of hybridity and even contagion that contact with Western culture brings. His inserting himself into the village forces the narrator to examine his own liminal identity.

This is an examination the narrator wants to avoid: "I forgot [Sa'eed] after that, for I began to renew my relationship with people and things in the village. I was happy in those days, like a child that sees its face in the mirror for the first time" (*SMN* 4). However, Sa'eed does not allow the narrator to maintain this comfortable misrecognition.[8] When the narrator tells Sa'eed that he has just finished a doctorate, having spent "three years delving into the life of an obscure English poet," Sa'eed laughs and tells him: "We have no need of poetry here. It would have been better if you'd studied agriculture, engineering or medicine" (*SMN* 9). The narrator, in retelling the disturbing life story of Mustafa Sa'eed to other listeners, suddenly becomes self-reflexive: "Look at the way he says "we" and does not include me, though he knows this is my village and that it is he—not I—who is the stranger" (*SMN* 9). This early interaction allows Salih to explore the ways tradition and modernity call each other into question, to illuminate the ways the "other" becomes crucial to a definition of the self, and to explore the continual fluctuation of the self between subject and object.

The narrator senses duplicity in Sa'eed; like an image in a mirror, Sa'eed exists in a space of nonbeing. He is a phantom to himself and a mocking double for the narrator. Both are trapped between cultures. Saree Makdisi notes that, while the narrator responds to the conflicted self that is the product of colonial relations by trying to wish the problem away, Sa'eed "does so not by becoming entirely European or entirely Arab, but by becoming both, but never at the same time, in the same place, or with the same people" (542). These contradictions are not only threaded into the conflicting voices and the unstable chronological shifts in the novel, but most importantly, they are found in the heterotopic environments of the novel, which house these virtual selves produced through perpetual performances. The narrator, who has accepted Mustafa Sa'eed's invitation to dine with other village notables at his home, discovers that even in the village, Sa'eed lives a divided life:

> When the conversation fell away and I found myself not greatly interested in it, I would look around me as though trying to find in the rooms and walls of the house the answer to the questions revolving in my head. It was, however, an ordinary house, neither better nor worse than those of the well-to-do in the village. Like the other houses it was divided into two parts: one for the women and the other containing the diwan or reception-room, for the men. To the right of the diwan I saw a rectangular room of red brick with green windows; its roof was not the normal flat one but triangular like the back of an ox. (*SMN* 11–12)

Mustafa Sa'eed's mysterious English building houses his worst and most intimate nightmares.

Meheimeed discovers this "English" Sa'eed a week later when Sa'eed, who has largely limited his participation in village life to farming and sharing his knowledge of Western science and law with the local agricultural committee, gets drunk at Mahjoub's and suddenly reveals a different self. He begins to recite "English poetry in a clear voice and with an impeccable accent" (*SMN* 14). The revelation, akin to a speaking in tongues, of this alien poetry dwelling inside this would-be fellah—"his eyes wandering off into the horizon within himself" (*SMN* 14)—horrifies Meheimeed. He tells the unseen audience: "I tell you had the ground suddenly split and revealed an afreet[9] standing before me, his eyes shooting out flames, I would not have been more terrified. All of a sudden there came to me the ghastly, nightmarish feeling that we—the men grouped together in that room—were not a reality but merely some illusion" (*SMN* 14–15). Sa'eed brings the devil of alterity into the village. Not only can Meheimeed not go home again, alien forms have appeared in the village space, a house with a roof "like the back of an ox" and a farmer who spouts English romantic lyrics, both representing the beginning of a descent into uncertainty. Meheimeed confronts Sa'eed, saying "It's clear you're someone other than the person you claim to be. . . . Wouldn't it be better if you told me the truth?" (*SMN* 15). Sa'eed responds, "I am this person before you, as known to everyone in the village" (*SMN* 16). Convinced that there is something hidden here, Meheimeed asks himself: "Should I speak to my father? Should I tell [my childhood friend] Mahjoub? Perhaps the man had killed someone somewhere and had fled from prison? Perhaps he—but what secrets are there in this village?" (*SMN* 16). Meheimeed swears he will get to the bottom of Sa'eed's mysterious past, but soon discovers it mirrors his own. Sa'eed is indeed the murderer that the narrator intuits, but his story only prefigures what is to come when the entire village becomes implicated in the double murder late in the novel of Hosna bint Mahmoud (Sa'eed's "widow") and Wad Rayyes whom she is forced to marry.

In his quest to unearth Sa'eed's past, Meheimeed discovers that while Sa'eed was living in London, he regularly seduced "innocent" young English girls, some of whom later committed suicide. Sa'eed seduces one of these girls, the Arabic-speaking Ann Hammond, after a lecture at Oxford he'd given on the poet Abu Nawas: "And so it was with us: she, moved by poetry and drink, feeding me with sweet lies, while I wove for her intricate and terrifying threads of fantasy" (*SMN* 145). She claims to see in his eyes "the shimmer of mirages in hot deserts" and to hear in his voice "the screams of ferocious beasts in the jungles" (*SMN* 145). He sees in the blueness of her eyes "the faraway shoreless seas of the North" (*SMN* 145–146). His house in London is "a lethal den of lies," a deliberate interior decoration assembling "lie upon lie:"

> the sandalwood and incense; the ostrich feathers and ivory and ebony figurines; the paintings and drawings of forests of palm trees along the shores of the Nile, boats with sails like doves' wings, suns setting over the mountains of the Red Sea, camel caravans wending their way along sand dunes on the borders of the Yemen, baobob trees in Kordofan, naked girls from the tribes of the Zandi, the Nuer and the Shuluk, fields of banana and coffee on the Equator, old temples in the district of Nubia; Arabic books with decorated covers written in ornate Kufic script; Persian carpets, pink curtains, large mirrors on the walls, and coloured lights in the corners. (*SMN* 146)

This heterotopia, a space of lies furnished with real artifacts, mirrors the way the English imagination has constructed Africa. As do Orientalist harem paintings hanging in museums in England or France, Sa'eed's exotic decor mimics a space that exists only in the colonial mindset. The hodgepodge of African and Oriental artifacts, placed in impossible juxtaposition, is reminiscent of the heterogeneously exotic landscapes Flaubert's Emma Bovary adored in her romantic keepsakes albums; those "dim scenes of fabulous lands, combining palm trees, pines, tigers on the right, lions on the left, Tartar minarets on the horizon, Roman ruins in the foreground, and kneeling camels for good measure. Framing each of these panoramas was a neat virgin forest, and somewhere a great perpendicular sunbeam was always shimmering on a lake where swans floated in the distance, a few white strokes against the steel-gray waters" (31). These scenes, mirroring the desires of Ann Hammond and Emma Bovary, reflect impossible landscapes made up of images looted—as were so many museum artifacts—from real places. The framing panoramic point of view of Emma's keepsake etching suggests a northern sensibility, romanticized in such a way as to disguise its appropriative nature. Not only have these looted symbols been disentangled from the faraway worlds they were a part of, they have been recombined in such a way as to displace the reality of those environments.

This Orientalist masquerade is reversed in Sa'eed's Sudanese dwelling, a simulacrum that brings real English spaces into question. Sa'eed's English house in the Sudan is constructed around seemingly everyday English artifacts: a fireplace, Persian rugs, Victorian chairs, oil portraits, and a substantial library. It is a heterotopia of the "real" space of English rooms where everyday "Englishness" is performed and British civilization archived. Sa'eed's library boasts many Western classics, including works by scholars of empire like Gibbon and soldiers of empire like Macaulay and Kipling, as well as scientific works by the psychologists of empire. He has a copy of *Totem and Taboo: Some Points of Agreement Between the Mental Lives of Savages and Neurotics* in which Freud constructs the racial "other" in culturally ethnocentric terms, theorizing non-Western societies as primitive on an evolutionary scale and immature on a psychological scale.[10] Freud writes:

> There are men still living who, as we believe, stand very near to primitive man, far nearer than we do, and whom we therefore regard as his direct heirs and representatives. Such is our view of those whom we describe as savages or half-savages; and their mental life must have a peculiar interest for us if we are right in seeing in it a well-preserved picture of an early stage of our own development.
>
> If that supposition is correct, a comparison between the psychology of primitive peoples, as it is taught by social anthropology, and the psychology of neurotics, as it has been revealed by psycho-analysis, will be bound to show numerous points of agreement. (1)[11]

Sa'eed also owns Octavo Mannoni's *Prospero and Caliban: The Psychology of Colonization*. As Frantz Fanon had pointed out in his critique of Mannoni's book in *Black Skin, White Masks*, ethnopsychiatry conveniently pathologized mental illness by attributing it to the genetic make-up of the colonized individual rather than to pathogenic colonial relations. When the Malagasy who had been invaded by the French colonial army recounted dreams of black bulls, black men and Senegalese *tirailleurs*, Mannoni interpreted these images as representing real and ancestral fathers. Guns, in this Freudian reading, became phallic symbols. Fanon points out that Malagasy dreams should be interpreted in relation to their historically specific context: 80,000 Malagasy, 1 out of every 50 natives, on the island had been killed by French forces. "The rifle of the Senegalese soldier is not a penis but a genuine rifle, model Lebel 1916" (83).[12] Just as the artifacts in Sa'eed's Orientalist chamber of lies provide the stage props for the acting out of exoticism in the English imaginary, the books in his English library hold a mirror up to the West's colonial imagination. Our young narrator, Meheimeed, asks himself in the midst of this room: "What play-acting is this? What does he mean?" (*SMN* 137). Sa'eed's own scholarly work includes four books: *The Economics of Colonialism*, *Colonialism and Monopoly*, *The Cross and Gunpowder*, and *The Rape of Africa*, titles that suggest a highly critical view of the colonial project, yet Sa'eed's library contains not a single Arabic book (*SMN* 137). The most telling sign of Sa'eed's confused identity is that even his Qur'an is an English translation.

The narrator tries to say what kind of space this room embodies by drawing analogies to similar spaces—all of them heterotopic: "A graveyard. A mausoleum. An insane idea. A prison. A huge joke. A treasure chamber. 'Open Sesame, and let's divide up the jewels among the people'"(*SMN* 137–138). Some of these analogical spaces are what Foucault calls heterotopias of deviation: "those in which individuals whose behavior is deviant in relation to the required mean or norm are placed" ("Of Other Spaces" 25). The hospital, the insane asylum, and the prison are among those heterotopias of deviation Foucault studies. These spaces of deviation play a significant role in Sa'eed's biography. Sa'eed himself makes this sort of ironic comparison when he says that his bedroom, a seductive den of lies, "was a graveyard" (*SMN* 30), was "like an operating theatre in a hospital" (*SMN* 31). Sa'eed's room, in fact, leads to a jumbled series of heterotopic analogies. As cemetery or mausoleum, it is a heterotopic space of the dead that mirrors the space of the living in ambiguous ways. As an ironic space, a huge joke, this room signifies both the rootlessness of our representations of reality, and also their power to have real effects. As transcultural space full of secrets to be discovered, Sa'eed's chamber is both the locus of truths and a den of lies: on the one hand, his library contains all the wealth of empire, the treasures of Western thought; on the other, it is merely the den of thieves whose distortions of and looting of indigenous knowledge will be exposed under the gaze of non-Western cultures.

Mustafa Sa'eed becomes enthralled by the power of language to create reality. In a lecture calculated to seduce his British audience, Sa'eed [mis]represents the hedonist poet, Abu Nawas, as "mystical" and "Sufi," and gets away with it. He is their cultural informant after all. He creates a room full of cheap Oriental splendor as the reflection of an English woman's fantasies in order to seduce her. In carrying out these heterotopic acts of mirroring, Sa'eed seduces not only Ann Hammond, but himself: "Though I realized I was lying, I felt that somehow I meant what I was saying and that she too, despite her lying, was telling the truth. It was one of those rare moments of ecstasy for which I would sell my whole life; a moment in which, before your very eyes, lies are turned into truths, history becomes a pimp, and the jester is turned into a sultan" (*SMN* 144). British Orientalists, in eroticizing such a vision of the East, produced the myth of a dangerous exotic masculinity that allows Sa'eed to attract their daughters and attain the illusion of dominance himself. As a creature of the margin, an orphan from Sudan and a "Black Englishman" in Britain (*SMN* 53), Sa'eed is fascinated by the instability of categories. Sa'eed, a person without a home, discovers a home of sorts; he dwells as an exotic self from an exotic land conjured up for him by the British. However, recognizing the discursive violence of the British, and even taking delight in beating them at their own game, does not mean that Sa'eed escapes from this representational hall of mirrors. Instead, when he returns to the Sudan, he builds his own "occidentalist" site that mirrors his ideal of an enlightened British self. Sa'eed builds for us an imagined England juxtaposed to an imagined Orient, both trapped in the violent discursive space of colonial relations.

Salih's novel is not content, however, to let us off this easily from coming to terms with postcolonial space. At novel's end, when Meheimeed enters the dark English room that has been closed since Sa'eed's disappearance into the Nile, he has a literal illumination:

> I struck a match. The light exploded on my eyes and out of the darkness there emerged a frowning face with pursed lips that I knew but could not place. I moved toward it with hate in my heart. It was my adversary Mustafa Sa'eed. The face grew a neck, the neck two shoulders and a chest, then a trunk and two legs, and I found myself standing face to face with myself. This is not Mustafa Sa'eed—it's a picture of me frowning at my face from a mirror. (*SMN* 135)

During the course of the novel, readers become aware that the narrator and Mustafa Sa'eed are doppelgängers. Meheimeed, like Sa'eed, is educated in Britain, is occasionally mistaken for Sa'eed's son, and falls in love with Sa'eed's widow, Hosna Bint Mahmoud, becoming her guardian as well as guardian of Sa'eed's two sons. Sa'eed and the narrator are refracted mirror images of one another, images that reflect the colonial condition as a series of hybrid, alienated subjectivities. This fact is brought to a culmination when the narrator enters the room with the roof like the back of an ox at the end of the novel. In the English room, he opens Sa'eed's notebook and reads, "My Life Story—by Mustafa Sa'eed," but the notebook is empty. In lieu of this autobiography, the narrator later comes across an unfinished lyric poem written by Sa'eed:

> The sighs of the unhappy in the breast do groan
> The vicissitudes of Time by silent tears are shown
> And love and buried hate the winds away have blown.
> Deep Silence has embraced the vestiges of prayer,
> Of moans and supplications and cries of woeful care,
> And dust and smoke the traveler's path ensnare.
> Some, souls content, others in dismay.
> Brows submissive, others . . . (*SMN* 152–153)

The narrator scratches out the last line and substitutes one written by himself: "*Heads humbly bent and faces turned away*" (*SMN* 153). This line echoes the thoughts the narrator had as he entered the room: "I must begin where Mustafa Sa'eed left off. Yet he at least made a choice, while I have chosen nothing. . . . If only I had told [Hosna bint Mahmoud] the truth [that I loved her] perhaps she would not have acted as she did. I had lost the war because I did not know and did not choose. . . . Now I am on my own: there is no escape, no place of refuge, no safeguard. . . . Where, then, were the roots that struck down into times past?" (*SMN* 134). By the end of the novel, the narrator has come full circle to the idea of lost rootedness, the illusion of wholeness, the recognition that the village is not without secrets and lies. In Salih's postcolonial world, then, we experience a discursive space that suggests none of us can go home again, neither to the certainties of positivism nor to the routines of tradition.

MUSTAPHA TLILI: *LION MOUNTAIN/A THOUSAND FUTURES LOST*

Mustapha Tlili is from Feriana on the pre-Saharan steppes of Tunisia between Kasserine and Gafsa along the Algerian border. In *Lion Mountain*,

Tlili juxtaposes the utopic space of ancestral myth and childhood memory to the heterotopia of modernization that emerges with the advent of the nation-state. The main events in the novel take place in the independence period. Tunisia had signed a convention of internal autonomy with France in 1955. The nationalist leader Habib Bourguiba had made a triumphal return to the country in June 1955, and his fellow nationalist Salah Ben Yusuf was given an equally enthusiastic greeting when he returned in September 1955. Bourguiba favored a gradual separation from France; Ben Yusuf a revolutionary one. Historian Kenneth Perkins writes: "At first, Bourguiba and Ben Yusuf occasionally appeared together, but their personal, political, and ideological differences made reconciliation impossible" (128). Confrontations between the two factions were leading Tunisia toward a civil war. Ben Yusuf fled to Cairo in January 1956, but resistance fighters from his rural region (the south and east where Tlili set his novel) fought on: "The magnitude of the support for Ben Yusuf appalled Bourguiba. Basking in the titles *al-za'im* (the leader) and *al-mujahid al-akbar* (the supreme combatant), he had persuaded himself that his combination of charisma and dedication to the nationalist struggle had ensured him the gratitude of all Tunisians" (130). Tlili's novel, then, is about the effects on the village of Lion Mountain of Bourguiba's crushing this rebellion and his forging a national unity and national identity embodied in himself as "President for Life."

When Tlili began writing his novel, he had planned to name it not after a particular, concrete landmark—Lion Mountain, the name of both the village and the mountain in the novel—but rather wanted the title to suggest a more abstract historical concept. In 1987 he published part of this novel in an anthology he put together with Jacques Derrida entitled *For Nelson Mandela.* His prefatory remarks, "The Future Itself," to this early excerpt read:

> The story of Horia, an old woman living alone on the Tunisian steppe, is from a novel in progress entitled (provisionally?) *A Thousand Futures Lost* and concerns an adamant struggle to keep a beloved horizon pure, and to keep sovereign a freedom felt as a native inalienable good.
>
> The frail, weak Horia, with the inflexibility of a powerful inner vision, unshakably resists larger forces. These forces rise up against the old woman and build constructions justified only by tricky schemes, but which deprive Horia of the open and unobstructed view, which she has always had from her ancestral home, of the ocher mountain proudly standing in the distance. *A Thousand Futures Lost* will be about resisting the intolerable. (75)

The early vision of the novel as focusing on a lost utopia gave way, in the writing, to a more complex heterotopic world in which the village is revealed to have its own secrets and lies. The narrator too is implicated in this turn of events as he is guilty of leaving Horia to face her fate alone and is impotent in the face of the human rights abuses he discovers. As the title of the novel suggests, *Lion Mountain* is at one and the same time about the *genius loci* of the narrator's home, and the narrator's participation in turning it into a *locus suspectus*.

The chronological frame of *Lion Mountain* begins in 1492 with the expulsion of the Muslims from Andalusian Spain, and more specifically with the narrator's ancestors who founded the village of Lion Mountain. It moves through the period of French colonial rule and ends with a modernization scheme, perpetrated by the independent state of Tunisia under Bourguiba, to make Lion Mountain a tourist attraction sometime in the 1970s. In choosing to entitle the novel *Lion Mountain* after the landmark that embodies the *genius loci* of the place, rather than "a thousand futures lost," Tlili valorizes the resilience of the social imaginary that defines this southern desert region and its people, rather than the many depredations of empire. The landscapes of the novel pair utopic and heterotopic spaces—the garden and the desert; the traditional village and the French town; Horia's courtyard and the battlefields of World War II; and Lion Mountain and the planned tourist complex that will block it from view. The historical disruptions experienced by Lion Mountain are mirrored in the shifts of narrative perspective, a mix of the protagonist's first person narration, free indirect discourse about the inhabitants of the village, and epistolary fragments containing Horia's voice. The novel's time line also echoes this migration of perspective as it is based on the comings and goings of a son (the narrator) who has emigrated to New York and who is telling this family saga to his brother, a revolutionary or visionary who may be in Paris, or Palestine, or Cambodia. Tlili captures both the cultural rootedness that sustains the narrator and the transcultural forces that are transforming the world and redefining the place where he was born. His time scheme illustrates how modernity arrived "bit by bit, over the *longue durée*" (Gaonkar 1). In his refracted method of telling the story, Tlili acknowledges the fragmentation that characterizes modernity, but he also resists allowing these landscapes to be defined by outsiders. Instead, he re-creates the force of the local mythology and challenges the predations of the powerful. Horia embodies home. Her moral compass and traditional Muslim perspective are steady enough to accommodate a changing world but grounded enough to resist and rebel against unacceptable outside interventions. Tlili captures the convergence of global forces and the divergence of social imaginaries as they have impinged on the place he calls home.

In a review of Tlili's novel *Lion Mountain*, Herbert Mitgang of the *New York Times* says that "the unnamed village could be in Albert Camus' Algeria, but it is more likely in Mr. Tlili's Tunisia" (12). Reading this comparison, one is, "struck by the stark impossibility of thinking *that*" (Foucault, *The Order of Things* xv). The imaginative differences between the North Africa of Camus and Tlili involve more than a simple border crossing here; Camus and Tlili grew up steeped in very different social imaginaries. In his story "The Guest," Camus places his protagonist, the teacher who is forced to keep watch over the Arab prisoner, in a village on one of these barren desert steppes:

> He had requested a post in the little town at the base of the foothills separating the upper plateaus from the desert. . . . He had been named to a post farther north, on the plateau itself. In the beginning, the solitude and the silence had been hard for him on these wastelands peopled only by stones. Occasionally, furrows suggested cultivation, but they had been dug to uncover a certain kind of stone good for building. The only plowing here was to harvest rocks. Elsewhere a thin layer of soil accumulated in the hollows would be scraped out to enrich palty village gardens. This is the way it was: bare rock covered three quarters of the region. Towns sprang up, flourished, then disappeared; men came by, loved one another or fought bitterly, then died. No one in this desert, neither he nor his guest, mattered. (97–98)

Camus desert environment is a barren and absurd landscape. In *Lion Mountain*, Tlili's village, Lion Mountain, on the other hand, is described as having the same harmonious depth as the mythical Wad Hamid in Salih's work or Kane's land of the Diallobé:

> A geography more than physical or human: sacred. At least until the tragedy. Yes, that's the way it really was for the villagers. In their vision of the world—above all in the eyes of the imam, that vigilant guardian of the Law—the natural order of things was profoundly at one with the moral and judicial orders. In this mystical topography, landmarks determining the rights of each and every individual were perfectly clear. (9)[13]

But like Wad Hamid and the land of the Diallobé, Lion Mountain has its own contradictions and secrets, its own jealousies and provincial limitations.

When the novel opens, the protagonists in Tlili's *Lion Mountain* inhabit the complex borderland between East and West, between tradition and modernity, between oral and written expression. We are brought into this borderland by the voice of Horia, the central character of the novel, a widow whose voice emerges "as spoken" in the letters the public scribe has written for her, to her elder son in America. These letters, refracted through the consciousness of that son—a professional writer—come to us as fragments, fragments that speak of tradition and stability in the midst of violent political change, first under French domination, then under the corrupt party politics of the independence movement, and finally under the modernizing initiatives of the developing postindependence nation. While Horia and her ancestors, like the desert mountain, persist and subsist despite the brutalities of change, her sons—one an intellectual, one a revolutionary—are caught in the contradictions between a disconnected past and an alienated present. As we listen to Horia's voice in the letters she has dictated and sent to her son, who recalls them for us and comments on them, we realize that the geography of identity in this novel is charted according to three conceptual coordinates: place, time, and space. The idea of place is deeply tied to that "unobstructed view" of Lion Mountain, where both the village and the landscape stand for clearly demarcated ways of doing and seeing. Time in the novel is a function of both a mythic past, when the founding Andalusian ancestors "galloped out of the unknown" (*LM* 4), and a secular present, understood as "a thousand futures lost" because of the narrow, instrumental, and corrupt mentalities of the new national leaders. Finally, space shapes the novel as the narrative is largely generated in epistolary fashion because Horia's two sons are far away.

The difference between having a "sense of place" and having only an "experience of space" in the novel illustrates the historical divide that separates Horia from her sons: she is the land and continuity; they are condemned rather to the borderlands: they speak multiple languages (Arabic, French, English), must deal with multiple governments ("first world/third world"; "developed/developing"; corrupt/corrupt), and experience multiple alienations from the place they were born. Patricia Yaeger, following the lead of environmental psychologist Jonathan Sime, has argued that what differentiates "place" from "space" is chiefly the way we identify with them. "'Place' is a term that 'implies a strong emotional tie . . . between a person and a particular physical location' while space is associated with an abstract or geometric environment" and is unsettlingly anonymous (5). An earlier theorist of environmental psychology, Yi-Fu Tuan, sees the relationship slightly differently: "Place is security, space is freedom: we are attached to the one and long for the other" (3). *Lion Mountain* explores the notion of "space" as a function of context. For Horia, space and place are found in her view of Lion Mountain from her home; she is geographically grounded. For her sons, place is what they lost in emigrating; space is what replaced it.

Tlili's novel opens with the idea that Lion Mountain is defined by heritage and hierarchy; Horia believed in a "clear and deliberate order of things" (*LM* 5): "For everyone, the imam is the voice of our ancestors, assuring their continuity as the latest in an unbroken line of religious leaders that stretches back for centuries. Knowledge and faith. Order and law. Peace and justice. If the mosque is the center of Lion Mountain, Imam Sadek is the center of the mosque" (*LM* 6). The mosque is "a dusty building, poignant in its simplicity, sparsely decorated and quite humble, with clumsy uneven lines of the utmost severity. . . . Walls and minaret of ocher, like the Mountain. Cupolas of a washed-out white, faded by the rains and sandstorms" (*LM* 3). The mosque shapes and is shaped by the lives and the landscapes it echoes.[14] The narrator of *Lion Mountain*, who has returned home following Horia's death, experiences a loss of "place." The landscapes of home so dear to Horia have been changed into alienating space for him on multiple levels: the voice in her letters comes now from the grave, he is rehearsing Horia's story, which happened when he was far away, and telling it to a brother who is a fugitive and who shares the guilt of having left their mother alone: "I'm writing this story for you as well, Little Brother. She loved you best of all. Where are you? Will you ever learn what happened to our mother? Oh, if only we'd been with her when she needed us most!" (*LM* 21). The narrator longs for a past and a homeland from which he is, nevertheless, a voluntary exile.

For traditional communities, place is so central to their identity that regional resistance to outsiders often presents itself as a passion for place. In the midst of a desolate, rock-strewn steppe, Lion Mountain had emerged at that place where, according to local legend, "a spring . . . gushed forth" (*LM* 4) just as the ancestors galloped out of the West over Lion Mountain. Thus, this "stony, semi-arid waste" "once favored by lions" (*LM* 12) became a fertile center; the spring irrigated "orchards of pomegranates, figs, almonds, mulberries, peaches, plums, apricots, and other fruit trees. Beneath their boughs, in square plots marked off by channels providing a thin but precious trickle of water, grow abundant tomatoes, and pimentos, parsley, carrots, and turnips, and all kinds of melons" (*LM* 4). Horia, a gifted farmer, is associated with all these blessings of the miracle of water. Like the Imam, she anchors the author's sense of place, just as the mosque and the mountain anchor hers. These people and places are the landmarks of place that persist through the social changes and political storms of this historical novel.

When the French colonizers arrived in Lion Mountain, they brought with them to this landscape the first indications of an alien concept of space. The villagers' resisted this invasion, and "after the initial crisis that sparked the village's defiant stand against the country's new rulers, Lion Mountain was left to itself" (*LM* 7). The French ignored the village, despite its location on Highway 15, the main route north–south. They built their own village just down the road which they called "the Spring." The French town lies in ruins when the narrator returns from the United States to bury both his mother and his memories. He describes the French village as "a few European buildings—the school, the post office, the former police station . . . now completely dilapidated . . . and the few surviving poplars from a magnificent row planted along the uphill side of the stream" (*LM* 8). The peaceful co-existence of the village Lion Mountain and the French town the Spring was an accident of fate; the particular French colonial official who happened to be assigned to Lion Mountain was willing to live and let live. He was, by historical chance, also largely ignored in his own turn by his superiors, assigned as he was to the dusty margins of the space of the metropole and overlooked by colonial power brokers.

Tlili's narrator describes a balanced environment where different places could exist in geometric harmony: "One could draw an almost perfect equilateral triangle between the Spring, Horia's house, and the small group of traditional dwellings. The old woman's house would be at the apex, while Highway 15 would form the base as it runs past, linking together the original village and the European neighborhood. Opposite Horia's house looms the Mountain" (*LM* 8). The sweep of the land between Horia's house and the mountain had, until the recent past, "remained intact, untouched by any cultivation or construction" (*LM* 9). This place is for the villagers "a geography more than physical or human: sacred" (*LM* 9). In dealing with the French outsiders, the villagers had been able, through their imam, to send the message that their will to resist any pollution of this sacred place was so strong—and the stakes for the colonizer so minimal in this poor, arid, borderland—that the French decided to turn their attention elsewhere, and Lion Mountain survived intact. Nevertheless, this equilibrium is quite temporary, Tlili suggests, because the two cultures involved conceive of their environments in very different ways. Lion Mountain appears to be an environment defined by extremes and contradictions: Lion Mountain, the land where "once . . . lions roamed the stony, semi-arid waste," is wild; its seasons are harsh, with "endless pitch-black [winter] nights of bitter cold" (*LM* 13) and summers "almost 50 degrees centigrade in the shade . . . still boiling hot late in the afternoon" (*LM* 48). Its days cover the extremes, "the cool dawn draped in a delicate, almost diaphanous crimson veil . . . the twilight, all ablaze, covering the Mountain and horizon with a thousand deep red tongues of flame" (*LM* 11). But space here is organized along a vertical axis of tradition and faith, so order and hierarchy bring it peace. The French, on the other hand, seem to organize space as if the land were a uniform and undifferentiated horizontal plane, like a graph. This is what Saad, Horia's Nubian servant, is struck by when he becomes a conscript during World War II: "the land of the Infidel. . . . Wide, straight, endless roads, lines of asphalt that seemed as though they might have been traced with a ruler. . . . People who all looked the same with their blue eyes, their wheat-straw hair . . . without any sense of shame or restraint" (*LM*

28). But it is not the French who break this temporary equilibrium, but rather their postcolonial students, the new leaders in the postindependence period who arrive to bring chaos to the land.

These "new masters" with their "arbitrary rules" and their "misdeeds" are "insiders " to Tunisia, but "outsiders" to the village, which they merely understand first as a voting district, and next as a link in the touristic infrastructure. As Mounira Charrad has argued, "the nationalist struggle in Tunisia culminated in the formation of a national state that was largely autonomous from the support of tribal areas" (201). At first, the new state authorities in Lion Mountain are intent upon substituting for older traditions of place, a new sense of national space defined as the Motherland, which is synonymous with Bourguiba's Neo-Destour party. The Delegate of the "New Masters," described as "petty malevolence made flesh and blood" (*LM* 59), comes to enroll all adult males in the Party with the threat that those who resist will lose their irrigation water. Thus, any resistance to the "national" space will result in damage to the traditional place. From the first day, our narrator remembers, the Delegate violates and pollutes the village as "he shows off at the wheel of a luxurious black Citroën, driving with ostentation and contempt through the narrow, stony streets of our poor little village at breakneck speed, making an incredible racket and leaving behind great clouds of dust" (*LM* 59). Representative of the "modernizing" party interested in eliminating religious customs and laws that are "obsolete," the Delegate narrates a new nation: "each visit, he tells us about a new episode in what he proudly calls the 'epic of the Party' or about another miracle by the man he calls, in a voice trembling with veneration, 'Monsieur the President,' who has returned in triumph to the country by way of the sea, on a white horse—or so he claims—like a prophet" (*LM* 85–86). This myth-making to establish the legitimacy of a new national leader is suspiciously reminiscent of the advent of Tunisian's first postindependence president to power, as described by Gilbert Grandguillaume: "The incarnation of the resistance, and then the State in a man who'd become the 'supreme combatant'—*Al-Mujahid al-akbar*—generated the Bourguiba myth in permanent cultivation and best symbolized by his triumphal return to Tunisia on June 1, 1955 [after negotiating the agreement on internal autonomy], that of a man who rode through the streets carried first by the crowd and then on a mounted on the horse of a fellow resistance fighter" (143). The Delegate explains to the villagers that outsiders are not the problem: "danger threatens from the Great South, source of all their [the Party's] problems. The enemy will attack any day now, and proceed up Highway 15 to the capital" (*LM* 99). The historical issue referred to here is the support dissidents from the "Great South" gave to Bourguiba's rival within the party, Salah Ben

Youssef, who favored fighting the French for full independence rather than negotiating with them about withdrawal from Tunisia as Bourguiba, the gradualist, was doing. The attempt is made, then, to convince the villagers to substitute this newly minted national epic with its secular "prophet" for the older hierarchical faith that has anchored Lion Mountain.

In actual fact, Bourguiba, inventor of his own mythic persona, would speak of himself to the public, in the third person. He reminded members of the new nation that they had been nothing but "individual particles like dust" before being united by his charismatic presence: "He was the one who created the country out of nothingness and to whom the country owes its position among nations . . . to his great actions, eminent service, brilliant successes. . . . He is a prestigious leader to whom people of all continents rush to seek advice. . . . He is a miracle of nature that doesn't occur often over the course of the centuries" (qtd. in Grandguillaume 144),[15] Bourguiba said of Bourguiba.

By the summer of 1958, the Party and its delegate in Lion Mountain have begun to tighten the screws on those who refuse to carry Party cards. Horia maintains that all things must be viewed from the perspective of eternal justice: "the truth is still the truth. Even the delegate can't claim to have the last word where truth and justice are concerned" (*LM* 56). Horia's Nubian worker Saad, who is like family to her, warns her that "this government, this political party, this Delegate, these people aren't afraid of anything. . . . We've now entered a time of tyranny" (*LM* 56). As the narrator learns much later, when Saad refused to sign up for the Party, he was treated to some first-hand experience of this new national space: "Saad shows me the cigarette burns on his arms. . . . I can see the stripes of a septic blue, mottled with blood, left by blows of a truncheon on his back . . . three months of torture . . . an entire week without food or water in a dank, coal-black cellar infested with rats and flooded with water, the basement of a dilapidated building in a big city, perhaps the capital" (*LM* 56).

This Delegate who causes dissension among some of the villagers and does bodily harm to others is finally chased from Lion Mountain by the Imam. The new authorities end up in retreat, finding, as did the French, that the stakes are too high. From this point on, the Party will administer the space of Lion Mountain from afar, via governmental agencies like the Post Office. The Post Office confiscates the letters sent between Horia and her son in New York. Horia circumvents this barrier by sending her letters through passing tourists who have come to capture in slides and pictures Lion Mountain's sense of place. She lives with and adjusts to these daily attempted invasions; her son far away does not have this mundane contact as a defense. Away at school for years, he counts on letters and short visits to protect his sense of place:

> I renewed my ties by listening to Horia's stories on long summer nights. With the melodious brook murmuring in the background, she would tell me of the latest torrential rains, the most recent sandstorms, and the thousand other events both great and small that had befallen our village, which nonetheless went on imperturbably, like the Mountain after which it was named. The essential bond was lost, however; the village I had left behind had abandoned me in turn. From that moment on I was an exile. A stranger. Was it so surprising that I should now be unable to understand what Horia was trying to explain to me? Was I right to blame myself for not understanding? (*LM* 74)

Unable to hear the silences in his mother's voice, and out of touch with daily life, the narrator clings to his utopia and only realizes with horror much later what Horia and Saad had been living through:

> Lion Mountain itself was already the great secret of my life, a secret that remained entirely separate from the orderly, rational life I led with my companions [in New York], as someone passionately engaged in the sacred pursuit of learning Horia had so desired for her sons. The secret was my magic world; I lived it apart from the real world, and I considered it my right to do so even with friends who loved me. And I lived this secret as though it were a privilege. Lion Mountain was my secret garden. I was secretly proud of it. It was that pride I lost when I was forced to harbor the other secret [of Saad's torture of which even the Imam is unaware]. My nights were filled with bad dreams. (*LM* 80)

Silenced by the unspoken threats of the modern nation, the narrator suggests he understands the cost of getting papers to return home again. Horia warns him: "I have only the two of you in this life. Your little brother and you. You will still have to return here. To this village. To this country. So, a reckless move . . . well-intentioned, but imprudent. Why provoke the Devil? Just imagine the consequences. . . . Better let the Devil destroy himself" (*LM* 72–73). Horia believes that "everything that is totally and basically corrupt is irrevocably doomed to perish. Of its own accord" (*LM* 72). The narrator has grown away from this steady belief, so "Lion Mountain" now merges the dream, the utopia of childhood memory, with the heterotopic nightmare of contemporary politics. He is a powerless and distant outcast.

In the end, it is the government's desire to capitalize on the flow of tourism that causes Horia's death. Invasion by the French, and physical coercion by the Party are succeeded by socioeconomic modernization. The Delegates again arrive at Lion Mountain, this time to inaugurate the construction of a new space that will be built on the great sweep of land between Horia's house and the ocher mountain. Monsieur le President has acted on the advice of "experts" and "chosen to endow Lion Mountain with a tourist area to be constructed on virgin soil at a geometric site . . . glass, concrete, shoddy flashiness out in the desert . . . the café-restaurant, the gas station, the crafts shop, the four story hotel" (*LM* 150–151). To defend her land, Horia and her faithful servant have mounted an old World War II machine gun on the roof, a weapon left as a remnant of the battles at the Kasserine Pass in a war that had largely passed Lion Mountain by. As security for the governmental groundbreaking, the national soldiers have placed tanks at the ceremonial site. The conflict results in the obliteration of Horia's house, blown to smithereens, and the death of Horia and faithful Saad. Lion Mountain is a place forever after fragmented. Returning months later, the narrator struggles to put the fragments of voices, landscapes and history back together, and reconstructing this geography of identity is the final purpose of his narrative, and of Tlili's as well. This is perhaps why Tlili finally calls his story *Lion Mountain* rather than *A Thousand Futures Lost*:

> Each of us carries with him, among his resources in life's struggle, a few deeply engraved images from his early years. They come—usually at their own bidding—to remind us of the many twists and turns in the long road already traveled. These images are beacons of light, safeguarding for all eternity those precious moments and loved ones we have lost, those parts of ourselves we treasure in secret, the better to preserve them from the banality of everyday life. The sorrowful or joyous events recounted in this narrative belong to this luminous heritage. (*LM* 71)

Scattered Identities: Mokeddem's *The Forbidden Woman* and *La Transe des Insoumis*

In a 1997 interview with Christiane Chaulet-Achour and Lalia Kerfa, Malika Mokeddem commented that she had moved from being in voluntary exile in France to being an expatriate:

> Crossing frontiers has been my deliverance. Is it because of my nomad heritage? Exile, I define in terms of a family, a tribe, but not in terms of a territory. And people who whine about exile all year long bore me terribly. Even if my first years in France weren't without pitfalls, I accomplished what I wanted. Because here there isn't that systematic will to break down individuals, to bully rebels and to undermine tenaciousness. . . . Two words that get my back up are "nationality" and "roots" . . . I know very well that it isn't necessary to deny anything to truly blossom.

> But I don't want to be fenced in by anything whatsoever. My grandmother would say: "Only palm trees have roots. We are nomads. We have a memory and some legs to walk with." I made that my motto. (32)[16]

That said, it is interesting that Mokeddem and her female characters who generally resemble her—for example, Yasmine in *Century of Locusts*, Sultana in *The Forbidden Woman*, and Kenza in *Of Dreams and Assassins*—still seem to spend much of their time evoking a nomadic culture that has disappeared, grieving for lost mothers, and longing for recognition from a culture they say they have left behind. At the same time, they lash out against the repression of individuality associated with tribalism, the gender-biased upbringing enforced first by mothers, and the colonial relationships that continue to define their second-class citizenship at home and abroad. These themes structure *The Forbidden Woman* (1993) and the autobiographical *La Transe des insoumis* (2003) and *Mes Hommes* (2005). Protagonists in both *Forbidden Woman* and *La Transe des Insoumis* shuttle between worlds in search of a place to call home. The chapters in *The Forbidden Woman* (*L'Interdite*) alternate between first person narratives by the expatriate Algerian Sultana and those by Vincent, a tourist from France. The chapters of *La Transe des insoumis* alternate between *Ici*, which is France where Mokeddem is writing the text, and *Là-bas*, which begins with the Algeria of her childhood. Mokeddem's projects—to establish her independence (her identity) through writing, to become part of a "community of writers" rather than part of a corrupt nation, to win the respect of her family—are transcultural inventions of the self. This section explores Mokeddem's world of words as a fictional space in which, like the mirror, the utopic and heterotopic (the *heimlich* and the *unheimlich*) meet in a place we call "home." In these books about returning home, "the non-place of language" is charged with mediating between her transcultural invention of a self and the all too real violence of the world.

Our participation in a social imaginary, like our experience of individual identity, involves a constant play between the *heimlich* (our at-homeness in a culture or a personal identity) and the *unheimlich* (our sudden estrangement from these parts of our unconscious lives through self-awareness). This dynamic is ironic in that it is through estrangement that we achieve conscious definition, but at the same time we are distanced from the self, or culture, through the very process of awareness. We all participate in social imaginaries, whether we choose to or not. And as we become aware of this or that building block of our social imaginary we may accept or reject it, but we cannot simply behave as if it did not exist, as if it did not shape our identities. Identity might be thought of as having different modes. First, there are the identity assumptions we inherit from the contingent facts of where and when we are born (our origins). Next, there are those situational elements of identity that emerge in particular contexts that interpellate us along the lines of race, or sex, or class, or religion, etc. In addition, there are those identifications we make with other people and things and even with our idea of our "self":

> Identifications are erotic, intellectual, and emotional. . . . They form the most intimate and yet the most elusive part of our unconscious lives. While we tend to experience our identities as part of our public personas—the most exposed part of our self's surface collisions with a world of other selves—we experience our identifications as more private, guarded, evasive. (Fuss 2)

Of course public identity and private identification are intimately and dialectically related identifications: perhaps identity is for us the history of our identifications.

We could safely argue that all of Mokeddem's works include significant autobiographical elements. Some works are directly autobiographical such as the recent *La Transe des insoumis* (2003) and *Mes Hommes* (2005); some are related more or less directly to her family history, such as *Les hommes qui marchent* and *Le siècle des sauterelles* (*Century of Locusts*); and some have protagonists who share many physical and emotional traits with Mokeddem herself, such as *L'Interdite* (*The Forbidden Woman*), *Des Rêves et des assassins* (*Of Dreams and Assassins*), *La nuit de la lézarde* and *N'zid.* In using writing to establish a transcultural identity, a place to feel at home, a community based on affiliation rather than filiation, Mokeddem often arouses in herself, and in readers, the *unheimlich*—a sense of scattered identities. Identifications are not the less central to identity for being based on misrecognition or fragmented insights.

Language is central to a transcultural invention of the self. Miriam Cooke explains in a chapter entitled "In Search of Mother Tongues" in *Women Claim Islam*:

> Autobiographies have become key sites for the questioning of norms and for the construction of alternative visions. As they examine the building blocks of their lives, writers, and especially women writers, are disentangling language, religion, place, and birth. They are asking what it means to call one particular language one's mother tongue when several languages are vying for primacy in establishing authentic identity. Arab writers in North Africa are examining the constructedness of language and of its supposedly natural links with identity and are showing how fragile are the connections said to undergird the unitary conception of identity. (29–30)

Cooke goes on to compare male writers such as Jacques Derrida and Albert Memmi with female writers such as Assia Djebar. As a Jewish Algerian, Derrida argues in the autobiographical works *Le monolinguisme de l'Autre* (*Monolinguism of the Other*) and *De l'hospitalité* that he grew up with no mother tongue. Critic Mustapha Marrouchi once addressed this issue in an essay on Derrida: "When asked whether he learned Arabic, [Derrida] dismissively replied: '[I'm] almost pathologically monolinguistic.' And yet despite Derrida's reply, the final question is: How can one whose ancestors resided in Algeria for centuries live in a country for almost a quarter of a century and not acquire the language of that country?" ("Decolonizing the Terrain" 9). Marrouchi was not alone in questioning Derrida's identifications, and Derrida did begin trying to situate himself in terms of his Algerian past. As Cooke summarizes his explanation:

> The story begins in 1870, when the French promulgated the Crémieux Decree that gave Algerian Jews French citizenship. They were thus distinguished from other Algerians who had been considered French nationals, although not citizens [i.e., the Berber and Arab Muslim population]. . . . From one day to the next, Jews—French or Arab or Berber—who had been assimilated into their Arabic or Berber communities stopped speaking Arabic or Berber. It was not that there was a law against learning Arabic, Berber, or even Hebrew; it was that these newly French Jews living on the borders of the Arab quarters—as did Derrida's grandparents—were steered away from those languages that they had spoken as *indigènes*. As newly French they were taught to despise these mother tongues. . . . Denied Algerianness because he was French, he was denied Frenchness because he was a Jew. What nation could he call his? What mother tongue offered itself? (44–45)

Derrida himself attributes not learning Arabic to what he calls provisionally an *interdict* although he says there was really no formal rule or law. Rather there were unwritten rules of segregation, run through the institutions of the colonial society. As the somewhat more privileged colonial subject living on the invisible border of an Arab neighborhood, Derrida explains this divorce from the language being spoken by his neighbors as a function of power in his book *Monolingualism of the Other*:

> Given all the colonial censorships—especially in the urban and suburban milieu where I lived—and given all the social barriers there, the racisms, a now grimacing, now "happy-go-lucky" xenophobia which was sometimes user-friendly or joyful, given the disappearance, then in progress, of Arabic as the official, everyday, administrative language, the one and only option was still the school, and the study of Arabic was restricted to the

> school, but as an alien language, a strange kind of alien language as the language of the other, but then of course, and this is the strange and troubling part, the other as the nearest neighbor. *Unheimlich.* (37)

Derrida's experience of language as absence of a mother tongue helps us to bring Mokeddem's views on language as a complex overlay of signals into relief. The oral Arabic of her paternal grandmother provides the mother tongue that anchors Mokeddem's imagination: "the flamboyance of oral Arabic left their mark on me long before French words got their hold on me. And, there really is a dichotomy for me between the speech of my grandmother—the flamboyant speech of an Arab nomad, her stories from this world she sensed was in danger, that she felt was threatened, so her speech was filled with urgency—and then the speech, the language of my mother; a real tongue, a tongue-lashing barking out orders at me" (*Malika Mokeddem: envers et contre tout* 41). The traditional Arabic of her parents she associates not only with rules and reprimands that curb her freedom but also with a form of gendered language that makes her a stranger in her own home. Her memoir *Mes Hommes* opens with a chapter called "the First Absence," which recalls the way the social imaginary reflected in her father's speech taught her about her identity:

> Father, my first man, through you I learned to measure love by the hurt I felt, by the absences I endured. At what age do words start their ravages? I begin to hunt down images from my earliest childhood. A few words come back to me, sketching out a black and white past . . . before reflection began, before I could even express myself. That point when language starts to make innocence bleed, and cutting words leave a permanent scar that throbs with pain. Later in life, we live with it or rebel against it.
>
> Talking to my mother you used to say "my sons" when you spoke of my brothers; "your daughters" when the conversation concerned my sisters and me. You always said "my sons" with pride. You had a touch of impatience, irony or resentment, sometimes even anger when saying "your daughters." The anger was when I disobeyed, as I often did—rebelling to rebel, and also because it was the only way to reach you. (11)

When Mokeddem suggests above that exile is about families and tribes not about territory, she is referring to this early attachment to her grandmother's nomadic speech and the stories of crossing wide-open spaces, on the one hand, and to this early lesson about the ways parental language can dislodge you from your home.

Asked about exile in an interview conducted by Najib Redouane, Yvette Bénayoun-Szmidt, and Robert Elbaz, Mokeddem explained that she felt at home, in her house (her personal space), in Montpellier:

> So, I've never felt exiled. It isn't a land that makes you have that feeling. It is the looks of others. . . . My relationship with my grandmother meant that I felt myself a nomad. . . . So, for me, territory, land is a beckoning, a beckoning with wide-open arms. It is a horizon with wide-open arms that breathes you in. It's the looks of others that puts you at the frontier. In the beckoning of a journey, there are no frontiers. ("Genèse d'une oeuvre" 294–295)

Likewise, she says that as the child of parents who did not read and write, "Knowledge was for [her] the first exile" (295) because it separated her from her family—but she maintains this was also "a deliverance" (294): "For me being put at the frontier happened very early. It began in Algeria. It began with my parents, with my own family. Is it because I am the descendant of a family of nomads? Exile is not about territory. It is about a tribe, and from the moment that tribe became suffocating, I became a stranger in relation to that tribe. But I was, at the same time, delivered from the weight of the taboos and the forbidden, and I took off toward open horizons" (295). When asked by Yolande Helm whether she felt her relationship to the French language was ambiguous, Mokeddem said it was rather a deliverance: "No way! No Way! I tell myself I cannot bite the breast that fed me, I cannot betray something that is part of me. My relation to language is that, I don't want anyone to think I reject Arabic; I reject the canned language of the government, of classical Arabic" ("Entretien" 42).

Mokeddem argues that she keeps what is a part of her, of her history, but she "battles against restrictions of whatever kind" (43). Much of Mokeddem's repertoire of creative themes is taken from a tribal social imaginary with which she is often at odds in crucial ways. She wishes to keep the nomadic lifestyle of her grandmother as a mythic grounding but reject the tribal customs that were part and parcel of that life: "in these tribes, conditions were difficult and so the rights of the individual, both men and women, were sacrificed to the survival of the clan" (46). She says that learning to read in French empowered her in two ways. First, as she explains in *La Transe des Insoumis*, it gave her a space her mother couldn't enter: "I was thrown into raptures of admiration before my open book, the notebook into which I recopied it. Overwhelmed by euphoria upon an unexpected discovery: my book, my notebook were indecipherable for my mother" (56). Second, it allowed her to escape from her immediate surroundings and their demands by replacing them with other worlds. But identifications can be unruly, as even Mokeddem admits sometimes. She recalls that she would read late into the night: "From my perch, I sneak a glance at Grandmother. Her abandoned silhouette breaks my heart. I console myself by claiming that I only agreed to that distancing out of a concern for her fragile sleep. A lame excuse that didn't absolve me even in my own eyes. Occasionally, I catch her circumspect gaze moving over me and my books. To escape her, I plunge back into my black and white beyond" (89). As Diana Fuss puts it in *Identification Papers*: "identifications are the origin of some of our most powerful, enduring, and deeply felt pleasures. They are also the source of considerable emotional turmoil, capable of unsettling or unmooring the precarious groundings of everyday identities" (2). A self generated around identification means identity is an on-going process, not a reified state of being. It also means that it is dependent on those beyond ourselves, on those who look back at us. Like the literary text, the self is created not only at the site of production, but at the site of reception as well.

The Forbidden Woman was the first of Mokeddem's works to attract a large audience, as she explains: "in the first place because I had arrived at a large publishing house, Grasset. And only secondarily because this book dealt with current news that was monopolizing attention. All of a sudden, being a woman, being an Algerian woman and a writer became emblematic. I see in that more danger than satisfaction. There is in that the risk of clichéd judgments, of reductive caricature" (Chaulet-Achour and Kerfa 28). Although I would argue that *The Forbidden Woman* is a much thinner and less grounded narrative than her earlier novels *Les Hommes qui marchent* [*Nomads*] and *Century of Locusts* based on the oral stories her grandmother told, it was also the first to be published in English, followed shortly after by *Of Dreams and Assassins*, a second novel about fundamentalist violence, brutal misogyny, and brutalized women in Algeria. The result has been that critics from abroad (France, Spain, Italy, and the United States, for example) have praised Mokeddem for her outspokenness and read her work through the lens of a Western social imaginary, as the product of a writer from the margins struggling to create a "brave new world" we might say. Meanwhile, readers who share her cultural social imaginary are much more leery about the manichean reading these novels encourage—as is Mokeddem herself.

The Forbidden Woman is the story of Sultana, a young doctor from Montpellier who travels back to her home village to in southern Algeria to bury her former lover, Yacine, who has been practicing medicine there since she broke off relations with him years earlier because she needed her freedom. When she arrives, she finds Yacine's old friend Salah there, and she makes a new friend, Vincent, who has come to Algeria to explore his own identity. Both of them fall in love with her. Vincent is the recent recipient of a kidney transplant; the donor is a young Algerian woman who has died in an auto accident:

> Gascon, Christian, and atheist by my father; Jewish by my mother, Polish and practicing out of solidarity; North African through my transplant and with no borders, through a "tissue identity," I nevertheless have gregarious and stubborn habits. My identity gathers nectar according to its own will, makes its honey, and crosses one old tannin with another. It mixes, accomodates. I don't reject anything. I'm an eclectic, a harlequin, as Michel Serres would say. (49)[17]

Like a kinder version of Conrad's Kurtz or a less innocent version of his Harlequin, Vincent is a mixture of all Europe and now, with the perfect match of this kidney, feels he is also North African and female—at least on the level of tissue. And as the allusion to Serres suggests, he embraces a sort of *métis* epistemology, which sets a playful ambiguity off against modernity's rage for order, its need for homogeneity.

Sultana's attempt at *métissage* is far less happy. Salah suggests she fashion her rebellion after that of "real" Algerian women who resist without using head-on tactics against "an almost totally unjust and monstrous society," women who go by way of knowledge, work, and financial autonomy as they persevere "in the shadow of men who stagnate and despair" rather than provoking confrontation (*FW* 111). Put simply, they work within the common social understandings that underpin value and legitimacy in their society. Sultana, who has challenged the conservative desert communities by smoking and drinking in public, leading a funeral procession, which is usually sex-segregated, and sleeping with a French tourist, describes her situation as more marginal than that of the "real" Algerian women or the cosmopolitan Vincent:

> "'Real Algerian women' don't have a problem with their identity. They're from an epoch, a land. They're whole. I've been many-faceted and torn apart. That's only been aggravated with age and exile. In France now, I'm neither Algerian nor even North African. I'm an Arab [Arab woman]. That's as much as to say nothing. Arab, this word dissolves you in the grayness of a nebula. Here, I'm no longer Algerian, nor am I French. I wear a mask. A Western mask? The mask of an emigré? The height of the paradox is that the two often merge. By virtue of always being elsewhere, you inevitably become different. Whether you are interesting, interrogating, or shocking, you are a moving peculiarity in time, in space, and in the diverse ideas that people can create out of 'the foreigner.' But would you believe that as uncomfortable as this foreign skin can be sometimes, it's nonetheless an invaluable source of freedom. I wouldn't exchange it for anything in the world! Also, I never hide anything. And the rumors and criticisms generally do nothing but urge on the jubilation that all transgressions provide me with." (*FW* 111–112)

Obviously, one of the problems with Sultana's speechifying is that her idea of freedom as transgression (a war on boundaries as such) is not unlike George Bush's war on "terrism" as such: it reduces complex forces into heroic narratives that pit the good hero/heroine against a thoroughly other, thoroughly evil enemy.

Mokeddem creates sympathy for Sultana by putting her in extreme circumstances: the fundamentalists are described as being every kind of disease and disaster:

> *They*, Everybody here says *they* when they're talking about members of the FIS [Front Islamique du Salut]. *They*, all at once grasshoppers [locusts], smallpox, typhus, cancer, leprosy, plague and AIDS of the mind. *They*, an endemic disease that has burst from the confines of the misery and confusion, and that encysts in the fatality and ignorance of the country. (*FW* 109)

These are the same people who drove Sultana out of the village as an orphan in the past, after sowing the seeds of suspicion that labeled her beautiful mother a whore and drove her father, an outsider as a Chaâmbi from the high plateaus, to kill her mother accidently, a crime of passion. At the tender age of five, she was like a leper:

> "It was rumored that we were a cursed family. For a long time I was convinced of it. When I'd walk down the street, children would run away from me as I approached. Hopping frogs scattered in panic. To escape from this I got myself a bell: for a few days I dragged an empty can, attached to a string, behind me. Then I withdrew from everything. I withdrew myself from present time. . . .
>
> Within two days, all of them abandoned me. I grew up alone, anorexic and hounded, with the soul of a tragic traveling performer." (*FW* 131)

The tragic immensity of Sultana's past wounds, and the evil infection of the present society are indeed stated in heightened terms. As Salah puts it:

> "Before it was only the party members, the pigs and the orderlies who poisoned our lives. Now, with the decay of the state's authority, any imbecile believes he's invested with a divine right and claims he can mete out justice according to his principles! Moronic populism and nationalism, these are the lifeblood of today's Algeria." (*FW* 125)

In the last chapter of the book, Sultana briefly joins forces with a dozen women from Ain Nekhla who are holding a war council in the hospital to fight the fundamentalist mayor Bakkar and his thugs. One of the women remembers when Sultana left the town as a girl: "Your eyes were terrible, terrible. . . . You stared at Bakkar and you said in a harsh voice, 'You and your band, you're the rot of this country. But I am going to study, and I'll be stronger than all of your cowardly and disgraceful acts. Look hard at me. I don't give a damn about you! And I'll come back one day to tell you so'" (*FW* 146).

This melodramatic depiction of truly tragic events has generated a wide range of responses from readers. A librarian from Oregon writing in *Library Journal* found "Mokeddem's sometimes effusive style is the only flaw in an otherwise worthy title documenting the oppression of women in this North African country" (Chadwell). At the other extreme, in *La Transe des insoumis*, Mokeddem quotes an expatriate Algerian journalist for *Le Nouvel Observateur* who described her work as not only bad literature: "but beneath . . . something worse is hiding: the dishonesty of surfing on the bloody Algerian wave. And that for once we must denounce!" (272–273). Jacalyn Duffin reviewing *The Forbidden Woman* for the "Literature, Arts and Medicine Database" describes the novel as

> thick on description and thin on understanding (or humor) . . . the florid prose occasionally becomes heavy handed: odd bits of slang jar in passages of solemn description, while children pronounce in ponderous parables like Biblical prophets.
>
> Occasionally the author's rage, rationalization, or narcissism cloud her message with a surprising Manichean simplicity: not all victims can be beautiful, strong, intelligent, and articulate. She seems to forget that even the ignorant, vile perpetrators—the petty mayors, the lecherous taxi drivers with their pus-filled eyes—are victims too. In the introduction, the translator [Melissa Marcus] comments on the "plethora" of adjectives and "incongruous metaphors," but defends Mokeddem's style for what it tells us of her pain and the suffering of all oppressed women. (Review)[18]

Like translator Melissa Marcus, Yolande Helm takes the more generous course situating Mokeddem's work in the larger global contexts that an international readership imposes. Transnational feminism creates a readership that identifies with the outrage at the gendered injustices that Mokeddem's semi-autobiographical protagonists suffer.

In her *Nomadic Voices of Exile: Feminine Identity in Francophone Literature of the Maghreb*, Valerie Orlando uses the idea of deterritorialization taken from Deleuze and Guattari and the notion of a Third Space as it is used by Homi Bhabha to indicate a "intersubjective and interstitial milieu" where "becoming" happens: "All relationships reside in that simple shifting fluid period where subject and object come together. In other words, all preconceived notions and stereotypes concerning subjectivity are wiped away. There is no dialectic between object and subject, master and slave, Other and colonizer; rather in this interstitial space, perception is confronted by its own limit and is placed in the midst of things" (4–5). This is a more *heimlich* or friendly version of interstices than we met in Foucault's ruminations about the *Chinese Encyclopedia*. Likewise it suggests a more consciously manageable subjectivity than Taylor or Bourdieu countenance in their notions of the social imaginary or the role of doxa in everyday life. It defines subjectivity as taking place in an intersubjective space rather than the intrasubjective realm of desire Fuss describes in *Identification Papers*. To the extent that working in the interstices suggests a Hegelian transcendence, a view of dialectic as something to be gone beyond, it also may mean a loss of that history of identifications, which, be they for good or ill, make us who we are. We recall Fanon reminding Sartre in *Black Skin, White Masks* that to deny someone the emotional weight of experience, even based on misrecognition and racism, is a terrible thing to do; Fanon claims the everyday experience of his black body, however purloined, misunderstood, or demonized it has been. Fanon objects to Sartre's "reminding me that my blackness was only a minor term. In all truth, in all truth I tell you, my shoulders slipped out of the framework of the world, my feet could no longer feel the touch of the ground, without a Negro past, without a Negro future, it was impossible for me to live my Negrohood" (138). Orlando embraces a "becoming-woman philosophy" that "has been born from a need to change the space of the feminine from one dominated by phallocentrism to that of agency and voice" (5–6). She argues that through texts like *The Forbidden Woman*, "Mokeddem sets out to draw the reading public's attention to the ongoing sociocultural and political strife of a country laid waste by inner conflict, factionalism, fundamentalism, and abuse of human rights. . . . That strife is often the product of the contemporary Arab world" (200). The difficulty where reception is concerned is that it is also the product of global interests outside the Arab world, and these interests are not synonymous with phallocentrism, though the overlap is significant.

Other feminist readers have seen this history through a lens that factors in the politics of reception as a major concern. Algerian sociologist Marnia Lazreg points out that "with few exceptions gender inequality is attributed to Islam's presumed influence upon the lives of men and women in North Africa and the Middle East. The unstated assumption is that religion is at once the cause of and the solution to gender inequality. Somehow, if religion is done away with, equality between men and women will ensue" ("Gender and Politics" 756). She argues in "Islamism and the Recolonization of Algeria" that the aim of the fundamentalists of the FIS

> is not to "re-Islamize" people as is often said. Rather it *recolonizes* private and public spaces by infusing them with new meanings and norms derived from ideational and behavioral sources that sound familiar to individuals because they are expressed in the Arabic language and refer to a monolithic 'Islam,' but in effect are alien to the historical and daily life experiences of individual Algerians. In the end, Islam as understood by Algerians, prior to the emergence of the Islamist movement, is transformed. . . . I am referring to this process as one of recolonization because of its targeting of Algerians' cultural space in a manner similar to the French who, in the nineteenth century, attempted to displace local norms and values to suit their political purposes. (44–45; emphasis added)[19]

The vocabulary of the FIS taps into a larger shared Muslim social imaginary, redefining it in its own image. This recolonization of Algerian cultural space on the inside of the country is matched by a neocolonial consumption of Algerian space on the outside, Lazreg argues in "The Triumphant Discourse of Global Feminism: should Other Women Be Known." Lazreg does not exclude transnational feminism from this paradigm, noting that many Western feminists believe that "they belong to perfectible societies, whereas Other women's societies are by definition 'traditional,' impervious to change from within, and unknowing of what is good for women"; the residue of these cultural roots from the enlightenment is manifest in two outcomes:

> On the one hand, they empower Western feminists when the latter encounter women from other societies, especially those from the Muslim world, whom they understand only through the reductive (and misunderstood) categories of religion. . . . On the other hand, they compel women from non-Western societies to speak from "Western women's perspectives," which means they must speak about their cultures while fleeing from them instead of perfecting them from within. (31)

Arguing along the same lines, Nada Elia, in a review of Mokeddem's *The Forbidden Woman*, notes that as a "short novel, 'exotic' and accessible, harshly critical of Islamic fundamentalism and patriarchy," this work will probably become a popular reading assignment for "women's studies or 'non-Western' literature courses. This is quite unfortunate, since, buried in the preface, is the otherwise important claim that Mokeddem was 'enchanted with her trip and her reestablishment of contact with the Algeria that she loves'" (Elia). And in fact, this same preface also notes that Mokeddem was "raised in a tolerant version of Islam" (vii). Gender, then, is only one lens (and a multifaceted one at that) through which Mokeddem's work is read and interpreted, and the issue of the politics of reception is raised by the uses to which a text opens itself.

In her essay "Malika Mokeddem: A New and Resonant Voice in Francophone Algerian Literature," Helm captures vividly the extreme characterization of the protagonist Kenza's father in Mokeddem's novel *Of Dreams and Assassins*:

> The protagonist's childhood is aborted by the absence of a mother who died and by the presence of a fissiste father who is abusive and odious. His occupation as a butcher allows his sexual voracity and predatory temperament to explode within a setting of mutilated carcasses of dead animals. An avid consumer of "flesh" he preys upon his female clients among the suspended cadavers. Kenza's father manipulates meat with a machiavellian and insane pleasure: his knife becomes a penis that rapes, digs into, and parts the tender and wounded flesh. (206)

This portrait of a father is certainly one of the most unforgettable images in the novel. Helm argues that this kind of extreme depiction will not be taken as characterizing all Muslim males: "One could accuse Malika Mokeddem of reinforcing the negative, stereotypical view of the Muslim male by presenting this vile and primal character. I believe, however, that a careful reader will not relegate him to a culturally authentic type" (206–207). Were literature just about classrooms and responsible close reading, this might be the case. But literature, especially this kind of engaged literature with a political message, has to be considered in the much larger, far more contentious frame of the distribution and consumption of the work.

Mokeddem has often echoed her protagonist Sultana's declaration: "My only real community is the community of ideas" (67). In a related way, Cooke points out that Derrida argued that "identity and human relationships are structured in terms of hospitality. In such a scheme no one belongs naturally anywhere but is always working out the rights and responsibilities of 'invitation, welcome, asylum, shelter'" (47). Ironically enough, when it comes to hospitality, Mokeddem remembers that she escaped being the daughter her mother wanted her to be (cooking, cleaning up after brothers, marrying young, having babies) by locking herself in the room in traditional Arab houses that is reserved only for *guests*. She would read all night and sleep late into the day, leaving the housework to her mother who depended on help from Mokeddem who was the oldest child in a large family. This egocentric behavior brought her into direct conflict with her mother:

> My appropriation of this room is the call to battle . . . between my mother and me. Every morning, she leaves her chores periodically to come pound angrily on the door: "Hey! *American*! There's work waiting for you. Get up! . . . Reading all night, living at a distance from others—*American*

> *style*—allowed me to escape as well from all the chores that devoured the days . . . to escape from being transformed into my brothers' slave. (*La Transe* 141)

Mokeddem trades her Algerian life for another she makes for herself in France among a community of the like-minded. But then she discovers the limits of this at-homeness, this hospitality, abroad:

> The Gulf War made me utter a word that I'd thought I'd never say: stateless. Stateless this time in my adopted country, France. I felt like vomiting for having taken that nationality. That France, the one belonging to the coalition of state terrorists, made me want to erase everything that smacked of the word France. But not the language. And I never considered the French population as a monolithic entity. Not even during the Algerian Revolution. Above all during the atrocities over there. Attachments to Jews as well as to Pieds Noirs had helped me to banish those frontiers in my head. Later and without denying anything of my origins, I formed the conviction that my true community was that of ideas. . . . The Gulf War was the repetition of the civilizing crusades of all the colonizing powers. . . .
>
> One evening, during a tumultuous discussion, I berated my best friend Matilde, for not recognizing clearly enough the devastation, the iniquity of that war. That sudden feeling of isolation, even among those I had chosen, those of my family of ideas, was more than I could bear. (98–100)

This sudden feeling of not being welcome, not being at-home, arises out of ethnic difference and identification that, for the moment, has displaced gender identification.

If hatred of misogyny is one optic through which literature is read and communities of ideas are formed, fear of xenophobia is another. Mokeddem tells an anecdote about a book signing for *Of Dreams and Assassins* that took place at the bookstore Fnac in Mulhouse, France some time after the first Gulf War. Mokeddem had written this book at a time when she was "homeless." As Mokeddem tells us in *La Transe des insoumis*, she ended up moving out of her home (moving in with the above-mentioned Mathilde), closing her medical practice in Montpellier, and living under police guard because of phone threats by Islamists. She wrote the book in a state of urgency to speak out against the violence in Algeria. Despite her earlier recognition of the xenophobia just beneath the surface in France, she is defensive about the reception of her book by an Algerian in the audience:

> —There was this guy in the audience. . . . He was an Algerian psychiatrist. Oh là, là! This guy was unbelievable. He had told me that in his

> practice a host of people had talked to him about *The Forbidden Woman*, especially the nurses. And he had read *Of Dreams and Assassins*. . . . I asked him, "What is the problem?"
> —He told me: "I would have liked . . . I am a psychiatrist . . ."—He never stopped repeating that to me—"I know that this kind of behavior exists in every society but I would have preferred that his portrait had been of a man in uniform, a cop or policeman or a . . . but not a poor devil."
> —I replied that there were a slew of poor devils who were like that.
> —"Fine," he said to me, "but . . . considering your role as a responsible writer, you've given the French reading public the image of a poor . . . this image of a poor devil of an Algerian. The image of the Algerian!"
> (I remember that at the time there was the Dutroux affair [a serial killer of young girls in Belgium], I think).
> —But listen, I told him: "I understand your point completely but one can't generalize and say, for example, that all Belgians are Dutrouxs." (*Malika Mokeddem* 277–278)

At the time of this reading, Le Pen and the National Front party (FN), running on a xenophobic platform, had a following in Mulhouse and Strasbourg that was the strongest in France (the FN garnered about 25% of the votes) (Bihr). For better or for worse, Dutroux was a Belgian among Belgians, not an Algerian in Alsace. The report *La Lutte contre le racisme et la xénophobie* (1997) by the Commission nationale consultative des droits de l'homme (CNCDH, National Consultative Commission on Human Rights), showed "that Arabs, followed by Gypsies, are the primary targets of racism" in France (*La Lutte*). While the Alsace Lorraine region does not have the typical characteristics that would explain the growth of a right-wing movement—it has low unemployment, a high standard of living, and a diverse population (Bihr), it does have a peculiar historical connection with North Africa, which helps to locate the source of its racism toward North Africans.

Following the loss of the provinces of Alsace and Lorraine in 1871, liberal politicians such as Jules Ferry and Eugène Etienne argued for the expansion of France's overseas colonies, which would in some measure make up for the loss of the provinces. To this idea, the xenophobic, conservative Déroulède replied: "I had two daughters and you are offering me twenty domestiques" (Jean Martin 19). Feeling they needed to emigrate from a German-controlled Alsace-Lorraine, 5,000 loyal French from Alsace-Lorraine migrated to the land confiscated from Algerians following the 1871 Mokrani revolt.[20] The lost provinces of Alsace and Lorraine were referred to as the "'twin sisters' without which the [French] nation could not be whole" (Boswell). In 1988, the National Front tapped into this nationalism and used the image of the Alsatian headdress, which had after 1918 become associated in the French social imaginary with loyalty and patriotism, on its election poster. This poster "depicted a sternly faced *alsacienne* in traditional black headdress (*coiffe*) whose face was covered by a Muslim veil in such a way that she appeared to be gagged; the minaret of a mosque was visible in the far background. Underneath the blunt caption read "Alsace, 'our' region. . . . For how much longer?" The allusion was clear: Muslim immigration posed a distinct threat to Alsatian identity and to the province's existence" (Boswell). It is in the context of this history of regional racism that the exchange between the Algerian psychiatrist and Mokeddem took place.

Mokeddem's roman à thèse, *The Forbidden Woman* has raised the same kinds of questions about the problem of reception. An identity politics demanding recognition on the basis of respect for difference needs to avoid the pitfalls of vague multiculturalism and of disconnection from real contexts and practices. Speaking of the content of *The Forbidden Woman*, the reviewer Elia finds that "laudable intentions notwithstanding, Mokeddem's message remains unconvincing, a promotion of multiculturalism that would somehow erase all differences. . . . In content if not in form, *The Forbidden Woman* fails to provide a valid model of what it seeks to promote: the equalizing 'benefits' of *métissage*" (Elia). *Métissage*, sometimes called creolization (borrowing from linguistics), refers to a racial and/or cultural mixing, most often in the context of the cultures of the Caribbean, the Americas, or the Indian Ocean. North Africans, both as colonized peoples and as contemporary immigrant populations, maintain their cultural specificity and connections to their countries of origin and cultures of origin. While the discourse of literary criticism slips easily from one context to the next moving over the surface of the texts, social imaginaries and social histories are rooted in specific contexts and practices that are less malleable. Critic Birgit Mertz-Baumgartner borrows from Caribbean writer Edouard Glissant's descriptions of the composite nature of creole culture and from Deleuze and Guattari's *Mille Plateaux* and their rhizomatic trajectories of identity, reading Mokeddem's novel in the light of postcolonial hybridity and feminist discourse (Mertz-Baumgartner 122–123). In "Exile and Its Discontents: Malika Mokeddem's *Forbidden Woman*," Mustapha Hamil, however, suggests that fundamentalism in Algeria needs to be understood in its complex historical context: "religious fundamentalism in Algeria, as in other parts of the Arab world, may be understood as a fin-de-millennium condemnation of a clumsy 'modernization' that has failed to transform the traditional cultural and mental structures of society" (53). Reading Mokeddem's *Forbidden Woman* as emblematic of this "deep-seated ideological crisis of contemporary Maghrebian discourse on identity and difference, modernity and tradition, East and West," Hamil posits that

> each intellectual project to define and circumscribe Maghrebian identity constitutes a sort of différance in the Derridean sense of something that is ceaselessly deferred. Given the never-ending suspension between Western and Arab-Islamic narrative of identity, Maghrebian cultural experience may be said to communicate a miserable Hegelianism: miserable because its dialectic seems to have no clear vision of its becoming, but a Hegelianism all the same. (58)

The focus on hybridity and scattered, suspended postidentarian subjectivities leads to a hamstrung Hegelianism in which one always falls short of the abstract goal of transcendental unity (or in terms of identity, at-homeness within the self and the world). Certainly identity is an on-going, contradictory, unfinished project for all of us, destined to be incomplete, but as Hamil points out, "when uncertainty becomes the prism through which postcolonial literature must now be examined" and when "fragmented identities have . . . become the absolute signifier of postcolonial subjectivities," then "it becomes almost impossible to talk about the political and psychological significance of collective identities" (60). In her essay "Malika Mokeddem," Yolande Helm notes in her conclusion: "Mokeddem claims to be 'une femme sans frontière.' Through her protagonists, she inscribes an ethnic-gender hybridity in her writing. She and her characters are women—and men—*en devenir*, in transitions, determined to survive. Their identities are split, not destroyed, and are evolving toward a new self" (208). Given the situational, contextual, and indentificational elements that contribute to ongoing identity construction, the different and often conflicting assumptions lodged in alternative social imaginaries, and the fact that identity is not simply something inscribed by the "I" producing it, but something received by interlocutors in whose mirror we perceive our "me," knowing where the borders are is no easy process. Is the new self she creates the product of a "miserable Hegelianism," and if so, what is the price of that compromise?

The relational self associated with Maghrebian societies, and especially important to the survival of nomadic peoples, has been displaced by a focus on individual identity—scattered and postidentarian—in Mokeddem's work. At the beginning of *The Forbidden Woman*, Sultana describes herself as "displaced" and "split . . . in two" (*FW* 3). She then describes herself as containing "dissident and different Sultanas"; one is all "emotions, exaggerated sensuality," and another is "sheer will," one who "coldly scrutinizes the landscape" (*FW* 6). Sultana looks at herself in the mirror in the final chapter of the novel and describes herself in the third person: "A flower of disdain tacked onto her smile and a side glance, she stares at me, contemplates me in scattered pieces on the chessboard of her will. Strengthened by the feeling of my recomposed complexity, I leave the bathroom" (*FW* 136). In addition, the gazes of all the other characters in the novel assign Sultana differing identities. And on top of this outside summing up, Mokeddem also invents characters who are echoes of Sultana in Dalila (the little girl who resembles Sultana and Mokeddem herself as a child), and Samia, Dalila's imaginary sister (who lives in LaFrance and shares traits with Mokeddem). Finally, because this novel is about memories of childhood through the eyes of an adult, it has the double retrospective point of view associated with autobiography where past memories are always produced through the perspectives of the present.

The scattered identities Sultana embodies do not coalesce to provide her a coherent political stance against a corrupt, authoritarian secular state, or a realistic defense against a narrow, bigoted, religious fundamentalism. Given the failure of the political process in Algeria to accommodate linguistic and religious differences [and we should add gender differences, too] following independence, Hamil comments that the Maghreb has "induced a mode of constructing ethnic and religious identity in terms of continuous temporality, rather than in term of historical discontinuities" (52). On the one hand, the government keeps traditional social and political power structures, giving them new modern facades—preferring "*salade niçoise*" to "couscous" (52); on the other hand, an equally unsustainable narrative is found in the fundamentalists' "attempt to reinstate in the present a pure Islamic condition of existence," an attempt that results in "a homogeneous essentialist discourse that is constantly defeated by the syncretic reality of the postcolonial moment" (57). With identity suspended in postmodern space, state practice reduced to a hollow facade, and religion hijacked by zealotry, where do we locate meaningful dialectical social transformation? Rebelling in the abstract, in the name of freedom against constraints, puts Sultana in the position of reacting as opposed to resisting creatively. She is haunted by the social imaginary she thinks she can choose to leave, and she is largely a foreigner to the Western social imaginary she has tried to adopt as her own: "the process of becoming de-identified and de-Algerianized in order to contest religious or State violence" leaves her with only the "illusive rhetoric of postidentarianism" (59). As the little girl Dalila says to Sultana: "you talk like a book. You're giving a lecture! . . . Westerners have contaminated you with their tchatche [gossip] and their highbrow poses" (*FW* 36). The community of women conjured up wholesale in the last chapter of *Forbidden Woman* to carry on the good fight seem like the product wishful thinking, at best.

Of Heterotopia and Health

This chapter opened by suggesting that Salih, Tlili, and Mokeddem, who were affiliated with rural areas where there was a particularly strong sense of community identification, were writing from positions of potential strength. The books they wrote about home became the heterotopic mirrors of the postcolonial identities they were able to imagine. Of the three, Salih succeeded in reflecting the situational ironies of postcoloniality, I would argue, without losing agency or settling for nostalgic solutions or a "miserable Hegelianism." Of the three, he is by far the most ironic in a therapeutic sense. We recall that Fanon claimed that "in the West Indies irony is a mechanism of defense against neurosis"; it encouraged "good conscience" (*Toward the African Revolution* 19). On the one hand, irony protected average West Indians from taking too seriously the image of themselves as reflected in the eyes of the Other who would do them harm. On the other hand, irony prevented them from taking themselves too seriously. Cultivating a sense of irony protected the West Indian from taking too seriously either the demonized self reflected in the mirror of colonialism, or the idealized self found in the mirror of Negritude. Salih, Tlili, and Mokeddem all experienced the destructiveness of colonialism and the fragmentation of postcolonial identity, yet Salih alone seems to have written a work in which irony is productive. In his novel, the self-reflexive "non-place of language" where truth can only be approached by way of a lie becomes a tool of agency of the author. Tlili's *Lion Mountain* is not without its occasional ironies, such as Horia's circumventing government censorship by asking the very tourists they are courting to mail her letters for her from their home addresses. But, written in French and told through the guilty consciousness of a son who left his mother to face decolonization alone, *Lion Mountain* tends to orient itself toward the past in establishing the narrative of what went wrong, how it all fell apart, how a "thousand futures" were "lost." Mokeddem's *The Forbidden Woman* also largely lacks a healthy irony, except in some of the dialogue attributed to young Dalila. Hamil suggests that Mokeddem is unable to reconcile "individual freedom and political resistance" because while "vindicat[ing] the plight of Algerian women as a group," on the one hand, she rejects the relational identity of tribal groups in exchange for "the freedom and 'apartness' of the individual, mainly writers like herself" (64). As Caren Kaplan argued convincingly in *Questions of Travel*, the postcolonial discourse of "nomadology" associated with Delueze and Guattari takes place in a European framework and may have little attachment to real struggle:

> In their effort to imagine differently the social spaces and sites of subjectivity, Deleuze and Guattari theorize alternative kind of identities and modes of dwelling that counter the fixed commodifications of capitalist relations. Unanchored to any specific historical formation, the radical displacement that is continually evoked in these texts is most often referred to as "deterritorialization." . . .

> The nomadic subject symbolizes displacement and dispersion. In Deleuze and Guattari's work, the site of the desert . . . is . . . empty, liberatory, and a margin for linguistic, cultural, and political experimentation. . . . The nomad is likened to the "immigrant" and the "gypsy." In all of these allusions, modernity and postmodernity collapse into undifferentiated cultures; Euro-American (or even solely European) culture structures the point of view, erasing temporal and spatial differentiations. (86–87)

As Kaplan goes on to explore, nomadology was picked up as a theoretical image by many subsequent postmodern and postcolonial theorists, with varying degrees of success, depending upon the context they applied it to and the claims made for it.

Christopher Miller in his discussion of Deleuze and Gutatari's *A Thousand Plateaus* in *Nationalists and Nomads* asks: "What, if anything, does this project of nomadology have to do with real and 'actual' nomads? 'Nothing' would be a compelling answer" (177). In a review of his book, Miller was severely taken to task for his critique by Eugene Holland who complained: "The crux of the matter, as Miller recognizes, is the *representational status* of their concept of nomadism. He claims it is representational; they insist it is not. He claims they are doing ethnography and representing people, i.e. actual nomads; they insist they are doing philosophy, and creating specifically philosophical concepts ("conceptual personae"), not (social) scientific ones" (163). Miller's replied to this charge, explaining that his essay was

> concerned with the question of what lies beyond the supposedly stable forms of identity that used to rule the world; more particularly, it examines closely the form of "postidentitarian" thought that is offered by *A Thousand Plateaus*. By scrutinizing the sources of Deleuze and Guattari's knowledge, and their use of those sources, particularly in their footnotes, I raised questions about their and their disciples' claims to operate on a plane that is somehow free from the burdens and the ethics of representation. My stated goal was "to read the referential within a universe that is supposed to be purely virtual." My conclusion was that the nomadology of *A Thousand Plateaus* was seriously compromised by its own gestures of reference, its "points of contact" with the world. I suggested that we would have to do better, that we needed "a more convincing ethic of flow" than that which Deleuze and Guattari described." ("We Shouldn't Judge" 129–130)

Miller's raising the question of the place of "ethics" in "postidentarian thought" is germane to our discussion of Mokeddem's work in the context of postcolonial literature and theory. Holland observed that "[Deleuze and Guattari's] concept of nomadism has had practically no impact whatsoever on the fields of colonial/postcolonial and francophone studies" (165); this claim is quite frankly puzzling. The work of Valérie Orlando cited above, as well as that of Réda Bensmaïa in *Experimental nations: Or, the Invention of the Maghreb* would suggest that deterritorialization is very much at the center of postcolonial thought and has been applied with varying degrees of success, depending on how it is contextualized.

What is interesting about Mokeddem's case is that here is a writer whose "actual" point of contact is a nomadic society and its social imaginary, whose representations of the desert are very much grounded in real experience of those landscapes, yet who, at the same time, has embraced in many ways the virtual world of Western "postmodern nomads who flow and float through and across cultural and linguistic frontiers without taking notice of how political and economic frontiers continue to be synchronized by global and local managements of power" (Hamil 64). Her autobiographical writing in *La Transe des insoumis* is more nuanced than the writing in *The Forbidden Woman* on issues like poverty, bourgeois privilege, and maldevelopment. In addition, the autobiography shows her to be far more ambivalent about claiming her freedom than she is in her novel. The themes of guilt about leaving and the desire for family and group recognition run like threads through her memoir. In her own judgment, the early novels *Les Hommes qui marchent* and *Le Siècle des sauterelles* are more deeply textured and in touch with the social imaginary she grew up in (*Malika Mokeddem* 289). Mokeddem, having a French education and having emigrated to France, opposes individual identity to group identity, feeling obliged to choose between them. A healthy sense of irony (enacted as humility and empathy) might open up a different path to escape this zero-sum game.

Tayeb Salih, by providing a nuanced perspective on the social imaginary he grew up with in his stories about Wad Hamid, seems to avoid this zero-sum game (which is not to say that his characters do). Writing in Arabic and echoing Arabic narrative conventions, such as the hakawati-style address at the opening of many chapters, keep him focused in *Season of Migration to the North*. Upon these local conventions, he weaves the conventional forms of Western literature like the courtroom scenes and the echoes of Conrad's narration. He evidences a complete control, not over meaning, but over the chiasmic relationship between the seemingly opposed parts of the narrative: England and the Sudan, males and females, truth and lies, past and present. Likewise, in the story Salih considers "one of the pillars of [his] work" (Hassan 37), "The Doum Tree of Wad Hamid," the old man who narrates the story is double-voiced in that he maintains an ironic reflexivity that allows him to be both derisive and humble (45). This irony is especially cogent at the end of the story when a young journalist visiting from the city asks him when modernity—the steamer, the water-pump, and the agricultural schemes the village has fought off throughout the period of colonization and decolonization in order to protect the doum tree and the marabout of Wad Hamid—will come to change the village. The old man replies that modernity will come when their children emigrate, and losing their identity, return to look at the village "with souls foreign to our own" (*Wedding of Zein & Other Stories* 19). The story ends with the young man's obscure inkling of what a communitarian identity means, and the old man's ironic yet humble plea that is focused on empathy. The old man points out sadly:

> "What all these people have overlooked is that there's plenty of room for all these things: the doum tree, the tomb, the water-pump, and the steamer's stopping place."
>
> When he had been silent for a time he gave me a look which I don't know how to describe, though it stirred within me a feeling of sadness, sadness for some obscure thing which I was unable to define. Then he said: "tomorrow, without doubt, you will be leaving us. When you arrive at your destination, think well of us and judge us not too harshly." (19–20)

CHAPTER FIVE

Epilogue

The Ends of Irony

> One good thing could come from this horror [9/11]: it could spell the end of the age of irony.
>
> —Roger Rosenblatt, "The Age of Irony Comes to an End," *Time*

> What strikes me as much more interesting [than 'a kind of absolute certainty and a total, seamless view of reality that recognizes only disciples or enemies] is how to keep a space in the mind open for doubt and for the part of an alert, skeptical irony (preferably also self-irony).
>
> —Edward Said, *Representations of the Intellectual*

One of the ends of irony (an alert, skeptical irony, self-irony) is to maintain good conscience in the face of a contradictory and evolving reality. In *Toward the African Revolution* and in his larger vision of a world not ruled by oppression, Fanon points to Jankélévitch's understanding of irony as "good conscience" because it creates that space in the mind that is tough and tender at the same time. Irony as "good conscience" encompasses both paradox and reconciliation; it is the enemy of illusion without destroying simplicity, and it joins wit to love.[1] In Fanon's view, then, oppression is not just a matter of physical force—"several policemen striking the prisoner at the same time; four policemen standing around the prisoner hitting him backward and forward to each other, while another burns his chest with a cigarette and still another hits the souls of his feet with a stick" (*The Wretched of the Earth* 280). Oppression is also a restriction of the space of thought; it is a crime against "humanity" as such, evidenced by "all the untruths planted in his being by oppression" (309). Fanon argued for a new humanism:

> It is a question of the Third World starting a new history of Man, a history which will have regard to the sometimes prodigious theses which Europe has put forward, but which will also not forget Europe's crimes, of which the most horrible was committed in the heart of man, and consisted of the pathological tearing apart of his functions and the crumbling away of his unity . . . [through] racial hatreds, slavery, exploitation, and above all the bloodless genocide which consisted in the setting aside of fifteen thousands of men.
>
> . . . .
>
> For Europe, for ourselves, and for humanity comrades, we must turn over a new leaf, we must work out new concepts, and try to set afoot a new man. (315–316)

Thirty years after the publication of Fanon's plea for a new humanism, Edward Said gave his 1993 Reith Lectures for BBC on "Representations of the Intellectual." He observed that the nemesis of the public intellectual today is not "mass society as a whole" as it had been for an earlier highbrow intelligentsia,

> but rather the insiders, experts, coteries, professionals who . . . mold public opinion, make it conformist, encourage a reliance on a superior little band of all-knowing men in power. Insiders promote special interests, but intellectuals should be the ones to question patriotic nationalism, corporate thinking, and a sense of class, racial or gender privilege." (*Representations* xiii)

The public intellectuals who refuse to join the gang and be admitted to the ranks of the social authorities are not "humorless complainers" but rather are dedicated to "a relentless erudition," are better at "wit and debate" than their opponents who are the sort of "hardheaded pragmatists and realists who concocted preposterous fictions like the New World Order or the 'clash of civilizations'"; as Said points out, circumstance fosters in public intellectuals a certain style: "there is something fundamentally unsettling about intellectuals who have neither offices to protect them nor territory to consolidate and guard; self-irony is therefore more frequent than pomposity, directness more than hemming and hawing" (xviii).

Immediately following September 11, 2001, while Robert Rosenblatt was eagerly announcing the end of irony and getting down to the pragmatic business of fighting enemies, Said was reassessing the ends of irony. In "The

Public Role of Writers and Intellectuals," which appeared in the *Nation* on September 17, 2001, he reflected that while he had tried in the Reith Lectures to pin down the role of intellectuals, "there have been major political and economic transformations since that time" requiring revisions and additions to his earlier views.[2] For one thing, "the realm of the political and the public has expanded so much as to be virtually without borders" (120). Whereas the Cold War had largely divided the globe into bipolar regions with clear borders, now infinite variations of position and location confound the writer's role making it difficult to find a clear position from which to challenge power, to establish just who one's audience is, to envision the literary means to achieve political ends. "My response to this," Said comments,

> is to stress the absence of any master plan or blueprint or grand theory for what intellectuals can do and the absence now of any utopian teleology toward which human history can be described as moving. Therefore one invents goals abductively—in the literal use of the Latin word "*inventio*" employed by rhetoricians to stress finding again, or reassembling from past performances, as opposed to the romantic use of invention as something you create from scratch. (140)

In this new political landscape, role of the public intellectual is to prevent the disappearance or convenient repackaging of the past, to construct fields of coexistence rather than battle fields as the outcome of intellectual labor, to stress the "need for the redistribution of resources" and to speak out against the "huge accumulations of power and capital that so distort human life" (142). Said suggests we have much to learn from the period of decolonization when the aims of freedom were quickly undercut by the reemergence of repressive rulers, as Fanon had warned would happen without a creative use of the past and the power to imagine a healthier future.

How does this transcultural invention to take place in North Africa? Réda Bensmaïa in *Experimental Nations* sees the new landscape as providing new possibilities for creative thought, despite the postcolonial nightmare Algeria has witnessed:

> Under today's postmodern conditions, it is not geographical or even political boundaries that determine identities, but rather a plane of consistency that goes beyond the traditional idea of nation and determines its new transcendental configuration. And it is in that sense I use the term *experimental nations*. My nations are experimental in that they are above all nations that writers have had to imagine or explore as if they were territories to rediscover and stake out, step by step, countries to invent and to draw while creating one's language. It is in

> this sense that these nations may be called virtual, without for all that being imaginary or unreal. The virtual, as we know, is opposed not to the *real*, but to the *actual*. (8)

In the effort to imagine the virtual nations that exist in tension with actual ones, Maghrebi writers should feel free to use all tools—"the *protocols of knowledge* and *forms of narrative*" from whatever provenance, to arm themselves with their multiple languages, to work with the material of their local histories and their international networks. Bensmaïa reminds us that Said himself has emphasized that "*literature has played a crucial role in the re-establishment of national cultural heritage, in the reinstatement of native idioms, in the reimagining and refiguring of local histories, geographies, communities*" (Said, "Figures" 1; Bensmaïa 7, his emphasis added). A literature of resistance is not merely reactive, it is equally a "shaper, creator, agent of illumination" ("Figures" 2). The challenge writers face today is how to engage with this new literary field that has taken on the contours of the planet, given an academic industry adept at turning liberatory aims into "ambiguous contests between ambivalent opponents"; how to contribute to the contest over "justice and human rights," given "the huge accumulations of power and capital that so distort human life" (Said, *Humanism* 142).

In *Transfigurations of the Maghreb: Feminism, Decolonization, and Literatures* written not long after the fall of the Berlin Wall, Winifred Woodhull addressed the same general problematic, finding that in the work of some writers concerned with North Africa, a "subversive poetics [had] gradually *replaced* work for change in the political field: for Lyotard, and for Khatibi as well, poetic language [had] come to be associated with an "other" politics radically divorced from social institutions and from material relations of domination" (x). Khatibi like most other writers from North Africa grappled with doing justice to the many languages and cultures that defined the territory: for him, "the effort to pluralize the Maghreb is synonymous with decolonization, [which is rather] a process requiring a double critique of Arab-Islamic institutions and culture on the one hand and of the universalizing, colonizing dynamics of Western metaphysics on the other" (ix). On the institutional level, corrupt government officials and interest groups within the country skewed the decolonization process. On the creative level, a literature of resistance was displaced by a literature of rumination, of nomadic poststructural wandering, of the chasing after Derridean traces. On the international level, the only remaining super power would soon be declaring a New World Order. It is in this context that Woodhull asked most appropriately, "Why should we assume that no politics is possible, other than a quiescent poetic one, because the world is writing memorials to Marxism?" (xvi). By looking at the way the figure of "woman" was deployed to contain, mediate and account for social divisions within the various figurations of North Africa, Woodhull aimed to demonstrate that a poststructuralist critique of the politics of representation should not in any way underwrite the wholesale dismissal of representational politics (198).

The landmark event that situates our time is 9/11, and now the stakes over representation are higher. The rise of the Israeli Wall of Separation not the fall of the Berlin Wall. The Project for the New American Century not the international Peace Dividend. The protracted miseries of the embargo and the U.S. invasion of Iraq not the cut-and-run Gulf War One. And in summer 2006, the destruction of Lebanon under the guise of constructing a lasting peace. One corrective to the symbolic domination of the global reach of Western technologies of war and commerce is irony from below. As reactionaries and radicals, politicians, professors, and pundits squabble over the terms of global trade agreements, environmental treaties, the law of the sea, and global warming, one form of irony below is the fact that brainless organisms have already made our decisions for us; today 90 percent of world goods are shipped by sea:

> In recent years, though, ships have switched to seawater [for ballast]. They'll drink up ballast in one port to spit it out in the next. That makes each boat a biological Trojan horse, with up to 7,000 invasive species hidden away in 11 billion tons of ballast water on any given day. Every nine weeks, a new marine bioinvader is set loose. The International Maritime Organization (IMO), which watches over the oceans, calls shipborne invaders "one of the most serious threats to the health of the world oceans." (Margolis 48–49)

Sometimes the rectifying sense of the ridiculous that speaks truth to power comes from those who have none. At the third meeting of the World Tribunal on Iraq[3] held in Istanbul (June 23–27, 2005), testimony was given by Dahr Jamail, who spent eight months in Iraq as an independent journalist from the United States and whose dispatches sent from the field became and important resource for the international press. He opened with this story of irony from below:

> In May of 2004 I interviewed a man who had just been released from Abu Ghraib. Like so many I interviewed from various US military detention facilities who'd been tortured horrifically, he still managed to maintain his sense of humor.
>
> He began laughing when telling me how CIA agents made him beat other prisoners. He laughed, he said, because he had been beaten

> himself prior to this, and was so tired that all he could do to beat other detained Iraqis was lift his arm and let it drop on the other men.
>
> Later, he laughed again as he told me what else had been done to him, when he said, "The Americans brought electricity to my ass before they brought it to my house." (Jamail)

In struggling to right priorities that have gone massively awry, writers have become public intellectuals not simply by reading their literary works as agents of illumination in a dark time. Many of the writers discussed in *Of Irony and Empire* are working in material ways to ensure the transcultural invention of a more just world. Cheikh Hamidou Kane, who some might assume to be a sort of nostalgic, failed visionary just as they see his character Samba Diallo as existentially hamstrung, has been a formidable force from the beginning, not only because of his steady moral compass but because of his grassroots vision of change. Blocked from continuing his studies beyond a certain level in the French schools in Senegal, Kane studied on his own keep up and was eventually granted admission. He struggled against the odds to get a law degree first in Dakar and then in Paris at the Sorbonne; this was followed by a degree in philosophy from the Sorbonne. As interviewer J. P. Little has commented: "It should also be noted that throughout the period in Dakar and in Paris, Cheikh Hamidou was politically active, being a founder member of the *Association des Elèves de Dakar* (Association of Dakar Students), where his militancy caused him to be threatened with the withdrawal of his bursary, and in Paris as a committed member of the FEANF (*Fédération d'Etudiants d'Afrique Noire en France*/Federation of Black African Students in France)" ("Autofiction" 82). Following school, he returned to Africa and worked as a government official for the new Senegalese government in various ministries before taking a number of posts for the United Nations and UNESCO in Ivory Coast, Nigeria, and Canada. As for Samba Diallo, Kane maintains that had his character lived, he would have returned to his native land to train his compatriots in agronomy and equally in matters of the spirit of tolerance: Muslim or not Muslim they are still Diallobe. They can be Muslim without being fundamentalist. They can modernize without losing the central traits of their local culture: consensus in decision making, oral dialogue, and tolerance (Little "Origins of Samba Diallo" 115).

Today near 80 years old, Cheikh Hamidou Kane was president of the activist, grass-roots, south-south nongovernmental organization ENDA (Environment and Development Action) until recently and is writing a third novel. On November 26, 2005, he delivered a lecture at a conference entitled "African Elites Face Their Responsibility" which launched the "Manifesto of the 121," a document signed by 121 intellectuals. The movement is an effort to counter Afro-pessimism over a hideous colonial past and a more hideous postcolonial present, in particular the shredding of Senegal by rival factions. Their guiding motto on their web site was from the opening of Fanon's essay on "National Culture" in *Wretched of the Earth*: "Each generation must out of relative obscurity discover its mission, fulfill it or betray it" (206).

In his speech, Kane held Western-educated African elites of his generation responsible for having betrayed their mission after independence. He congratulates the younger generation of intellectuals for coming together from all their various political perspectives and various trainings in Western disciplines, noting: "In the general climate of pessimism, failure and stalemate prevailing in Black Africa, less than fifty years after the responsibility of directing ourselves was nominally returned to us, I saw the Manifesto of the 121 launched by Senegalese intellectuals on the global network as a rainbow of sorts unfurled across the horizon before us, a promising sign announcing the end of this period of wandering and distress" (Lecture). Intellectuals shaped by Western modernity, Kane pointed out, have returned from "their ignorance, their biases, their scorn and denigration of the way and the values of African civilization" (Lecture). African intellectuals had wrongly thought they could "build a modern Africa divorced from their own cultural roots, sustained only by imitated Western values, which were often enough either perverted or incorrectly applied, as is often true of imitations"; Kane concluded by saying there were two necessary and possible conditions to be met in order to fulfill rather than betray this new mission:

> First, the return to the indigenous values of Africa needed to be revisited, reinterrogated, and reappropriated by the intellectual elite, and used once more to guide the way, without xenophobia or chauvinism, and also without any complexes.
>
> Next, the realization of these goals needed to be the decisive and deliberate reintegration and reunification of Africa, based on real facts and real steps, not mere incantations.
>
> The most decisive way to put an end to colonialism is to destroy the frameworks that served as its foundations, that allowed it to cut apart the living flesh of the continent, in order to mark out sectors for the foreign masters to exploit for profit. The forms of power that we've been fighting over among ourselves for fifty years like starving, wild beasts are only the scraps left on a table that's already been cleared. (Lecture)

Given the immense wealth of Africa's human and material resources, Kane ends by pointing out that the problem to be addressed is not Africa's dispossession but its disunity. The "Manifesto of the 121," and the Web site that hosted it, provided a new kind of forum for Africa's intellectual elites where they could carry out the work of public intellectuals.

Tayeb Salih has worked as a public intellectual in two competing modes. His work, Waïl Hassan argues, must be "read dialectically in the context of his twin careers as a novelist and a columnist who can intervene directly in the sphere of politics": "To the extent his fiction seems to withdraw from the material world of history and politics, Salih seems to withdraw from fiction" (180). Salih shifted from literature to journalism in January 1989 when he left the BBC's Arabic Service, Hassan notes, and began contributing regular columns to the Arabic-language weekly magazine *Al-Majalla*:

> In addition to political commentary and literary criticism, his articles . . . have focused on topics like colonial history in Africa . . . Asia and Australia (a series of articles on the conditions and mythology of the Aborigines); the Sudanese civil war; the slave trade; socioeconomic conditions in East Asia (for example, prostitution in Bangkok); literacy in the Arab world; and the perennial anti-Arab racism of the Western media. (175–176)

When a fundamentalist government came to power in Sudan in June 1989, toppling a democratically elected government, Salih was one of the strongest voices denouncing it (174). As Salih explained in his lecture given at the American University in Beirut in 1980, he has always been torn between the need to write and the feeling that intervention in the world should be more direct:

> I should confess that when I am writing a sense of futility invades me. I feel I should be doing something else, that I should be somewhere else. A writer is somehow superfluous and this feeling may be due to the fact that I grew up in the Sudan. It needed doctors, engineers and teachers. However, you get committed against your will. You write and writing starts exercising its own life. (14–15)

So, in addition to writing journalism for ten years, Salih also began working for UNESCO. A steady critic of gender-bias and of patriarchal ideology, Salih also valorizes a mystical religious tradition as "an alternative form of religiosity to fundamentalism . . . as well as an ethical alternative to the radical secularism that, for many progressive Muslims intellectuals in the 1990s, lies at the root of Western imperialism" (Hassan 180).

Anouar Majid argues that writers like Cheikh Hamidou Kane and Tayeb Salih are best read as rooting their identities "in Islamic consciousness, not in blackness, or some other colonial category":

> The Islamic continuum in Africa bridges temporal, spatial, and gender gaps remarkably well, and thus points to new cultural, economic, and

> political configurations that might serve as alternatives to the failed nation-state model that has brought the continent to the brink of ruin. Writers who underestimate this Islamic component and privilege either color or nation as better defining components of their identity tend to reiterate colonial prejudices, despite their best intentions and revolutionary rhetoric. (*Unveiling Traditions* 74–75)

In arguing an identity politics that foregrounds Islamic culture (as opposed to religion in the narrower sense), Majid is hardly discouraging the need to deal with gender inequality. Both women's claims for recognition and for redistribution of power in very material forms are taken seriously: "Although the widely held assumption that women have been historically persecuted by all patriarchal cultures is, to a large extent, incontestably true, the discourses of Western feminism, largely shaped by gender relations in Christian capitalist cultures and by the exhausted paradigms of Western social thought, have hindered a more subtle appreciation of women's issues under Islam" (99). Indigenous models of equality in Islamic culture, in the context of recent debates over feminism, human rights, and democracy, have emerged as promising avenues of change in the transcultural invention of Muslim Africa. The Islamic normative tradition, as Mustapha Tlili has noted, focuses on issues of just governance. He explained this idea to the *Philadelphia Inquirer* this way: "Islam, in its central teachings embodies and embraces constitutional, democratic, just and accountable electoral government. . . . Non-Islamist authoritarian regimes, many of them friends of the United States, would have a harder time fishing for objections to the administration's call for democratization if Washington simply offered technical assistance toward making their countries' elections better run, and eventually freer, fairer and more credible" ("Vote for Starting Small").

Living in New York and working for the United Nations, Tlili is clear about the fact that 9/11 changed his life forever as he watched the horrific events transpire from his living room window. As a fellow at the World Policy Institute, he founded the "UN Project," which "seeks to advance the dialogue between the United States and the United Nations and to renew the commitment of the United States, particularly its policymakers, academics, and media professionals, to the values of interdependence and multilateralism" ("United Nations Project"). Clearly he has his work cut out for him. As President Bush already explained in a 2003 news conference: "It's important for [the United Nations'] words to mean what they say, and as we head into the 21st century . . . when it comes to our security, we really don't need anybody's permission" ("President George Bush discusses Iraq"). As a former UN chief of the Anti-Apartheid, Decolonization, and Palestine Programs," Tlili doesn't give up easily. He said soon after 9/11: "As a Muslim, and one who is proud of his faith, although I consider it strictly my personal domain, I then resolved to devote every fiber of my energy and intellectual commitment to playing whatever part I could so that what happened that day would never happen again" ("Opening Statement"). As part of this effort, he is the founder and director of Dialogues: Islamic World-U.S.-the West, a program at New York University supported by funding from the Carnegie Corporation, the MacArthur Foundation, the Rockefeller Brothers Foundation, el Legado Andalusi, Majlis El Hassan and the State of Qatar. As their mission statement notes,

> with the attacks focusing the world's attention on extremist movements in the Middle East and Islamic Asia, political commentators have been seeking, and often failing, to explain the political and social roots of these movements and their accompanying grievances against the West and the United States. The program has been launched as a structured forum for sustained dialogue involving voices from the various religious, intellectual, economic, and political sectors of Islamic and American/Western societies, including those non-elite Islamic figures with proven credibility in their communities who are too often unheard in the West. Dialogues is largely focused on Muslim claims and viewpoints, as well as on efforts to understand various Islamic social and political movements. But the program also involves a discussion of the Western value system, for true dialogue cannot be constructed as a one-way street. ("Dialogues")

Tlili has been clear in coordinating these dialogues and workshops that he is not interested in joining the "industry of dialogue" that emerged to discuss the "clash of civilizations" after 9/11. Nor does he support the industry of "dissecting Islam" to establish what went wrong (Abdel-Latif). Asserting that dialogue and tolerance were the hallmarks of fora in both the Muslim world and the West at the best of times—in Umayyad Damascus, Baghdad in Abbasid time and in Córdoba, Sevilla, and Granada in the time of al-Andalus and in the tradition of Socrates' symposium or France's eighteenth-century salons, Tlili maintains the public intellectuals must move forward through dialogue. Woodhull notes in *Transfigurations of the Maghreb* that while "every symbolic order founds itself by means of exclusions," theorists as diverse as Gayatri Spivak, Edward Said, and Martin Bernal have refused "to view any given set of exclusions . . . as inevitable" (199). In this spirit of openness, Tlili states: "we intended to exclude no one, no particular trend or political tendency from either the Muslim world of the Western world. There can be no real dialogue where exclusion of any sort is practiced" ("Opening Statement").

The issue of how we understand the politics of exclusion and how we frame the staking of claims for recognition and for redistribution of power and resources is perhaps the most vexed and interesting debate in contemporary feminist and human rights transnational inquiry. Valentine Moghadam, in "Gender, National Identity and Citizenship: Reflections on the Middle East and North Africa," focuses on the contemporary global context of these struggles":

> Women's struggles in various parts of the "modernizing" world for equality, autonomy, and empowerment—struggles that originated in the early twentieth century but have taken a global and more ambitious turn in the late twentieth century—have been directed at laws, policies, and cultural understandings that exclude women or privilege men. Women's social movements in Africa, Asia, and Latin America have sought the elaboration or extension of civil, political, and social rights for women. These have often taken place in a national context far less congenial than that in the early part of the century, but in a new global context that provides opportunities, support, and legitimation for the advancement of women. At the same time, women's social movements and non-governmental organizations operating across national boundaries are helping to create a "global civil society" and concepts of "global citizenship." (138)

It is in context of the particular history of Algeria and this larger frame of transnational feminism and human rights that the work of Malika Mokeddem opens important questions about how identity politics and recognition play out in a world of ambiguous interests and complex agendas.

Malika Mokeddem, as discussed earlier in the context of her novel *The Forbidden Woman*, became politically engaged primarily through this transnational vector of feminist networks and in response to the assassinations of writers, artists, and journalists in Algeria in the early 1990s. Her book was dedicated not only to the memory of slain journalist and writer Tahar Djaout, but also to a women's nongovernmental organization, the Groupe Aïcha [also Aïsha]. The Arab Women's Forum Aïsha, founded in 1992, is a network of democratic Arab women's organizations promoting women's legal rights, gender equality, and participation in social and economic decision making. These organizations also work to stop abuse and fight discrimination against Arab women. These affiliated organizations have headquarters in Palestine, Egypt, Lebanon, Jordan, Tunisia, Morocco, Sudan, and Algeria. In an interview with Yolande Helm concerning women's rights in Algeria, Mokeddem comments that while one could not really say significant social change has happened through the on-going struggles in Algeria around modernization, still "there is a transformation happening and women are really at the pivot point of those changes" ("Entretien" 47). Nadje Al-Ali summarizes the way alternative modernities intersect with gender, using the example of women in Egypt: "Caught between the pursuit of modernization, attempts at liberalization, a pervasive nationalist rhetoric of 'authenticity' and ongoing imperialist encroachments, women are often the focus of conflicting and ambiguous interests" (1).

Too often, fully justified condemnations of the ways women's rights have been handled by particular nation states in Muslim Africa have quickly been turned into wholesale condemnations of Muslim culture. This is a danger especially when the stories are recounted in hyperbolic terms and consumed by a public whose assumptions about the culture are overdetermined in the first place. For example, Mokeddem's *The Forbidden Woman* routinely arouses the "I'm so glad I'm not a woman in a Muslim culture" response from a mainstream female Western readership. Mokeddem herself recognized the unfortunate articulation between her novels *The Forbidden Woman* and *Of Dreams and Assassins* and the larger transcultural industry interested in inventing North Africa as backward and savage:

> Continuing to write in this fashion is only bringing grist to the mill of Western media who report nothing about the country other than the barbaric. This would be an extra injustice inflicted on a people who are resisting in spite of everything and, in spite of everything, will rediscover one day their love of life. That doesn't mean we should pass over this tragedy in silence, no! In any case, how could we? But finding other forms besides this style of urgency and . . . finding a joyful writing. That's our freedom. (Chaulet-Achour and Kerfa 31)

While conflicting and ambiguous interests make identity politics a rough terrain, all indications are that we have hardly gone beyond them, nor should we. Identity politics have usefully generated struggle around and theorizing of the structures that perpetuate injustice. And whatever the shortcomings, they have focused attention on the discourses and practices that underpin exclusion and oppression. If, as Said suggested above, "one invents goals abductively—in the literal use of the Latin word "*inventio*" employed by rhetoricians to stress finding again, or reassembling from past performances," then understanding past exclusions is crucial is to struggles around equality and human rights.

Fanon's insights into the sources of oppression and into the dynamic of identity and recognition provide continuing sources of illumination. Toward the end of *Black Skin, White Masks*, Fanon sums up some of the discoveries he has made along the way about the sociogenesis of oppression. When he states that "the body of history does not determine a single one of my actions," and "I am my own foundation," he is saying neither that the past doesn't matter nor that he is a free agent in some ahistorical way, but rather that past practice should not be a prison: "As a man of color . . . [I] do not have the right to lock myself into a world of retroactive reparations" (231). In a fine chapter on "The Politics of Recognition: Sartre, Fanon, and Identity Politics," Sonia Kruks argues that contemporary "identity politics" are related to but different from the earlier form of a politics of recognition described by Charles Taylor.[4] Taylor posits, in Kruks view, that "the collapse of ascribed identities and social hierarchies" associated with feudalism, for example, led to "modern, universalist claims about equal human dignity":

> With modern notions of dignity, equality, and freedom also emerged the notion of the 'authentic' self: that is, the self as a unique and 'inner' being that can find its fulfillment only in personal self-expression. . . . The authentic self, which demanded recognition from others, was above all a moral self: a self of sentiments, values and judgments, a self that was the seat of the "soul" and a self that was (and still is) intimately linked to Western individualism. . . . Indeed, as Taylor rightly observes, "Not only contemporary feminism but also race relations and discussions of multiculturalism are undergirded by the premiss that denied recognition can be a form of oppression." (84)[5]

Feminists, migrant workers, black power advocates among others espousing this more recent version of identity politics are not begging to be recognized as human in order to assimilate into the mainstream of Western culture through access to education, the workplace, or the political process. Insisting on their embodied identities and the historical experiences that formed them, they are not interested in gaining recognition only to lose themselves. "This demand for recognition," Kruks clarifies, "is made irrespective of whether identities are viewed in essentialist terms . . . or whether they are viewed as socially, culturally, or discursively constructed. The demand is not for inclusion within the fold of 'universal humankind,' on the basis of shared human attributes; nor is it for respect 'in spite of' ones's differences. Rather, what is demanded is respect for oneself *as* different" (85). Kruks maintains we "need to seek for non-exclusionary affirmations of difference and for forms of universalism that can accommodate particularity: no easy task" (95).

Identity politics and politics of recognition as modes of activism have raised thorny questions on both the national and international levels. Nancy Fraser, working largely within the context of U.S. and Western social and economic history, has argued that recognition claims have displaced the struggle around redistribution claims, such that social acceptance on the expressive level has replaced the struggle for access to and control over material goods and resources. A multiculturalism that focuses on cultural inclusion but does not factor in sufficiently the economic exploitation and political exclusions that continue to foster inequality would be a case in point ("From Redistribution to Recognition?" 68).[6] In the area of literary production, Mokeddem creates hybrid characters such as Vincent, using imagery to suggest a relatively painless and even pleasurable continuum between the physical transplant he receives and an expressive rewiring of his prejudices and practices through this medical multiculturalism: "But this tolerance [of the kidney] couldn't keep me from thinking that with this organ, surgery had implanted in me two seeds of strangeness, of difference: the other sex and another 'race.' And the feeling of this double *métissage* of my flesh became deeply rooted in my thoughts and pushed me uncontrollably toward women and toward this other culture, which until then I had haughtily disregarded" (*FW* 21). While the thinking behind Mokeddem's transcultural invention of Vincent is atheoretical and too mechanical, Fraser's dichotomy between recognition and redistribution is too starkly theoretical. As Iris Marion Young points out, there is little use for a theoretical framework that opposes culture and economy: "Fraser denies that this dichotomy describes reality. What, then, justifies its use in theory?" (150).

The discussion of recognition claims that Fraser initiates, Iris Young challenges, and Kruks summarizes so well is a discussion that is detailed and meticulous—but limited to a set of assumptions that are part and parcel of a Western social imaginary. When we enter a transcultural space, competing social imaginaries are at play and alternative modernities provide the historical contexts. Here, we need to turn our attention to the difference between individualist identity construction and relational identity construction. As mentioned above, the "authentic" self as a moral, atomistic, free-floating particle in a social ambience is central to a Western social imaginary but exists in contradiction to the notions of self in many other societies: "The former conceptualize people/citizens as self-interested autonomous individuals while the latter view individual identity as being defined through relations with others and embedded in community" (Nyamu-Musembi 7). Human rights discourse as embodied in international treaties has been seen, by some, as downplaying the importance of community and seeking to impose an individualist model of rights "at odds with non-Western ways of life" (6).[7] The debate that plays out here is really one about conceptions of identity rather than about bearers of rights; that is, "the debate is really between an abstracted view of the right-bearing individual as a universal construct, and a contextual view of the individual as defined by his/her ethnic, cultural, or religious community" (7). Those who hold an abstracted view of identity tend to set up the debate over the universal and the particular in human rights discourse as being about a contradiction or competition between individual rights, on the one hand, and group rights or national rights, on the other. Issues of violence against women—a topic that tends to elicit clear bonds among women—is often a woefully ambiguous territory. As Jacqueline Bhabha demonstrates in "Embodied Rights: Gender Persecution, State Sovereignty and Refugees," individual rights trump cultural or nation-state's rights when it suits the political agendas or fits with the cultural prejudices of the courts, and vice-versa. After the Iranian revolution in 1979 when the specter of fundamentalism cast a shadow over U.S. ideas about Muslim countries, a U.S. court ruled that a Jordanian woman's fear of domestic violence should she be deported was a well-established fear of persecution because she had "*continued to express her belief in Western values through her actions*" (183). On the other hand, a Chinese woman who had had a number of abortions, because she already had a son and her husband did not want her sterilized, applied for asylum in Canada, with her unplanned daughter, on the grounds that she would be forcibly sterilized if she returned to China. The courts found that China was dealing with a difficult population issue, and the judge ruled: "*I do not feel it is my purpose to tell the Chinese government how to run its economic affairs*" (185). Given the contradictions between individual and state's rights in these cases, Bhabha notes that feminists are often in a double bind: "relativist conceptions of human rights, while anti-imperialist in intent and rhetoric and sensitive to the need to contextualize social and cultural norms, in the asylum context easily become vehicles for a discriminatory hierarchization of human rights protection and an uncritical reinforcement of exclusionary state practices" (189). In this face-off between individual and group (sovereign state) rights, Bhabha concludes" "Paradoxically, protection of individual asylum seekers' right to differ, to their right to challenge the norm, is best served by articulating and upholding notions of human rights which do not accommodate to the particular" (189). From the standpoint of liberal individualist formulations of human rights, perhaps this makes sense. But why should we participate in this zero-sum game between individuals and the groups to which they belong?

Another perspective holds that there is no need to frame the human rights issue as one that pits the individual against the group. A contextual view of human rights holds that there are group rights that are not simply the sum total of the rights of aggregated individuals. If individuals are seen as building their identities as members of communities, then community rights can be understood as being constitutive of individual human rights. In this view, some rights might be primarily individual such as the rights to dignity, legal status, information, freedom of association, movement, and work; collective rights would include the right to self-determination (which is very difficult to understand as in any way individual), the right to resources (water, for example), the right to social and cultural development. And some rights are both individual and collective, such as the right of freedom from genocide. And finally, some rights are about community treasures such as medicinal lore or oral traditions that no one owns individually but which can have great value. Thus,

> contrary to the dominant tendency in liberal human rights discourse, which is to present state-citizen relations in abstracted individualist terms, people are constantly negotiating between an internal moral system (shaped by factors such as culture and religion, and represented by institutions such as kinship) and the formal legal regime of the liberal state. Far from subsuming individual concerns under community interests, "situated analyses of rights" point to people's own experience of these concerns and interests as overlapping and intertwined, *sometimes in harmony and sometimes in tension*. (Nyamu-Musembi 8; emphasis added).

The idea of a contextual approach to human rights, which recognizes the role that society plays in the health and well-being of the individual and recognizes the dialectical relationships between them, is deeply rooted in the theories of Frantz Fanon.

Fanon's intellectual mentors, Hegel and Sartre, both were Western in their approach to identity. Hegel, in offering "an a-social, primarily ethico-existential, account of the struggle for selfhood" (Kruks 84), and Sartre, in positing that "the other is always a threat to my own experience of self" (91), build on models of abstracted, individualist rights that Fanon did not end up sharing. Fanon's third world status, his cultural upbringing, his raced experience in the construction of self, his work as a student with Tosquelles on therapeutic communities, and his engagement in anti-colonial struggle and communal rights—all these things, in my view, make his standpoint on recognition different from those who were his teachers. Kruks argues that in his philosophizing of modern identity, Sartre was hampered by "his lack of a grasp of social mediations, of the dynamics through which issues of interpersonal recognition and identity pass into (and from) the domain of concrete institutions and social structures" (96). Kruks concludes her essay on identity politics and the politics of recognition by finding that Fanon, like Sartre, leaps in the final pages of *Black Skin, White Masks*, "from a nuanced analysis of lived experience to . . . abstract universalism"; he argues that "freedom is always oriented toward the future" (Kruks 103). As evidence, she cites the following passage:

> The Negro is not. Any more than the white man. Both must turn their back on the inhuman voices which were those of their respective ancestors in order that authentic communication be possible. . . . Superiority?

> Inferiority? Why not the simple attempt to touch the other, to feel the other, to explain *the other* to myself? (*Black Skin, White Masks* 231; emphasis added)

Kruks sees Fanon as abandoning the social grounding of his analysis up to this point, and rushing into a vague universalism here. I would argue that it is crucial that he does not urge us to "explain ourselves to the other" but rather (as the words I have emphasized suggest) insists on the dialectic between self and the world by asking us to do the more empathetic, therapeutically ironic move of explaining the other to ourselves. Beyond that, analyses of Fanon's work need to go far beyond a focus on Fanon's first book and his early experience as a student in France. Kruks argues that Fanon, in *Black Skin, White Masks*, lacked the

> tools with which to theorize the interconnections between the realm of existential experience, in which the dynamics of nonrecognition and self-affirmation are played out, and the broader world of processes and structures, in which the particular dynamics [he] describes are embedded. Both [Sartre and Fanon] lack a conception [and a politics] of mediations that can enable them to examine the articulations between the experiential dimensions of oppression and resistance and the wider social processes in which they are enmeshed. (104)

I would submit that we see in Fanon's work—his training, his clinical studies, his teaching, and his writing—a continual effort to locate his thinking precisely at the point of articulation between the individual experiences and the social processes in which they are enmeshed.

Fanon's earliest published works were "L'Experience vécu du noir" ("the Lived Experience of the Black Man," *L'Esprit*, May 1951, later included in *Black Skin, White Masks*) and "Le syndrome Nord-Africain" (The North African Syndrome," *L'Esprit*, February 1952, later included in *Toward the African Revolution*),[8] both pieces employing the irony of self-conscious speech acts to say one thing and suggest another. Fanon takes on a voice to illustrate the socially constructed discursive regimes of various individual speakers. Macey notes in his biography of Fanon:

> [*Black Skin, White Masks*] was and is an elusive book, not least because it is so difficult to categorize in terms of genre. It is difficult to think of any precedent for it, and it did not establish any new genre or tradition. It had no sequel. Fanon did not write the study of "Language and Aggressivity" which was, he claimed, in preparation, and the style of his later writings is very different. Although written largely in the first person and although a rich biographical source, [*Black Skin, White Masks*] is not a

> pure autobiography: the "I" that speaks in it is often a persona. . . . The opacity of the language, and the constant shifts in register as Fanon moves from medical discourse to poetry and back again, often make the text uncomfortably difficult to read. (161–162)

It seems to me that Fanon maintains the style of exploring the articulation between the individual and society through voice and silence, through shifts of register, and ironic speech acts. He always looks for the social as opposed to the merely biological or psychic causes of sickness.

It was during this same period that he was in the psychiatric residency program at Saint Alban Hospital in France. His supervisor was Professor François Tosquelles who was committed to a thorough-going form of milieu therapy and the idea of the therapeutic community:

> Saint-Alban was the laboratory for the first experiments in what has come to be known in France as institutional psychotherapy. Its general principles are well described by Félix Guattari, who was in some ways a product of the school: "Its main characteristic is a determination never to isolate the study of mental illness from its social and institutional context, and, by the same token, to analyze institutions on the basis of interpreting the real, symbolic and imaginary effects of society upon individuals." The basic ambition of Tosquelles and the Saint-Alban group was to humanize their institution by recognizing and promoting . . . the human value of its inmates. (150)

The residency with Tosquelles gave Fanon further evidence of the importance of social inclusion for the well-being of the individual. But Fanon went beyond diagnosing and treating the alienated individual. By reintegrating them into society, he focused attention on the ways society produced alienated individuals through material exploitation, institutional injustice, and emotional exclusion. In addition, he would increasingly explore the ways the medical establishment was placed between a criminalized patient and a society that normalized the violence of nonrecognition and exclusion.

Essays such as "the North African syndrome" and "Conduites d'aveu en Afrique du Nord" (Confession in North Africa), a clinical paper written with R. Lacaton in 1955, put recognition at the center of the inquiry. These essays explore the expressive life of the North Africans in question. They deconstruct the alienating institutions and attitudes of the dominant society. They also focus on how we participate in this reproduction of misery and inequality through nonrecognition. But always implicit beneath the mockery and the ironic mimicry of the discourse is the transgressive message that we could free ourselves to do otherwise, could refuse to be prisoners to a disastrous past, refuse to reenact that past in the present, refuse to project the inhumanity of nonrecognition as our future. "The North African Syndrome" explores the gulf of nonrecognition between the immigrant patient and the medical establishment:

> [The North African] knocks. The door is opened. . . . And he tells about *his pain*. Which becomes increasingly his own. He now talks about it volubly. He takes hold of it in space and puts it before the doctor's nose. He takes it, touches it with his ten fingers, develops it, exposes it. It grows as one watches it. He gathers it over the whole surface of his body and after fifteen minutes of gestured explanations the interpreter (appropriately baffling) translates for us: he says he has a belly ache.
>
> All those forays into space, all those facial spasms, all those wild stares were only meant to express a vague discomfort. We experience a kind of frustration in the field of explanation. The comedy, or the drama, begins all over again: approximate diagnosis and therapy. (*Toward the African Revolution* 5–6)

Translating the North African's unintelligible dialect, probing the silences (circumstantial, structural, and strategic), Fanon imagines the racist attitudes that diagnose this patient before the doctor ever encounters him, the stereotypes of malingering and lying; he imagines the immigrant's isolation, the sidelong stares in the bus, the criminalization in the mass media, the perpetual insecurity and surveillance on the job, the distance from loved ones and physical contact: "And what is more pathetic than this man with robust muscles who [says to] us in his truly broken voice, 'Doctor, I am going to die'?" What therapy or cure can be offered to a man who endures "a daily death"?

> A death in the tram
> a death in the doctor's office,
> a death with the prostitutes,
>
> a death on the job site,
> a death in the movies,
> a multiple death in the newspapers,
> a death in the fear of all decent folk of going out after midnight.
> A death,
> yes a DEATH. (13)

Fanon takes us repeatedly back to recognition: to harm the other is to destroy the self. If the patient is sick, it is because the society is pathogenic. Fanon's suggestion for a cure begins with a "physician cure thyself" scene:

> Your solution, sir?
>
> Don't push me too far. Don't force me to tell you what you ought to know, sir. If YOU do not reclaim the man who is before you, how can I assume that you reclaim the man that is in you?
>
> If YOU do not want the man who is before you, how can I believe the man that is perhaps in you?
>
> If YOU do not demand the man, if YOU do not sacrifice the man that is in you so that man who is on this earth shall be more than a body, more than a Mohammed, by what conjurer's trick will I have to acquire the certainty that you, too, are worthy of my love? (16)

Irony, the trope based on dialectic in which A returns as non-A, is at the heart of Fanon's virtuoso performances. He captures with perfect pitch the telling notes and half-notes that make up the discursive chorus of regimes of power, such that the even the tone-deaf recognize the tune. And then, as above, having located the dissonant chords and revealed the false notes, he tells us "Physician, heal thyself."

The ends of irony are to offer ethical correctives to the status quo of the powerful, to provide new hope in desperate times. Fanon has resurfaced at the turn of the millennium in the face of the distortions in human relations brought about by the increasingly violent uses of power around the globe. Fanon used ironic speech acts to capture the enormity of global events on an imaginative stage that was human in scale and that held humans accountable. As Ato Sekyi-Otu exclaims at the end of his book on *Fanon's Dialectic of Experience*:

> With what immensely complex and compelling force Fanon's texts speak to us when we read their contents as speech acts in the moving body of a dramatic narrative! For then these contents reveal themselves to us not as self-enclosed propositions stamped on each and every occasion with the author's discrete assent and unmistakable imprimatur. Rather, they are grasped now as enactments of positions assumed, stances staged, claims advanced by typical characters in a story of experience; now as ironic commentaries, admonitions, exhortations interjected into the utterances and activities of these characters; but always as products of that dialectical movement by which the enacted event or figure is compelled to disclose its incompleteness, the fatal shortcomings of its moral consequences, and thereby made to yield a vision of suppressed and transgressive possibilities. (236)

Irony is still today a necessary corrective to Empire. And far from finding that irony has become outmoded in the 9/11 era, we find it more pertinent than ever.

This study ends with Said's concept of the public intellectual's role in exposing the reductive tropes of imperialist thinking and in turning transcultural inventions toward the ends of good conscience. As Mustapha Marrouchi noted when discussing *Culture and Imperialism* in his recent book *Edward Said at the Limits* detailing Said's role as a public intellectual:

> Said does not confine himself to canonical texts of imperial literature. He is equally engaged in readings of resistance cultures and postimperial writers and is in continuous dialogue with Frantz Fanon as a figure in postcolonial discourse both as a theorist and as an icon. He serves as the conduit for Said's reading of colonialism. "When Fanon wrote his books, he intended to talk about the experience of colonialism as seen by a Frenchman, from within a French space hitherto inviolable and now invaded and re-examined critically by a dissenting native" (1993: 224). (103)

As Said noted in the epigraph to this chapter, skeptical irony and self-irony clear a space for dialectical thought. The first protects us from the exclusionary, repressive operations of imperialist epistemologies; the second has the therapeutic benefit of inducing humility. In "Empowering Inquiry: Our Debt to Edward Said," a talk delivered to the Transnational Foundation for Peace and Future Research shortly after Said's death in 2003, human rights advocate Richard Falk concluded:

> Said embraces a view of reason that engages the emotions rather than confines itself to a realm of conceptual abstraction traced back to the formative influence of Descartes on the modern mind, and the rejection of modernist claims of certainty that feed tendencies toward "secular fundamentalism." His affinity with the Romantic tradition enables Said to combine the passionate with the rigorous to constitute a powerful type of academic scholarship that sustains a pervasive concern with struggles to overcome suffering and injustice in the lifeworld, whether these manifest themselves in relation to the health of the person or of the body politic. Said acts as both guide and exemplary figure in this troubling birth of a globalizing world, not only helping us to understand its contradictory currents that are flowing by us on all sides, but also illuminating paths of constructive action and attitude that provide firm ground for taking stands and steps forward, especially on behalf of those being most marginalized and victimized. ("Empowering Inquiry")

Like Fanon, Said embraced a tough-minded humanism, grounded in empathy, able to move us beyond transgression to transformation because we see the other in ourselves and are empowered by that ironic recognition.

Notes

Chapter 1

1. Fanon's discourse presents many challenges for translators. While both Constance Farrington's 1963 translation and Richard Philcox's 2004 translation of *The Wretched of the Earth* have their strengths, we opted to use the Farrington translation because of the critical history it brings with it. The Philcox translations of *The Wretched of the Earth* and *Black Skin/White Masks* (2007) open a new chapter in this ongoing debate over how to capture Fanon's voice. The chart Keller cites here was developed by a French psy op in his report, "Memento de l'Officier d'Action Psychologique en Algérie," which summarized his research into Muslim "character traits" and suggested how this research might be useful in psychological warfare.

2. "The social imaginary," as Charles Taylor explains it, "is not a set of ideas; rather it is what enables, through making sense of, the practices of a society" ("Modern Social Imaginaries" 91).

3. The authors focused on in this study come from rural Saharan areas not the more Mediterranean-oriented, urban areas in the Maghreb or of Sub-Saharan Africa south of the sahel.

4. This English translation is from Harrow, *The Marabout & the Muse* xxi.

5. "The simple methodological and epistemological distinction between closed systems and open systems often provides us with the first chapter of a guidebook with which to question the ideological function of closure in the discourse of science. Simply stated, a closed system is one for which its context is effectively irrelevant or defined as such (e.g., the solar system, the cosmos as a whole); an open system, in contrast, is one that depends on its environment for its continuing existence and survival (e.g., an organism, a population, a society)" (Wilden xxxi).

6. W. H. Auden, *Prose*, vol. 2: 347; for variants see 160, 180, 424.

7. See Dipesh Chakrabarty, "Postcoloniality and the Artifice of History: Who Speaks for 'Indian' Pasts?" 1–26. Chakrabarty calls for a decentering or a "provincializing" of Europe in the writing of history: "Insofar as the academic discourse of history . . . is concerned, 'Europe' remains the sovereign, theoretical subject of all histories, including the ones we call 'Indian,' 'Chinese,' 'Kenyan,' and so on. There is a peculiar way in which all these other histories tend to become variations on a master

narrative that could be called 'the history of Europe'" (1). In a critique of Chakrabarty's view that the social imaginary of Europe as an epistemo-political perspective has saturated the discourse of history, making Europe the primary habitus of the "modern," Neil Lazarus argues for the need to retain a Marxist "modern narrative of modernity." In his view, capitalist modernity is different from all previous universalizing projects: "To propose the 'provincializing' of 'Europe' is both to dematerialize capitalist modernity and to misrecognize its world-historical significance" (*National and Cultural Practice in the Postcolonial World* 28–29).

8. Ethiopian proverb cited as an opening epigraph in James C. Scott, *Domination and the Arts of Resistance: Hidden Transcripts* n.p.

9. For an account of the forms of racial segregation and color and origin coding in the French military establishment experienced by Fanon and his two friends Pierre Marie Claire Mozole and Marcel Manville, all of whom had eagerly signed up to go defend France during World War II, see Manville's *Les Antilles sans fard* 42–44.

10. Fanon biographer David Macey notes that in a letter to his parents written before going on a dangerous mission during the war, Fanon wrote: "It is a year since I left Fort-de-France. Why? To defend an obsolete ideal. . . . Nothing here, nothing justifies my sudden decision to defend the interests of farmers, who don't give a damn" (*Frantz Fanon* 103–104). As Macey goes on to explain: Fanon rarely spoke of his wartime experience, even when he was with friends, but on a number of occasions he did cite a very bitter passage from Césaire's "discourse on colonialism" of 1951. Here, Césaire speaks of the need to explain to "the very distinguished, very humanistic and very Christian bourgeois of the twentieth century" that a Hitler slumbers within him and that what he cannot forgive Hitler for is not his crimes in the abstract, but "the crimes against the white man, the humiliation of the white man, the fact that he applied to Europe the colonial practices that had previously been applied only to the Arabs of Algeria, the coolies of India and the negroes of Africa" (*Frantz Fanon* 111).

11. Giambattista Vico, *De Italorum sapienta*, *Opere* 1.181 (qtd. in Mooney 3–4).

12. Giambattista Vico, *De constantia jurisprudentis* (qtd. in Mooney v).

13. See Charles Taylor, "Two Theories of Modernity," and Dilip Parameshwar Gaonkar, "On Alternative Modernities," in *Alternative Modernities*.

14. On Lyotard's connections to Algeria and Algerian literature, see the "Introduction" to Woodhull's *Transfigurations of the Maghreb: Feminism, Decolonization, and Literatures*.

15. Although the rise in ironic approaches that Rorty refers to did take place, it is not my contention here that it has displaced the cultural role claimed by religion, for example. Rorty's arguments stem from a Western social imaginary that does not take into account other social imaginaries. His argument has embedded within it a set of assumptions about the evolutionary course of human thought and about the place elite culture holds in this narrative (projected into a global context) that I do not share.

16. See, for example, Gee, "The New Literacy Studies" 180–183; 190. See also Gee, *Social Linguistics and Literacies: Ideology in Discourses*, and especially *The Social*

Mind: Language, Ideology, and Social Practice (xvii), for extended arguments positing that things often considered individual in the West—meaning, memory, values—are not in the brain or the mind but out in the social space of action and interaction.

17. See Said, *The World, the Text, and the Critic.*

18. For an example of the way North African emigrant workers are "thingified" in France, see Fanon, *Toward the African Revolution* 14; for a discussion of "thingification," see Césaire, *Discourse on Colonialism.*

19. See also, Edward Said, *The World, the Text, and the Critic* 290.

20. See also, Esposito, *The Islamic Threat* 15–16, 22–23.

Chapter 2

1. To understand how great the gap was between discourse and reality where conscription was concerned, one needs only to compare the words of General Mangin, author of the Black Army idea, and those of historians like Suret-Canale (for sub-Saharan Africa) and Ageron (for North Africa). Mangin in his report to the *Comité de l'Afrique Française* represented African tribes as eager to sign up, but Ageron says forcing local communities to furnish a quota of volunteers was referred to as "des procédés de recrutement au lasso" ("recruitment by lasso"; see *Histoire de l'Algérie contemporaine*, vol. 2: 256), and Suret-Canale enumerates the number of uprisings and migrations that took place across French West Africa to protest recruitment (see *French Colonialism in Tropical Africa 1900–1945* 140–143). M. Le Hérissé, colonial administrator working with Mangin to find conscripts, testified: "Their loyalty is undeniable; led by their chiefs, they flock to our sides, to the service of France, which many have already learned to think of as [their] country" (*Mission* 29).

2. The work of E. F. Gautier is illustrative of this tendency on the part of French scholars of the North African colonies to see the local peoples as unaware of their own pasts, stagnating and lagging behind Europe. As he put it in his 1927 history of the *Les siècles obscurs du Maghreb: l'islamisation de l'Afrique du Nord*: "the history of the Maghreb is almost virgin territory. . . . In the Maghreb, the stone age lasted much longer than in Europe: lots of dolmens are made of stones with Roman inscriptions on them; the Maghrebi, of all the white races of the Mediterranean, is surely the laggard, trailing far behind the others" (2–3).

3. Emmanuel Dongala, a writer from Republic of Congo with first-hand experience of civil war, refugee camps, and displacement, puts the following speech in the mouth of Katelijne, a Belgian journalist covering relief efforts, in his novel *Johnnny Mad Dog*: "The world is completely ignorant of the tragedy unfolding here. An appalling civil war that has caused nearly ten thousand deaths, half a million displaced persons and refugees, a humanitarian catastrophe—and not a single word in the American or European media. Obviously, this isn't Kosovo or Bosnia. Africa is far away, right? Who cares about Africa? Tantalum—okay. Oil, diamonds, hardwoods, gorillas—yes. But the people don't count. They're not whites, like us" (145).

4. In an article in the *Revue de Paris* (c. 1909), Colonel (later General) Mangin, the founder of the Black Army idea, wrote: "The drop in birthrate in France and the reduction of military training to two years have caused considerable falling off in the total strength of the army, which is getting worse" (qtd. in Suret-Canale, *French Colonialism in Tropical Africa* 134).

5. Gobineau enjoyed fame in Germany, based in large part on his racial theories, but he was little known in France. However, Gobineau was well-known to two influential French intellectuals: Ernest Renan and Alexis de Tocqueville. When he arrived in Paris in 1837, Gobineau made the acquaintance of the Scheffer family, one of whom—Cornélie, Scheffer's niece who later became Mrs. Ernest Renan—was a lifelong friend and correspondent. Both Ernest Renan and de Tocqueville read Gobineau's *Essai* when it appeared and wrote to Gobineau expressing their reactions to his racial theories. Renan was equivocal about Gobineau's conclusions, but he seems to accept his premises about race. De Tocqueville's letter to Gobineau, on the other hand, focuses on the fatalism and political divisiveness of Gobineau's racial theory:

> You continually speak about races regenerating or degenerating, losing or acquiring through an infusion of new blood social capacities which they have not previously had. (I think these are your own words.) I must frankly say that, to me, this sort of predestination is a close relative of the purest materialism.
>
> And be assured that should the masses, whose reasoning always follows the most beaten tracks, accept your doctrines, it would lead them straight from races to individuals and from social capacities to all sorts of potentialities. . . .
>
> The consequences of [your] theories is that of a vast limitation, if not a complete abolition, of human liberty. Thus I confess that after having read your book I remain, as before, opposed in the extreme to your doctrines. I believe that they are probably quite false; I know that they are certainly very pernicious." (de Tocqueville 227)

6. See Lorcin, "The Soldier Scholars of Colonial Algeria."

7. As Lorcin notes, Rinn's "Essai d'études linguistiques et ethnologiques sur les origines bèrberes" was published in the *Revue Africaine*, vols. 25–33 (1881–1889). Rinn's theory had clear precursors and sequels: "In the Middle Ages [this classification] was applied to a social order: the serfs were descendants of Ham, the clerks of Shem and the nobles of Japheth. In nineteenth-century Germany, Japheth had sired the Germans, Shem the Semites" (Lorcin 280).

8. In *Colonizing Egypt*, Timothy Mitchell discusses, in the case of Egypt, how the colonizing process extended the world-as-exhibition; it was a mode of ordering and containing local knowledge confronted around the world. Schneider gives the example of ethnographic exhibitions, popular after 1875, run by private promoters who would bring up troupes of natives to perform simulated battles, dances, etc. (5).

9. For discussions of the centrality of Western notions of masculinity to the discourse of civilization in the period leading into World War I, see Gail Bederman's *Manliness & Civilization: A Cultural History of Gender and Race in the United States,*

1880–1917 and Patrick Brantlinger's *Rule of Darkness: British Literature and Imperialism, 1830–1914*.

10. See *Images et colonies* (86–96) for popular French depictions of soldiers from Africa; see Stanley, *What Did You Do in the War, Daddy?* and Zeman *Selling the War* for the images used on propaganda posters during World War I and World War II.

11. As Adam Hochschild's account of European colonization in the Congo, *King Leopold's Ghost*, so amply demonstrates, the reversals that colonial racial mythology is able to contain are quite astounding. In the Congo, the atrocities committed by the colonizers included the severing of thousands of hands and feet. Five to eight million Africans died. Bertrand Russell would term what happened in the Belgian Congo the first holocaust of the twentieth century (see note 13).

12. The poetic imagery is from Léon Bosquet and Ernest Hosten, *Un fragment de l'épopée sénégalaise: le tirailleurs sur l'Yser* (Brussels: G. Van Oest, 1918), 21.

13. See Bertrand Russell, "Murder for Money: Congo." In addition to Russell's text in electronic form, there is discussion of just how negative, or ironic, Russell's use of "savages" might be.

CHAPTER 3

1. All subsequent references to the English translation of the novel will be indicated parenthetically in the text by the abbreviation *SMN*.

2. See also, Spurr, *Rhetoric of Empire* 63; and Mary Louise Pratt, *Imperial Eyes: Travel Writing and Transculturation*, especially Chapter 2: "Science, Planetary Consciousness, Interiors."

3. All subsequent references to the English translation of the novel will be indicated parenthetically in the text by the abbreviation *AA*.

4. J. P. Little's "Autofiction and Cheikh Hamidou Kane's *L'aventure ambiguë*" is an essay largely based on material from two interviews she conducted with Kane, one on December 16, 1997 (which Little later published as "The Origins of Samba Diallo: An Interview with Cheikh Hamidou Kane") and one on February 14, 1998.

5. Chinua Achebe writes: "We may have been talking about individualism as if it was invented in the West or even by one American, Emerson. In fact individualism must be, has to be, as old as human society itself. From whatever time humans began to move around in groups the dialogue between [the Western psychiatrist Octave] Mannoni's polarities of 'social being' and 'inner personality' or, more simply, between the individual and the community must also have been called into being. It is inconceivable that it shouldn't. The question is not whether this dialectic has always existed but rather how particular peoples resolved it at particular times" ("The Writer and His Community" 56).

6. I am thinking here of the Sudanese writer Tayeb Salih's *Season of Migration to the North*, dealt with later in this study, which, like *Ambiguous Adventure*, involves

both the return of a student to a village and ends with a similar immersion into water. Salih's protagonists lack the steady, secure faith of Kane's characters, and Salih focuses rather on the spiritual degradation fostered by colonial systems.

7. In their arguments about these issues, Eickelman and Piscatori comment:

> Sociologists and political scientists who have predicated the success of development upon secularization find the idea of center and periphery as the key to their analysis of national and state authority. Indeed, the prevailing orthodoxy of the social sciences from the 1950s through the 1970s was modernization theory. It presupposed that a prerequisite of political development, and sometimes of political liberty, was the integration of outlying regions to national and international, political and economic networks through a common educational, economic, and communications system. These ideas have percolated into the study of Islam within both the social sciences and the humanities in such forms as the dichotomy of "great tradition" and "little tradition" . . . the division between 'central' and outlying lands, as in the *Cambridge History of Islam* . . . and the idea of *l'Islam périphérique* among some French scholars [for example, the entire issue of *Archipel*, 29 (1985)]. . . . Our basic point is that although there doubtless is a powerful tendency in modern societies towards the establishment and maintenance of central authority, there is a persistence of other networks of value and authority which are independent, or at least partially independent, of that authority, and do not appear to be on the wane. Thus, the straightforward distinction between center and periphery is called into question. (12–13).

8. In "The Obligation to Migrate: the Doctrine of *hijra* in Islamic Thought," in *Muslim Travellers*, Muhammad Khalid Masud notes that scholars like Ibn 'Arabi based their interpretation of *hijra* on verse 4:100 of *The Holy Qur'an* (42). That verse reads:

> He who forsakes his home
> In the cause of Allah,
> Finds in the earth
> Many a refuge,
> Wide and spacious:
> Should he die
> As a refugee from home
> For Allah and his Messenger,
> His reward becomes due
> And sure with Allah:
> And Allah is oft-forgiving,
> Most Merciful.

9. The close relationship between grandfather and grandson, and ancestor worship involving what is sometimes referred to as "reincarnation" in English, are elements of the syncretism between Sufi Islam and Traditional African religion. In "Reincarna-

tion: An Impossible Concept in the Framework of African Ontology," Innocent Onyewuenyi explains that the influence of the ancestors is more a matter of powerful spiritual influence and aid, rather than reincarnation per se:

> The vital force of an ancestor is comparable to the sun, which is not diminished by the number and extent of its rays. The sun is present in its rays and heats and brightens through its rays; yet, the rays of the sun singly or together are not the sun. In the same way the "vital force" which is the being of the ancestor can be present in one or several of the living members of his clan, through his life-giving will or vital influence, without its being diminished or truncated. Just as the sun is the causal agent of his descendants who are below him in the hierarchy. This vital influence is subordinate and distinct from the creative influence which is the domain of God." (In *African Belief in Reincarnation: A Philosophical Reappraisal*, Enugu: University of Nigeria Press, 1996: 33–45; see also, http://www.afrikaworld.net/afrel/atr-reincarnation.htm).

In the 1997 interview conducted by J. P. Little, Kane comments: "To a certain extent I think that Samba Diallo, for me, is a sort of reincarnation and continuation of the life and the being of the man who was my great-great-grandfather, Abdoulaye. . . . I think that perhaps unconsciously in my mind, Samba Diallo is a sort of reincarnation" ("Origins of Samba Diallo," 118). The conversations Samba Diallo carries on at the graves of "Old Rella" and Thierno suggest a communication across the dimension of the living and the dead that is typical of African traditional religion of the Muslim practice of *ziyara*.

10. Maryse Condé's historical novels *Segu* (New York: Ballantine, 1988 [1984]) and *The Children of Segu* (New York: Viking, 1989 [1984]) trace the historical moment when the animist tribes of the Bambara came into conflict with first Usuman dan Fodio and then al Hajj 'Umar.

11. The "Memorial" was a piece of parchment remembering and recording Pascal's spiritual crisis and miraculous conversion on the night of November 23, 1654. The "Memorial" was found sewn into Pascal's clothes upon his death, and he had apparently carried it with him since his revelation. See #913 (*Pensées* 309–310).

12. Qtd. in Krailsheimer (25). See also Pascal's *On the Art of Persuasion*.

13. See also Dunn who discusses the "lonely crowd" motif in Western philosophy, especially as it informs Descartes' experience.

14. See Aire "Mort et Devenir" 758; Harrow "The Power and the Word" 76 and "Camara Laye, Cheikh Hamidou Kane, and Tayeb Salih" 296; and Mortimer 66.

15. Marita Knicker, in "Le Coran comme modèle," cites many connections to Islamic references but does little more with the connection.

16. See also, George Lang, "Through a Prism Darkly: 'Orientalism' in European-Language African Writing" in which he discusses the depth of Kane's adherence to Muslim practices for his philosophical insights (*Faces of Islam* 302).

17. The spelling Koran is kept in quotations where it appeared in the original; otherwise, the spelling Qur'an is used.

CHAPTER 4

1. Michel Foucault"s "Of Other Spaces," translated Jay Miskoweic, was published by *Diacritics* (Spring 1986), 22–27. These notes from a lecture given in March 1967 were published under the title "Des Espaces Autres" by the French journal *Architecture-Mouvement-Continuité* in October 1984. Although not reviewed for publication by the author, thus not part of the official corpus of his work, the manuscript was released into the public domain for an exhibition in Berlin shortly before Foucault's death (22).

2. See Waïl S. Hassan, *Tayeb Salih: Ideology & the Craft of Fiction* (Syracuse: Syracuse University Press, 2003). Hassan includes as an appendix to this study of the corpus of Salih's work a useful "Chronology of the Wad Hamid Cycle" based both on Raja' Ni'ma's earlier chronology and on other clues in Salih's works.

3. The interview with Salih is from Ahmad Sa'eed Muhammadiyya's *Al-Tayyib Salih: 'abqari al-riwaya al-'arabiyya* (Beirut: Dar al-'awda, 1976).

4. See also M. M. Bakhtin, *Problems of Dostoevsky's Poetics* 194–195.

5. In a discussion of the "clash of civilizations" thesis, Emran Qureshi and Michael Sells point out that historians such as Bernard Lewis "[refer] to 'our Judeo-Christian civilization' as self-evident fact. Yet for thousands of years, up through the Holocaust, Jews were, at best, tolerated evils in the view of the dominant Christian ideologies." They note that, if one is to be exact, it needs to be recognized that Jews have contributed at least as much to civilizations ruled by Islam as they have to those ruled by Christianity. Thus a clash of civilizations would need to be seen as a clash between Judeo-Christianity and Judeo-Islam. So, while the three Abrahamic religions define themselves, in part, by their difference from one another, it is equally important to keep the history of their productive co-existence in mind and to understand the clash thesis as more about political stakes than about religious conflicts. (6)

6. This style of narration so reminiscent of Marlow's narration in Conrad's *Heart of Darkness* is one reason *Season of Migration to the North* is seen as a postcolonial rewriting of Conrad's text.

7. For an extended discussion of hybridity in the novel, see Patricia Geesey, "Cultural Hybridity and Contamination."

8. The most cited example of mirror as embodying a dynamic of recognition/misrecognition is Lacan's description of the mirror-stage when an infant, fragmented by realizing its separateness from the world around it, recognizes with jubilation the unity of its reflection in a mirror. This is also a moment of misrecognition as the child is not that whole, autonomous being reflected in the mirror. The utopia of the mirror image is supplanted by the heterotopia of the mirror itself, which makes us painfully aware that our experience of what Lacan calls the Real is always mediated by the Symbolic. See Lacan, "The Mirror-Stage" 1–7.

9. The *afreet* is "a demon or spirit from the Djinn world, of great strength and cunning; often a snatcher of women" (Bushnaq xxvii).

10. For a discussion of this process, Fuss 35; and Fabian, *Time and the Other*.

11. As Edward Said points out in *Freud and the Non-European*, Freud's perspective was that of a "Viennese-Jewish scientist, philosopher and intellectual who lived and worked his entire life in either Austria or England" (13).

12. For a more extended discussion of the import of Fanon's critique, see Macey, *Frantz Fanon: A Biography* 188–192.

13. All subsequent references to the English translation of the novel will be indicated parenthetically in the text by the abbreviation *LM*.

14. In Feriana, the Tlili lineage is the maraboutic tribe descended from Sidi Ahmed Tlili. See *Villes et territoires au Maghreb*. There is an annual festival in honor of Sidi Ahmed Tlili, and a zaouia named after him in the center of town.

15. See also *Politique-Hebdo*, no. 107 (December 1973).

16. This interview by Christiane Chaulet-Achour and Lalia Kerfa, "Portrait de Malika Mokeddem," was first published in *Algérie Littérature/Action*, no. 14 (October 1997), 185–195.

17. All subsequent references to the English translation of the novel will be indicated parenthetically in the text by the abbreviation *FW*.

18. On the issue of depicting the complex social, economic, gender, and political forces that led people to join fundamentalist groups, the more ironic, humorous presentation provided by Merzak Allouache *Bab El-Oued* might serve as an alternative model.

19. See also Chapter 11, "Between God and Man," of Lazreg's *The Eloquence of Silence*.

20. By the time of the 1878 World's Fair held in Paris, one of the exhibitors was the Society for the Protection of the People of Alsace-Lorraine with a display of three types of rural houses built for the entire villages who had emigrated to North Africa as settlers. See Florica Dulmet, "La Métropole à l'heure de l'exotisme," *Historia spéciale*, 130.

Chapter 5

1. See Jankélévitch, *L'Ironie* 191–199; see also Wilson O. Clough's "Irony: A French Approach," 183.

2. This essay, which originally appeared in *The Nation*, later became the final essay of Said's final book. See Edward Said, "The Public Role of Writers and Intellectuals," *Humanism and Democratic Criticism*.

3. WTI is a horizontal network of local groups and individuals worldwide that work together in a nonhierarchical system. The project consists of commissions of inquiry and sessions held around the world investigating various issues related to the war on Iraq, such as the legality of the war, the role of the United Nations, war crimes, and the role of the media. See: http://www.worldt ribunal.org/main/?b=1.

4. See for example, Taylor's *Multiculturalism: Examining the Politics of Recognition.*

5. See also, Charles Taylor, *The Ethics of Authenticity* 48.

6. See also, Nancy Fraser, "Recognition without Ethics?" in *Recognition and Difference.*

7. In "The Imperialist Epistemological Vision," Al-Masseri writes: "We can see the persistent rhetoric on 'human rights,' now led by the most imperialist administration in the world (that of the United States) is, in essence, an onslaught on humanity and human nature. The individual, whose rights are allegedly defended, has become an independent entity unrelated to a family, community, or state. In this sense, he or she is a set of abstract needs defined specifically by monopolies, advertisement and fashion companies, and by several entertainment industries. In this context, the individual is no more than a unit reduced to a receptor of heavy instructions from public institutions that have no individuality and no value other than augmenting profit. These institutions resemble an absolute state that has appointed itself as an absolute power and that has remodeled individuals so that they could play the roles or perform the functions assigned to them. To talk of human rights (in the abstract) is, therefore, to continue the original assault on the intermediary institutions that began in the Renaissance and left humanity completely naked before the state and its institutions" (412–413).

8. Macey provides the following background for these early publications: "Fanon's literary career began quietly with the appearance of his essay on 'the lived experience of the black man' in the May 1951 issue of the journal *Esprit*, which took as its theme 'the lament of the black man.' There was no indication that it was a chapter from a forthcoming book. The second of Fanon's contributions to the journal came in February 1952, when his article on "The North-African syndrome" appeared as part of a dossier on 'The North-African Proletariat in France.' It was complemented by M'Hamed Ferid Ghazi's statistically based article on the growing immigrant population, which argued that the Algerian community was 'the most proletarian' and the most underprivileged of all the foreign communities—Italian, Spanish, and Polish—that coexisted within the 'French' proletariat. Founded in 1932 by the philosopher Emmanuel Mounier, the monthly *Esprit* had been relaunched in 1944 as the main platform for the Catholic left and was widely regarded as one of the great expressions of the spirit of wartime Resistance. Rather like Sartre's *Les Temps modernes*, it provided a non-aligned or 'new left' alternative to the Communist press. Jean-Marie Domenach and Francis Jeanson were co-editors of the 'Esprit' series of books." Macey, *Frantz Fanon* 154–155.

Bibliography

Abdel-Latif, Omayma. "Bridging the Divide," *Al-Ahram*, no. 611 (November 7–13, 2002). http://weekly.ahram.org.eg/2002/611/focus.htm.

Abrams, M. H. *A Glossary of Literary Terms*. New York: Holt, Rinehart, and Winston, c.1988.

Abul Qasem, Muhammed. *The Recitation and Interpreatation of the Qur'an: Al-Gazali's theory*. A translation of Book 8 of Abu Hamid Muhammad Al-Ghazali's *Revival of the Religious Sciences* (*Ihya' 'Ulum ad-Din*). London: Kegan Paul, 1982.

Achebe, Chinua."The Writer and His Community (Nov 1984)." *Hopes and Impediments: Selected Essays, 1965–87*. New York: Doubleday, 1990.

African Literature and the Universities. Ed. Gerald Moore. Ibadan: Ibadan University Press, 1965.

Ageron, Charles-Robert. *Histoire de l'Algérie contemporaine*. Vol. 1, *La Conquête et les débuts de la colonisation*. Vol. 2, *De l'Insurrection de 1871 au déclenchement de la guerre de libération* (*1954*). Paris: Presses universitaires de France, 1964.

Aire, Victor O. "Mort et devenir: Lecture thanato-sociologique de *L'Aventure ambiguë*." *The French Review* 55, 6 (May 1982): 752–760.

Al-Ali, Nadje. *Secularism, Gender and the State in the Middle East: The Egyptian Women's Movement*. Cambridge: Cambridge University Press, 2000.

Al-Ghazali, Abu Hamid Muhammad. *Revival of the Religious Sciences* (*Ihya' 'Ulum ad-Din*). Book 8, *The Recitation and Interpretation of the Qur'an*. Trans. Muhammad Abul Qasem. London: Kegan Paul, 1982.

Ali, A. Yusuf. Translation and Commentary. The Holy Qur'an. N.P.: American Trust Pub., 1977.

Allouache, Merzak. *Bab El-Oued*. Boulder: Lynne Rienner, 1998.

Alloula, Malek. *The Colonial Harem*. Trans. Myrna Godzich and Wlad Godzich. Introduction by Barbara Harlow. Minneapolis: University of Minnesota Press, 1986.

Al-Masseri, Abdulwahab. "The Imperialist Epistemological Vision." *American Journal of Islamic Social Scientists* 11 (Fall 1994): 403–415.

Al-Tabari, Muhammad ibn Jarir. *Jami' al-Bayan 'an Ta'wil Ay al-Qur'an*. London: Oxford University Press, 1987–.

Alternative Modernities. Ed. Dilip Parameshwar Gaonkar. Durham: Duke University Press, 2001.

Amin, Samir. *The Maghreb in the Modern World: Algeria, Tunisia, Morocco*. Trans. Michael Perl. Harmondsworth: Penguin, 1970.

Amyuni, Mona Takieddine. "Introduction." *Season of Migration to the North by Tayeb Salih: A Casebook*. 11–25.

"Atlas Shrugged: A Novel by Ayn Rand." http://www.atlasshrugged.tv/book.htm.

Auden, W. H. *Prose*. Vol. 2, 1939–1948. Ed. Edward Mendelson. *The Complete Works of W.H. Auden*. Princeton: Princeton University Press, 2002.

Austin, J. L. *How To Do Things With Words*. Cambridge: Harvard University Press, 1962.

Ayoub, Mahmoud. *The Qur'an and Its Interpreters*. 2 vols. Albany: State University of New York Press, 1984.

Bachelard, Gaston. *The Poetics of Space*. Trans. Maria Jolas. Boston: Beacon Press, 1969.

Bakhtin, M. M. *Problems of Dostoevsky's Poetics*. Trans. Caryl Emerson. Minneapolis: University of Minnesota Press, 1984.

Balesi, Charles John. *From Adversaries to Comrades-in-Arms: West Africans and the French Military, 1885–1918*. Waltham, MA: Crossroads Press, 1979.

"Banania: History of the 'Y'a bon Banania' Character." http://www.museedelapub.org/pubgb/virt/mp/banania/. Accessed July 13, 2005.

Bederman, Gail. *Manliness & Civilization: A Cultural History of Gender and Race in the United States, 1880–1917*. Chicago: University of Chicago Press, 1995.

Benayoun-Szmidt, Yvette, Robert Elbaz and Najib Redouane. "Genèse d'une oeuvre." *Malika Mokeddem*. Ed. Redouane. 275–326.

Bensmaïa, Réda. *Experimental Nations: or, the Invention of the Maghreb*. Princeton: Princeton University Press, 2003.

Bhabha, Homi K. *The Location of Culture*. London: Routledge, 1994.

———. *Nation and Narration*. London: Routledge, 1990.

———. "Signs Taken for Wonders: Questions of Ambivalence and Authority under a Tree Outside Delhi, May 1917." *"Race," Writing and Difference*. Ed. Henry Louis Gates. Chicago: University of Chicago Press, 1986. 163–184.

Bhabha, Jacqueline. "Embodied Rights: Gender Persecution, State Sovereignty and Refugees." *Women, Citizenship and Difference*. Ed. Nira Yuval-Davis and Pnina Werbner. London: Zed, 1999. 178–191.

Bihr, Alain. "Alsace, Exception to the Rule." *Le Monde diplomatique*, English language edition (May 1998). http://mondediplo.com/1998/05/07bihr.

"The Black Troops on the Rhine." *The Nation* (March 9, 1921): 365–366.

Blair, Dorothy S. *African Literature in French: A History of Creative Writing in French from West and Equatorial Africa*. Cambridge: Cambridge University Press, 1976.

Booth, Wayne C. *A Rhetoric of Irony*. Chicago: University of Chicago Press, 1974.

Bosquet, Léon and Ernest Hosten. *Un Fragment de l'épopée sénégalaise: le tirailleurs sur l'Yser*. Brussels: G. Van Oest, 1918.

Boswell, Laird. "Right-wing Extremism in Frontier Regions: The French National Front and the Crisis of Alsatian Identity." *Twenty-First Century Papers: On-Line Working Papers from The Center for 21st Century Studies University of Wisconsin—Milwaukee*, No. 5 (May 2005). http://www.uwm.edu/Dept/21st/workingpapers/boswell.pdf.

Bourdieu, Pierre and Terry Eagleton. "Doxa and Common Life: An Interview." *Mapping Ideology*. Ed. Slavoj Zizek. London: Verso, 1994. 265–277.

Boyd-Buggs, Debra. "Marabout-Masters: Maraboutism and the Problem of Education in the Senegalese Novel." *The Postcolonial Crescent: Islam's Impact on Contemporary Literature*. Ed. John Hawley. New York: Peter Lang, 1998. 185–214.

Brantlinger, Patrick. *Rule of Darkness: British Literature and Imperialism, 1830–1914*. Ithaca: Cornell University Press, 1988.

Brench, A. C. *The Novelists' Inheritance in French Africa: Writers from Senegal to Cameroon*. London: Oxford, 1967.

Brown, Ella. "Reactions to Western Values as Reflected in African Novels." *Phylon* 48, 3 (1987): 216–228.

Bulhan, Hussein Abdilahi. *Frantz Fanon and the Psychology of Oppression*. New York: Plenum Press, 1985.

Burke, Kenneth. *A Grammar of Motives*. 1945. Berkeley: University of California Press, 1969.

Bushnaq, Inea. *Arab Folktales* New York: Pantheon, 1986.

Caillier, Bernadette. "L'Aventure ambiguë: autobiographie ou l'histoire d'un peuple." *The French Review* 55, 6 (May 1982): 742–751.

Camus, Albert. *Exile and the Kingdom*. Trans. Justin O'Brien. New York: Knopf, 1958. First Vintage edition, 1991.

Certeau, Michel de. *The Practice of Everyday Life*. Trans. Steven F. Rendall. Berkeley: University of California Press, c.1984.

Césaire, Aimé. *Discourse on Colonialism*. Trans. Joan Pinkham. New York: Monthly Review, 1972.

Chadwell, Faye. "Mokeddem: The Forbidden Woman." *Library Journal* 123, 5 (March 15, 1998). EBSCO 1475879.

Chakrabarty, Dipesh. "Postcoloniality and the Artifice of History: Who Speaks for 'Indian' Pasts?" *Representations* 37 (1992): 1–26.

Charrad, Mounira. *States and Women's Rights: The Making of Postcolonial Tunisia, Algeria, and Morocco.* Berkeley: University of California Press, 2001.

Chaulet-Achour, Christiane and Lalia Kerfa. "Portrait de Malika Mokeddem." *Malika Mokeddem: Envers et contre tout.* 21–34.

Chittick, William C. *The Sufi Path of Knowledge: Ibn al-'Arabi's Metaphysics of Imagination.* Albany: State University of New York Press, 1989.

Clough, Wilson O. "Irony: A French Approach." *Sewanee Review* 48 (1939): 175–183.

Comaroff, John L. "Ethnicity, Nationalism, and the Politics of Difference in an Age of Revolution." *The Politics of Difference.* Ed. Wilmsen and McAllister. 162–183.

Comaroff, John and Jean Comaroff. *Ethnography and the Historical Imagination.* Boulder: Westview Press, 1992.

Condé, Maryse. *The Children of Segu.* New York: Viking, 1989.

———. *Ségu.* New York: Ballantine, 1988.

Condorcet, Antoine-Nicolas de. *Sketch for a Historical Picture of the Progress of the Human Mind.* Introduction by Stuart Hampshire. New York: Noonday Press, 1955.

Cooke, Miriam. *Women Claim Islam.* New York: Routledge, 2001.

Corliss, Mary. "Palms Up for Michael Moore, Thumbs Down for Bush." http://www.time.com/time/arts/article/0,8599,641252,00.html.

Coundouriotis, Eleni. *Claiming History: Colonialism, Ethnography, and the Novel.* NY: Columbia University Press, 1999.

Crowder, Michael. *Colonial West Africa: Collected Essays.* London: Frank Cass, 1978.

Dailly, Christophe. "The Novelist as a Cultural Policy-Maker." *Présence Africaine* 125 (1983): 202–213.

Davidson, Basil. *The Black Man's Burden: Africa and the Curse of the Nation-State.* New York: Times Books, 1992.

Déjeux, Jean. *Le Sentiment réligieux dans la littérature maghrébine de langue française.* Paris: L'Harmattan, 1986.

De Man, Paul. *Blindness and Insight: Essays in the Rhetoric of Contemporary Criticism.* Minneapolis: University of Minnesota Press, 1983.

Derrida, Jacques. *Monolingualism of the Other, or, the Prosthesis of Origin.* Trans. Patrick Mensah. Stanford: Stanford University Press, 1998.

Descartes, René. "Discourse on Method." *The Philosophical Writings of Descartes.* Trans. John Cottingham, Robert Stoothoff and Dugald Murdoch. Cambridge: Cambridge University Press, 1985. 111–151.

de Tocqueville, Alexis. *The European Revolution and Correspondence with Gobineau.* Ed. John Lukacs. Garden City, NY: Doubleday, 1959.

Diallo, Bakary. *Force-Bonté.* 1926. Paris: Agence de Coopération Culturelle et Technique, 1985.

"Dialogues: Islamic World-U.S.-The West." http://www.islamuswest.org.

Dongala, Emmanuel. *Johnny Mad Dog*. Trans. Maria Louise Ascher. New York: Farrar, Straus and Giroux, 2005.

Douglas, Allen. "Between Racism and Antimilitarism: The *Canard enchaîné* and France's Colonial Wars of the 1920s." *Franco-Arab Encounters*. 70–92.

Doyle, Michael W. *Empires*. Ithaca: Cornell University Press, 1986.

Duffin, Jacalyn. Review of *The Forbidden Woman* by Malika Mokeddem. Literature, Arts and Medicine Database. http://endeavor.med.nyu.edu/lit-med/lit-med-db/webdocs/webdescrips/mokeddem11909–des-.html.

Dulmet, Florica. "La Métropole à l'heure de l'exotisme." *Historia spéciale* 25 (Sept.-Oct. 1993): 126–130.

Dunn, Kevin."'A Great City is a Great Solitude': Descartes's Urban Pastoral." *Yale French Studies* 80 (1991): 93–107.

Eboussi, Fabien. "L'Aventure ambiguë de Cheikh Hamidou Kane: Quelques instants d'entretien avec Cheikh Hamidou Kane." *Abbia* 6 (1964): 207–215.

Echenberg, Myron. *Colonial Conscripts: The Tirailleurs Sénégalais in French West Africa, 1857–1960*. Portsmouth, NH: Heinemann, 1991.

Eickelman, Dale F. and James Piscatori. "Social Theory in the Study of Muslim societies." *Muslim Travellers*. 3–25.

Elia, Nada. Review of *The Forbidden Woman*, by Malika Mokeddem. *World Literature Today* 72, 4 (Autumn 1998). EBSCO Accession number 1475879. http://0–search.epnet.com.oasis.oregonstate.edu:80/login.aspx?direct=true&db=aph&an=1475879.

El Moudden, Abderrahmane. "The Ambivalence of *rihla*: Community Integration and Self-Definition in Moroccan Travel Accounts, 1300–1800." *Muslim Travellers*. 69–84.

Esposito, John. *Islam: The Straight Path*. Oxford: Oxford University Press, 1998.

———. *The Islamic Threat: Myth or Reality?* New York: Oxford University Press, 1992.

Fabian, Johannes. *Time and the Other: How Anthropology makes its Object*. New York: Columbia University Press, 1983.

Faces of Islam. Ed. Kenneth Harrow. Portsmouth, NH: Heinemann, 1991.

Falaturi, Abdoldjavad. "Experience of Time and History in Islam." *We Believe in One God*. Ed. Annemarie Schimmel and Abdodjavad Falaturi. 63–76.

Falk, Richard. "Empowering Inquiry: Our Debt to Edward Said." Transnational Foundation for Peace and Future Research, 2003. http://www.transnational.org/forum/meet/2003/Falk_DebtSaid.html.

———. *Human Rights Horizons: The Pursuit of Justice in a Globalizing World*. New York: Routledge, 2000.

Fanon, Frantz. *L'An Cinq, de la Révolution Algérienne*. Paris: François Maspero, 1959.

———. *Black Skin, White Masks*. Trans. Charles Lam Markmann. New York: Grove Press, 1967.

———. *Les Damnées de la terre*. Préface de Jean-Paul Sartre (1961). Paris: Editions François Maspero, 1961.

———. *Les Damnées de la terre*. Préface de Jean-Paul Sartre. Postface de Alice Cherki et de Mohammed Harbi (2002). Paris: Editions La Découverte & Syros, 2002.

———. *A Dying Colonialism*. New York: Grove Press, 1965.

———. *Peau noire, masques blancs*. Paris: Editions du Seuil, 1952.

———. *Pour la Révolution africaine: Ecrits politiques*. Paris: François Maspero, 1969.

———. *Toward the African Revolution: Political Essays*. Trans. Haaki Chevalier. New York: Grove Press, 1967.

———. 1963. *The Wretched of the Earth*. Preface by Jean-Paul Sartre. Trans. Constance Farrington. New York: Grove Press; *The Wretched of the Earth*. Forward by Homi Bhabha. Preface by Jean-Paul Sartre. Trans. Richard Philcox. New York: Grove, 2004.

Fellous, Gérard. "Michel Foucault: 'La Philosophie "structuraliste" permet de diagnostiquer ce qu'est aujourd'hui.'" *La Presse de Tunis*, April 12, 1967, 3.

Felski, Rita. *The Gender of Modernity*. Cambridge: Harvard University Press, 1995.

Flaubert, Gustave. *Madame Bovary*. Trans. Merloyd Lawrence. Boston: Houghton Miflin, 1969.

Foucault, Michel. "Of Other Spaces." Trans. Jay Miskoweic. *Diacritics* (Spring 1986): 22–27.

———. *The Order of Things: An Archeology of the Human Sciences*. New York: Vintage, 1973.

———. "Questions on Geography." *Power/Knowledge: Selected Interviews & Other Writings 1972–1977*. Ed. Colin Gordon. Trans. Colin Gordon, Leo Marshall, John Mephan, and Kate Soper. New York: Pantheon, 1980.

Franco-Arab Encounters: Studies in Memory of David C. Gordon. Ed. L. Carl Brown and Matthew S. Gordon. Beirut, Lebanon: American University of Beirut, 1996.

Fraser, Nancy. "From Redistribution to Recognition? Dilemmas of Justice in a 'Post-Socialist Age." *New Left Review* 212: 68–93.

———. "Recognition without Ethics?" *Recognition and Difference*. 21–42.

Freud, Sigmund. *Totem and Taboo. The Standard Edition of the Complete Psychological Works of Sigmund Freud*. Vol. 13. London: Hogarth Press [1953–].

———. *The Uncanny. The Standard Edition of the Complete Psychological Works of Sigmund Freud*. Vol. 17. London: Hogarth Press [1953–]. http://ogch.tripod.com/tusf.html.

Fuss, Diana. *Identification Papers.* London: Routledge, 1995.

Fussell, Paul. "The Initial Shock . . . A Conversation with Paul Fussell."*Humanities* 17, 5 (November/December 1996). http://www.neh.gov/news/humanities/1996–11/fussell.html.

———. *The Great War and Modern Memory.* Oxford University Press, 1975.

Gaonkar, Dilip Parameshwar. "On Alternative Modernities." *Alternative Modernities.* Ed. Gaonkar. 1–23.

Gautier, E. F. *Les Siècles obscurs du Maghreb: L'Islamisation de l'Afrique du Nord.* Paris: Payot, 1927.

Gee, James Paul. "The New Literacy Studies: From the 'socially situated' to the work of the social." *Situated Literacies: Reading and Writing in Context.* Ed. David Barton, Mary Hamilton and Roz Ivanic. London: Routledge, 2000. 180–196.

———. *Social Linguistics and Literacies: Ideology in Discourses.* London: Taylor & Francis, 1996.

———. *The Social Mind: Language, Ideology, and Social Practice.* New York: Bergin & Garvey, 1992.

Geesey, Patricia. "Cultural Hybridity and Contamination in Tayeb Salih's *Mawsin al-hijra ila al-Shamal* (*Season of Migration to the North*)." *Research in African Literatures* 28, 3 (Fall 1997): 128–140.

Girault, Arthur. *Principes de colonisation et de législation coloniale.* Paris: 1st edition, 1895; 2nd edition, 1903; 3rd edition, 1907; 4th edition, 1921; 5th edition, 1927, 6th edition, 1943.

Gobineau, Arthur-Joseph de. *Essai sur l'inégalité des races humaines.* Paris: P. Belfond, 1967.

———. *The Inequality of Human Races.* Trans. Adrian Collins. New York: Putnam, 1915.

Graham, William. *Beyond the Written word: Oral Aspects of Scripture in the History of Religion.* New York: Cambridge University Press, 1987.

Grandguillaume, Gilbert. *Arabisation et politique linguistique au Maghreb.* Paris: Editions G.-P. Maisonneuve et Larose, 1983.

Hamed-Touati, M'Barka. *Immigration maghrébine et activitiés politiques en France de la première guerre mondiale à la veille du front populaire.* Tunis: Université de Tunis I, 1994.

Hamil, Mustapha. "Exile and Its Discontents: Malika Mokaddem's *Forbidden Woman.*" *Research in African Literatures* 35, 1 (Spring 2004): 52–65.

Harrow, Kenneth. "Camara Laye, Cheikh Hamidou Kane, and Tayeb Salih: Three Sufi Authors." *Faces of Islam.* Ed. Kenneth Harrow. 261–298.

———, ed. *The Marabout & the Muse: New Approaches to Islam in African Literature.* Portsmouth, NH: Heinemann, 1996.

———. "The Power and the Word: *L'Aventure ambiguë* and The Wedding of Zein." *African Studies Review* 30, 1 (March 1987): 63–77.

Hart, William D. *Edward Said and the Religious Effects of Culture.* Cambridge: Cambridge University Press, 2000.

Hassan, Waïl S. *Tayeb Salih: Ideology & the Craft of Fiction.* Syracuse: Syracuse University Press, 2003.

Hegel, G. W. F. *Phenomenology of Spirit.* Trans. A. V. Miller. Oxford: Oxford University Press, 1977.

Helm, Yolande. "Entretien avec Malika Mokeddem." *Malika Mokeddem: envers et contre tout.* 39–52.

———. "Malika Mokeddem: a New and Resonant Voice in Francophone Algerian Literature." *Maghrebian Mosaic.* 195–211.

Hochschild, Adam. *King Leopold's Ghost.* NY: Houghton Mifflin, 1998.

The Holy Qur'an. Trans. with Commentary by A. Yusuf Ali. N.P.: American Trust Pub., 1977.

Holland, Eugene. "Representation and Misrepresentation in Postcolonial Literature and Theory." *Research in African Literatures* 34,1 (2003): 159–173.

Horne, Alistair. *The Price of Glory.* London: Macmillan, 1962.

Hourani, Albert. *A History of the Arab Peoples.* New York: Warner, 1991.

Hutcheon, Linda. *Irony's Edge: the Theory and Politics of Irony.* New York: Routledge, 1994.

Images et colonies: Iconographie et propagande coloniale sur l'Afrique française de 1880 à 1962. Paris: Collection des publications de la BDIC [Bibliothèque de documentation internationale contemporaine] dirigées par Joseph Hue et Publications de l'ACHAC [Association Connaissance de l'Histoire de l"Afrique Contemporaine] dirigées par Nicolas Bancel, Pascal Blanchard et Armelle Chatelier, 1993.

"Is the Black Horror on the Rhine Fact or Propaganda?" *The Nation* (July 13, 1921): 44–45.

Jamail, Dahr. "Testimony on War Crimes and the Recent Situation in Iraq." http://www.worldtribunal.org/main/?b=1. Accessed July 19, 2005.

Jankélévitch, Vladimir. *L'Ironie.* Paris: Flammarion, 1964.

JanMohamed, Abdul R. "The Economy of the Manichean Allegory: The Function of Racial Difference in Colonialist Literature." *"Race," Writing and Difference.* Ed. Henry Louis Gates. Chicago: University of Chicago Press, 1986. 78–106.

Kane, Cheikh Hamidou. *Ambiguous Adventure.* Trans. Katherine Woods. Oxford: Heinemann, 1963.

———. *L'Aventure ambiguë.* Paris: Juillard, 1961.

———. Lecture. "African Intellectuals Face their Responsibility." www.congopage.com/article.php3?id_article=3081.

Kaplan, Caren. *Questions of Travel: Postmodern Discourses of Displacement.* Durham: Duke University Press, 1996.

Keller, Richard. "*Action psychologique*: French Psychiatry in Colonial North Africa, 1900–1962." PhD diss., Rutgers University, 2001.

Knicker, Marita. "Le Coran comme modèle littéraire dans *L'Aventure ambiguë* de Cheikh Hamidou Kane." *Nouvelles du Sud* 6 (1986–87): 183–190.

Kotchy, Berthelemy. "Interview de M. Cheikh Hamidou Kane, écrivain sénégalaise." *Etudes littéraires* 7 (1974): 476–486.

Krailsheimer, A. J. *Pascal.* New York: Hill and Wang, 1980.

Kruks, Sonia. *Retrieving Experience: Subjectivity and Recognition in Feminist Politics.* Ithaca: Cornell University Press, 2001.

Lacan, Jacques. "The Mirror-Stage as Formative of the I as Revealed in Psychoanalytic Experience." *Ecrits: A Selection.* Trans. Alan Sheridan. London: Tavistock, 1977.

Lacaze, Marcel-Eugène. "La Guerre européenne et le tirailleur sénégalais." Thesis Faculté de Médecine, Université de Bordeaux, 1920.

Lang, George. "Through a Prism Darkly: 'Orientalism' in European-Language African Writing." *Faces of Islam.* Ed. Kenneth Harrow. 299–312.

Laremont, Ricardo René. *Islam and the Politics of Resistance in Algeria, 1783–1992.* Trenton: Africa World Press, 2000.

Lash, Scott and Mike Featherstone. "Recognition and Difference: Politics, Identity, Multiculture." *Recognition and Difference.* 1–20.

Lawler, Nancy Ellen. *Soldiers of Misfortune: Ivoirien Tirailleurs of World War II.* Athens: Ohio University Press, 1992.

Layoun, Mary. "Fictional formations and Deformations of National Culture." *The South Atlantic Quarterly* 87:1 (Winter 1988): 53–73.

Lazarus, Neil. *Nationalism and Cultural Practice in the Postcolonial World.* Cambridge: Cambridge University Press, 1999.

Lazreg, Marnia. *The Eloquence of Silence: Algerian Women in Question.* New York: Routledge, 1994.

———. "Gender and Politics in Algeria: Unraveling the Religious Paradigm." *Signs* 15, 4 (1990): 755–80.

———. "Islamism and the Recolonization of Algeria." *Arab Studies Quarterly* 20, 2 (Spring 1998): 43–58.

———. "The Triumphant Discourse of Global Feminism: Should Other Women Be Known." *Going Global: The Transnational Reception of Third World Women Writers.* Ed. Amal Amireh and Lisa Suhair Majaj. New York: Garland, 2000. 29–38.

Le Bon, Gustave. *The Psychology of Peoples*. New York: Arno, 1974.

Lewis, Martin Deming. "One Hundred Million Frenchmen: the 'Assimilation' Theory in French Colonial Policy." *Comparative Studies in Society and History: An International Quarterly* 4, 2 (January 1962): 129–152.

Lings, Martin. *What Is Sufism?* Berkeley: University of California Press, 1975.

Little, J. P. "Autofiction and Cheikh Hamidou Kane's *L'Aventure ambiguë*." *Research in African Literatures* 31, 2 (2000): 71–90.

———. "The Origins of Samba Diallo: An Interview with Cheikh Hamidou Kane." *International Journal of Francophone Studies* 2, 2 (1999): 112–120.

Lorcin, Patricia. *Imperial Identities: Stereotyping, Prejudice and Race in Colonial Algeria*. London: I. B. Tauris, 1995.

———. "The Soldier Scholars of Colonial Algeria. Arabs, Kabyles and Islam: Military Images of France in Algeria." *Franco-Arab Encounters*. 128–150.

La Lutte contre le racisme et la xénophobie 1997: Exclusion et droits de l'homme. Commission nationale consultative des droits de l'homme. 1997. Originally accessed as "France." "Antisemitism and Xenophobia Today"(AXT). http://www.axt.org.uk/antisem/archive/archive2/france/france.htm. Accessed June 25, 2005.

Lyantey, General Hubert. "Du rôle social de lòfficier dans le service militaire universel." *Revue des Deux Mondes* (15 mars 1891), 443–459.

M . . . , Muhammad. Personal Interview. Tunisia, 17 July 1997.

Macey, David. *Frantz Fanon: A Biography*. New York: Picador USA, 2001.

———. *The Lives of Michel Foucault: A Biography*. New York: Pantheon Books, 1993.

Maghrebian Mosaic: A Literature in Transition. Ed. Mildred Mortimer. Boulder: Lynne Rienner, 2001.

Majid, Anouar. *Freedom and Orthodoxy: Islam and Difference in the Post-Andalusian Age*. Stanford: Stanford University Press, 2004.

———. *Unveiling Traditions: Postcolonial Islam in a Polycentric World.* Durham: Duke University Press, 2000.

Makdisi, Saree S. "The Empire Renarrated: *Season of Migration to the North* and the Reinvention of the Present." *Colonial Discourse and Post-colonial Theory: A Reader*. Ed. Patrick Williams and Laura Chrisman. New York: Columbia University Press, 1994. 535–550.

Malak, Amin. *Muslim Narratives and the Discourse of English*. Albany: State University of New York Press, 2005.

Malika Mokeddem. Ed. Najib Redouane, Yvette Bénayoun-Szmidt and Robert Elbaz. Paris: L'Harmattan, 2003.

Malika Mokeddem: Envers et contre tout. Ed. Yolande Aline Helm. Paris: L'Harmattan, 2000.

Mangin, Lieutenant-Colonel. *La Force noire*. Paris: Hachette, 1910.

———. *La Mission des troupes noires: compte-rendu*. Paris: Comité de l'Afrique Française, 1911.

Mannoni, Octave. *Prospero and Caliban: The Psychology of Colonization.* Trans. Pamela Powesland. New York: Praeger, 1964.

Mantran, Robert. *Les grandes Dates de l'Islam.* Paris: Larousse, 1990.

Manville, Marcel. *Les Antilles sans fard.* Paris: L'Harmattan, 1992.

Maran, René. *Batouala.* Portsmouth, NH: Heinemann, 1987.

Marcus, K. Melissa. Preface. *The Forbidden Woman.* By Malika Mokeddem. vii–xiv.

Margolis, Mac, Tom Masland, Sudip Mazumdar and Liat Radcliffe. "Invasion of the Critters." *Newsweek* (Pacific Edition), 144, 8 (August 23, 2004): 48–49.

Marrouchi, Mustapha. "Decolonizing the Terrain of Western Theoretical Productions." *College Literature,* June 1997: 1–34.

———. *Edward Said at the Limits.* Albany: State University of New York Press, 2004.

Martin, B. G. *Muslim Brotherhoods in Nineteenth-Century Africa.* Cambridge: Cambridge University Press, 1976.

Martin, Jean. "Une Spectaculaire expansion coloniale." *Historia spéciale* 25 (Sept.–Oct. 1993): 8–27.

Masud, Muhammad Khalid. "The Obligation to Migrate: The Doctrine of *hijra* in Islamic Law." *Muslim Travellers.* 29–49.

"Memento de l'officier d'action psychologique en Algérie." Appendix five: "La Psychologie de coeur." Centre des Archives d'Outre-Mer, Aix-en-Provence (CAOM), SAS/DOC/5.

Mendelson, Edward. "We are all here to help others." The W. H. Auden Society. http://www.audensociety.org/vivianfoster.html.

Mercier, Roger and M. and S. Battestini. *Cheikh Hamidou Kane.* Paris: Fernand Nathan, 1967.

Mertz-Baumgartner, Birgit. "Identité et écriture rhizomatiques au féminin dans *L'Interdite* de Malika Mokeddem." *Malika Mokeddem.* Ed. Redouane. 121–136.

Miller, Christian T., Ann M. Simmons, et al. "Relief Camps for Africans and Kosovars: Worlds Apart." *Los Angeles Times,* May 21, 1999. http://www.transnational.org/features/contrasts.html.

Miller, Christopher. *Nationalists and Nomads: Essays on Francophone African Literature and Culture.* Chicago: University of Chicago Press, 1998.

———. "'We Shouldn't Judge Deleuze and Guattari': A Response to Eugene Holland." *Research in African Literatures* 34, 3 (2003): 129–141.

Mitchell, Timothy. *Colonizing Egypt.* Berkeley: University of California Press, 1991.

Mitgang, Herbert. "The Time of Tyrants in a North African Village." *The New York Times* (June 16, 1990): 12.

Moghadam, Valentine M. "Gender, National Identity and Citizenship: Reflections on the Middle East and North Africa." *Comparative Studies of South Asia, Africa and the Middle East,* 19, 1 (1999): 137–156.

Mokeddem, Malika. *Century of Locusts.* Trans. Laura Rice and Karim Hamdy. Lincoln: University of Nebraska Press, 2006.

———. *The Forbidden Woman.* Trans. K. Melissa Marcus. Lincoln: University of Nebraska Press, 1998.

———. *Les Hommes qui marchent.* Paris: Grasset et Fasquelle, 1997.

———. *Interdite.* Paris: Grasset et Fasquelle, 1993.

———. *Mes Hommes.* Paris: Grasset & Fasquelle, 2005.

———. *My Men.* Trans. Laura Rice and Karim Hamdy. Lincoln: University of Nebraska Press, forthcoming.

———. *Of Dreams and Assassins.* Trans. K. Melissa Marcus. Charlottesville: University of Virginia Press, 2000.

———. *Des Rêves et des assassins.* Paris: Grasset & Fasquelle, 1995.

———. *Le Siècle des sauterelles.* Paris: Ramsay, [1996], 1992.

———. *La Transe des insoumis.* Paris: Grasset et Fasquelle, 2003.

Mooney, Michel. *Vico in the Tradition of Rhetoric.* Princeton: Princeton University Press, 1985.

Mortimer, Mildred. *Journeys Through the French African Novel.* Portsmouth: Heinemann, 1990.

Muhammadiyya, Ahmad Sa'eed. *Al-Tayyib Salih: 'abqari al-riwaya al-'arabiyya.* Beirut: Dar al-'awda, 1976.

Muslim Travellers: Pilgrimage, Migration, and the Religious Imagination. Ed. Dale F. Eikelman and James Piscatori. London: Routledge, 1990.

Nelson, Keith. "The 'Black Horror on the Rhine': Race as a Factor in Post-World War I Diplomacy." *The Journal of Modern History* 42 (1970): 606–627.

Nott, Josiah C. *Two Lectures on the Natural History of the Caucasian and Negro Races.* Mobile: n.p., 1844.

Nusseibeh, D. Sari. "Israel as a Foreign State: The Arabs' Intellectual Dynamics." http://www.hashd.org/english/oxford1.htm.

Nyamu-Musembi, Celestine. "Towards an actor-oriented perspective on human rights." IDS Working Paper 169. Brighton: Institute of Development Studies, 2002.

Onyewuenyi, Innocent. "Reincarnation: An Impossible Concept in the Framework of African Ontology." *African Belief in Reincarnation: A Philosophical Reappraisal,* Enugu: University of Nigeria Press, 1996: 33–45; see, http://www.afrika-world.net/afrel/atr-reincarnation.htm.

Orlando, Valérie. *Nomadic Voices of Exile: Feminine Identity in Francophone Literature of the Maghreb.* Athens: Ohio University Press, 1999.

Pascal, Blaise. *Pensées.* Trans. A. J. Krailsheimer. New York: Penguin, 1966.

Perkins, Kenneth. *A History of Modern Tunisia.* Cambridge: Cambridge University Press, 2004.

The Politics of Difference: Ethnic Premises in a World of Power. Ed. Edwin N. Wilmsen and Patrick McAllister. Chicago: Chicago University Press, 1996.

Politique-Hebdo. 107 (December 1973).

Porter, Bernard. "We Don't Do Empire." *History Today* 55, 3 (March 2005): 31–33.

Pound, Ezra. "Hugh Selwyn Mauberly." Section 5, "E.P. Ode pour l'éléction de son sépulchre." *Selected Poems of Ezra Pound.* New York: New Directions, 1926.

Pratt, Mary Louise. *Imperial Eyes: Travel Writing and Transculturation.* New York: Routledge, 1992.

"President George Bush Discusses Iraq in National Press Conference." March 6, 2003. "The White House." Accessed July 3, 2005. http://www.whitehouse.gov/news/releases/2003/03/20030306–8.html.

"A Quiet Joke at Your Expense." *The Economist* (December 16, 1999). http://www.economist.com/displayStory.cfm?story_id=268955.

Qureshi, Emran and Michael A. Sells. "Introduction: Constructing the Muslim Enemy." *The New Crusades: Constructing the Muslim Enemy.* Ed. Emran Qureshi and Michael A. Sells. New York: Columbia University Press, 2003.

Recognition and Difference: Politics, Identity, Multiculture. Ed. Scott Lash and Mike Featherstone. London: Sage Publications, 2002.

Remarque, Erich Maria. *All Quiet on the Western Front.* Trans. A. W. Wheen. Boston: Little, Brown and Co., 1929.

Renan, Ernest. *De la Part des peuples sémitiques dans l'histoire de la civilisation: Discours d'ouverture du cours.* Paris: M. Lévy Frères, 1862.

———. Lettre à Gobineau. *Correspondances, 1845–1892.* Vol. 10. *Oeuvres complètes de Ernest Renan.* Paris: Calmann-Lévy, 1947–. 203–205.

———. *De l'Origine du langage.* Vol. 8. *Oeuvres complètes de Ernest Renan.* Paris: Calmann-Lévy, 1947–. 9–123.

Rinn, Louis. *Marabouts et khouan.* Alger: A. Jourdan, 1884.

———. *Les Origines berbères: études linguistiques et ethnologiques.* Alger: A. Jourdan, 1889.

Robinson, David. "An Approach to Islam in West Africa." *Faces of Islam.* Ed. Kenneth Harrow. 107–130.

Rorty, Richard. *Contingency, Irony, and Solidarity.* Cambridge: Cambridge University Press, 1989.

Rosenblatt, Roger. "The Age of Irony Comes to an End." *Time* (24 September 2001). http://www.time.com/time/covers/1101010924/esroger.html.

Rushdie, Salman. *The Satanic Verses.* London: Viking, 1988.

Russell, Bertrand. "Murder for Money: Congo, 1st Genocide of the 20th Century." http://www.tenc.net/analysis/russell.htm. Accessed July 23, 2006.

Said, Edward. *Culture and Imperialism.* New York: Vintage, 1994.

———. "Figures, Configurations, Transfigurations." *Race & Class* 32, 1 (1990): 1–16.

———. *Freud and the Non-European.* London: Verso, 2003.

———. *Humanism and Democratic Criticism.* New York: Columbia University Press, 2004.

———. *Orientalism.* New York: Pantheon, 1978.

———. *Representations of the Intellectual: The 1993 Reith Lectures.* New York: Pantheon Books, 1994.

———. *The World, the Text, and the Critic.* Cambridge: Harvard University Press, 1983.

Salih, Tayeb. Lecture delivered at the American University in Beirut on May 19, 1980. *Season of Migration to the North by Tayeb Salih: A Casebook.* 14–16.

———. *Mawsim al-hijrah ila al-shamal.* Beirut: Dar al-'Awda, 1967.

———. *Season of Migration to the North.* Colorado Springs: Three Continents Press, 1980.

———. *Urs az-Zayn wa sab' qisas.* Beirut: 1966.

———. *The Wedding of Zein and Other Stories.* Trans. Denys Johnson-Davies. Washington, DC: Three Continents Press, 1985.

Schimmel, Annemarie. "Creation and Judgment in th Koran and in Mystico-Poetical Interpretation." *We Believe in One God.* Ed. Annemarie Schimmel and Abdoldjavad Falaturi. 149–177.

———. *Deciphering the Signs of God: A Phenomenological Approach to Islam.* Albany: State University of New York Press, 1994.

———. *Islam: An Introduction.* Albany: State University of New York Press, 1992.

Schneider, William H. *An Empire for the Masses: The French Popular Image of Africa, 1870–1900.* Westport, CT: Greenwood, 1982.

Schuon, Frithjof. *Understanding Islam.* Bloomington: World Wisdom Books, 1994.

Scott, James C. *Domination and the Arts of Resistance: Hidden Transcripts.* New Haven: Yale University Press, 1990.

Season of Migration to the North by Tayeb Salih: A Casebook. Ed. Mona Takieddine Amyuni. Beirut: American University of Beirut, 1985.

Sekyi-Otu, Ato. *Fanon's Dialectic of Experience.* Cambridge: Harvard University Press, 1996.

Senghor, Leopold Sedar. *The Collected Poetry.* Charlottesville: University Press of Virginia, 1991.

———. "Foreword." *Leo Frobenius—An Anthology*. Ed. Eike Haberland. Weisbaden: Franz Steiner Verlag, 1973. vii–xiii.

Shaka, Femi Okiremuete. "Vichy Dakar and the Other Story of French Colonial Stewardship in Africa: A Critical Reading of Ousmane Sembène and Thierno Faty Sow's *Camp de Thiaroye*." *Research in African Literatures* 26, 3 (1995): 67–77.

Shakespeare, William. "As You Like It." *William Shakespeare: The Complete Works*. Ed. Ralph M. Sargent. Baltimore: Penguin, 1969.

Siddiqui, Ataullah. *Christian-Muslim Dialogue in the Twentieth Century*. New York: Palgrave Macmillan, 1997.

Smith, Adam. *Lectures on Rhetoric and Belles Lettres—Considerations concerning the First Formation of Languages*. Vol. 4. *The Glasgow Edition of the Works and Correspondence of Adam Smith (1981–1987)*. The Online Library of Liberty. Liberty Fund, Inc. http://oll.libertyfund.org.

Spurr, David. *The Rhetoric of Empire: Colonial Discourse in Journalism, Travel Writing, and Imperial Administration*. Durham: Duke University Press, 1993.

Stanley, Peter. *What Did You Do in the War Daddy? A Visual History of Propaganda Posters*. New York: Oxford University Press, 1983.

Stovall, Terry. "Colour-blind France? Colonial Workers during the First World War." *Race & Class* 35, 2 (Oct.–Dec. 1993): 35–55.

Suret-Canale, Jean. *French Colonialism in Tropical Africa 1900–1945*. New York: Pica, 1971.

Tambiah, Stanley J. "The Nation-State in Crisis and the Rise of Ethnonationalism." *The Politics of Difference*. Ed. Wilmsen and McAllister, 124–143.

Taylor, Charles. *The Ethics of Authenticity*. Cambridge: Harvard University Press, 1991.

———. *Modern Social Imaginaries*. Durham: Duke University Press, 2004.

———. "Modern Social Imaginaries." *Public Culture* 14, no. 1 (2002): 91–124.

———. *Multiculturalism: Examining the Politics of Recognition*. Ed. Amy Gutmann. Princeton: Princeton University Press, 1994.

———. "Two Theories of Modernity." *Alternative Modernities*. Ed. Gaonkar. 172–196.

Tlili, Mustapha. "The Future Itself." *For Nelson Mandela*. Ed. Jacques Derrida and Mustapha Tlili. New York: Henry Holt and Co., 1987. 73–81.

———. *Lion Mountain*. New York: Little, Brown & Co, 1990.

———. *La Montagne du lion*. Paris: Editions Gallimard, 1988.

———. "Opening Statement." "Clash of Civilizations or Clash of Perceptions? In Search of Common Ground for Understanding." Dialogues: Islamic World—U.S The West Conference, Granada, Spain, (October 28–31, 2002). http://www.islamuswest.org/events.html.

———. "United Nations Project." "World Policy Institute." http://www.worldpolicy.org/projects/un/index.html.

———. "A Vote for Starting Small." *The Philadelphia Inquirer*, April 4, 2004. http://www.islamuswest.org/press_10.html.

Todorov, Tzvetan. *On Human Diversity: Nationalism, Racism, and Exoticism in French Thought*. Cambridge, MA: Harvard University Press, 1993.

Tuan, Yi-Fu. *Space and Place: The Perspective of Experience*. Minneapolis: University of Minnesota Press, 1977.

Tuccille, Jerome. *Alan Shrugged: Alan Greenspan, World's Most Powerful Banker*. Hoboken: John Wiley & Sons, 2002.

Turner, Bryan. *Marx and the End of Orientalism*. London: George Allen & Unwin, 1978.

Van Oort, Richard. "Performative-Constative Revisited: The Genetics of Austin's Theory of Speech Acts." *Anthropoetics* 2, 2 (January 1997). http://www.anthropoetics.ucla.edu/Ap0202/Vano.htm.

Vico, Giambattista. *The New Science of Giambattista Vico*. Trans. from 3rd edition (1744) by Thomas Goddard Bergin and Max Harold Fisch. Ithaca: Cornell University Press, 1948.

———. *On the Study Methods of Our Time*. Trans. Elio Gianturco. Indianapolis: Bobbs-Merrill, 1965.

Villes et territoires au Maghreb: Itinéraire d'une recherche. Cahiers de l'IRMC, no. 1, 2000. Institut de Recherche sur le Maghreb Contemporain. http://www.irmc-maghreb.org/publicat/cahiers1/IRMC_cahiers1.PDF.

Der Völkerzirkus Unserer Feinde. Mit einem Vorwort von Leo Frobenius. Berlin: Eckart-Verlag, 1917.

We Believe in One God: The Experience of God in Christianity and Islam. Ed. Anne Marie Schimmel and Abdoldjavad Falaturi. New York: Seabury Press, 1979.

Weisberg, Jacob. "Bushisms of the Day." Slate. html://www.slate.com/id/2097136

White, Hayden. *Metahistory: The Historical Imagination in Nineteenth-Century Europe*. Baltimore: Johns Hopkins Press, 1973.

———. *Tropics of Discourse: Essays in Cultural Criticism*. Baltimore: Johns Hopkins University Press, 1978.

Wilden, Anthony. *System and Structure: Essays in Communication and Exchange*. 2nd Ed. London: Tavistock, 1980.

Wilson, Woodrow. "Fourteen Points." *Our Documents*. http://www.ourdocuments.gov/doc.php?doc=62&page=transcript.

Wolf, Eric R. *Europe and the People Without History*. Berkeley: University of California Press, 1982.

Woodhull, Winifred. *Transfigurations of the Maghreb: Feminism, Decolonization, and Literatures*. Minneapolis: University of Minnesota Press, 1993.

Yaeger, Patricia. "Introduction: Narrating Space." *The Geography of Identity*. Ed. Patricia Yaeger. Ann Arbor: University of Michigan Press, 1996. 1–39.

Yazdi, Mehdi Ha'iri. *Principles of Epistemology in Islamic Philosophy: Knowledge by Presence.* Albany: State University of New York Press, 1992.

Young, Iris Marion. "Unruly Categories: A Critique of Nancy Fraser's Dual Systems Theory." *New Left Review* 222 (March April 1997): 147–160.

Young, Robert J. C. *Colonial Desire: Hybridity in Theory, Culture and Race.* London: Routledge, 1995.

———. *Postcolonialism: An Historical Introduction.* Oxford: Blackwell Publishers, 2001.

———. *White Mythologies: Writing History and the West.* London: Routledge, 1990.

Zeman, Zbynek. *Selling the War: Art and Propaganda in World War II.* London: Orbis, 1978.

INDEX

SUNY series,
Explorations in Postcolonial Studies

Emmanuel C. Eze and Arif Dirlik, editors

Anjali Prabhu, *Hybridity: Limits, Transformations, Prospects*

M. T. Kato, *From Kung Fu to Hip Hop: Globalization, Revolution, and Popular Culture*

Natascha Gentz and Stefan Kramer (eds.), *Globalization, Cultural Identities, and Media Representations*

Sandra Ponzanesi, *Paradoxes of Postcolonial Culture: Contemporary Women Writers of the Indian and Afro-Italian Diaspora*

Sam Durrant, *Postcolonial Narrative and the Work of Mourning: J.M. Coetzee, Wilson Harris, and Toni Morrison*

Patrick Colm Hogan, *Empire and Poetic Voice: Cognitive and Cultural Studies of Literary Tradition and Colonialism*

Olakunle George, *Relocating Agency: Modernity and African Letters*

Elisabeth Mudimbe-Boyi (ed.), *Beyond Dichotomies: Histories, Identities, Cultures, and the Challenge of Globalization*

John C. Hawley (ed.), *Postcolonial, Queer: Theoretical Intersections*

Alfred J. Lopez, *Posts and Pasts: A Theory of Postcolonialism*

S. Shankar, *Textual Traffic: Colonialism, Modernity, and the Economy of the Text*

Patrick Colm Hogan, *Colonialism and Cultural Identity: Crises of Tradition in the Anglophone Literatures of India, Africa, and the Caribbean*